MW01470922

Table of Contents

Introduction 13
Air Fryer Breakfast Recipes 14
   Thyme Potato Breakfast Mix 14
   Chicken and Spinach Breakfast Casserole 14
   Sausage Bake 15
   Breakfast Chicken Burrito 15
   Fruity Breakfast Casserole 16
   Smoked Bacon and Bread Mix 16
   Cheesy Hash Brown Mix 17
   Roasted Peppers Frittata 17
   Blackberries and Cornflakes Mix 18
   Simple Scrambled Eggs 18
   Creamy Mushroom Pie 19
   Carrots and Cauliflower Breakfast Mix 19
   Pesto Breakfast Toast 20
   Sausage Omelet 20
   Polenta Cakes 21
   Vanilla Toast 21
   Chili and Parsley Soufflé 22
   Air Fried Mushroom Mix 22
   Parmesan Breakfast Muffins 23
   Tomato and Eggs Mix 23
   Italian Eggplant Sandwich 24
   Corn Pudding 25
   Breakfast Potatoes Mix 26
   Breakfast Sausage Rolls 26
   Breakfast Biscuits 27
   Chorizo Omelet 27
   Oregano Artichoke Omelet 28
   Potato Frittata 28
   Simple Cheese Toast 29
   Green Beans Omelet 29
   Cod Tortilla 30
   Cheese and Ham Patties 30
   English Tuna Sandwiches 31
   Creamy Peas Omelet 31
   Vanilla Oatmeal 32
   Pear Oatmeal 32
   Breakfast Rice Pudding 33
   Squash Breakfast Mix 33
   Herbed Omelet 34

Zucchini and Chicken Breakfast Tortillas 34
Kale Sandwich 35
Breakfast Pancakes.. 35
Tofu and Quinoa Bowls 36
Black Bean Burritos 36
Veggie and Tofu Casserole 37
Yam Pudding.. 37
Breakfast Cauliflower Mix 38
Easy Mushroom Fritters.. 38
Tofu and Bell Peppers Breakfast 39
Stuffed Peppers 39
Peppers and Lettuce Salad 40
Breakfast Spinach Pie 40
Eggplant and Zucchini Breakfast Mix... 41
Herbed Tomatoes Breakfast Mix 41
Simple Pumpkin Oatmeal... 42
Apple Oatmeal 42
Carrot Oatmeal 43
Strawberry Oatmeal.. 43
Beans Oatmeal 44
Apple Bran Granola 44
Air Fryer Lunch Recipes 45
Greek Sandwiches... 45
Chicken and Mushroom Pie 46
Chicken Pizza Rolls 47
Chinese Pork Bites 47
Old Bay Chicken Wings 48
Dijon Hot Dogs... 48
Lentils Lunch Cakes.. 49
Beef Meatballs and Sauce.. 49
Beef Meatball Sandwiches 50
Cod Fillets and Kale Salad 50
Simple Lunch Turkey 51
Cod Meatballs... 51
Beef and Potato Stew 52
Shrimp Pasta 52
Cheese Ravioli 53
Cod Curry 53
Chicken Lunch Casserole.. 54
Creamy Potato Lunch.. 54
Chinese Beef and Cabbage Bowls 55
Veggie Pudding... 55
Coconut Zucchini Mix.. 56

Simple Chicken, Kale and Mushroom Mix 56
Chicken and Beans Casserole 57
Cod and Warm Tomato Mix 57
Chicken and Cauliflower Bake 58
Japanese Pork Mix 58
Sea Bass Stew 59
Bourbon Lunch Burger 60
Air Fryer Lamb 61
Lunch Broccoli Mix 61
Lunch Tomato and Okra Stew 62
Veggie Stew 62
Black Beans Lunch Mix 63
Beans and Quinoa Stew 63
Green Beans Lunch Stew 64
Chickpeas Stew 64
Lentils Lunch Curry 65
Delicious Eggplant Stew 65
Simple Okra Lunch Salad 66
Lunch Green Beans Casserole 66
Italian Chicken Mix 67
Honey Chicken Thighs 67
Lunch Baby Carrots Mix 68
Quinoa and Spinach Pesto Mix 68
Greek Quinoa Salad 69
Quinoa and Spinach Salad 69
Chicken and Cabbage Curry 70
Potatoes and Calamari Stew 70
Salsa Chicken Mix 71
Corn Stew 71
Butternut Squash Stew 72
Air Fryer Side Dish Recipes 73
Creamy Potatoes 73
Sweet Potato Side Salad 73
Mayo Brussels Sprouts 74
Green Beans and Shallots 74
Italian Mushroom Mix 75
Simple Eggplant Mix 75
Creamy Tomatoes 76
Brussels Sprouts Side Dish Delight 76
Simple Zucchini Fries 77
Mixed Peppers Side Dish 77
French Carrots Mix 78
Maple Parsnips Mix 78

Simple Air Fried Beets 79
Cauliflower and Mushroom Risotto 79
Moroccan Eggplant Side Dish 80
Air Fried Cauliflower Mix 80
Simple Rosemary Potatoes 81
Parsnips and Carrots Fries 81
Easy Mushroom Mix 82
Yellow Squash and Zucchini Mix 82
Cheesy Mushroom Salad 83
Lime Corn 83
Garlic Potatoes 84
Creamy Cabbage Mix 84
Wild Rice Mix 85
Parsley Quinoa 85
Creamy Risotto 86
Spiced Pumpkin Rice 86
Mashed Sweet Potatoes 87
Saffron Rice 87
Mint and Cherries Rice 88
Broccoli Risotto 88
Artichoke Rice 89
Air Fried Beans Mix 89
Black Beans Mix 90
Pineapple Rice 90
Beans Mix 91
Mashed Cauliflower 91
Parsnips Mash 92
Carrot Puree 92
Butternut Puree 93
Parmesan Asparagus Mix 93
Simple Air Fried Fennel 94
Minty Peas 94
Lemony Artichokes 95
Citrus Cauliflower Mix 95
Garlicky Beets 96
Fava Beans Mix 96
Simple Cabbage Mix 97
Bell Pepper and Lettuce Side Salad 97
Cheesy Spinach 98
Roasted Rhubarb 98
Herbed Potatoes Mix 99
Endives and Rice Mix 100
Turmeric Cabbage Mix 100

Tomato Endives Mix..101
Mung Beans Mix 101
Brown Lentils Mix..102
Indian Red Potatoes..102
Air Fryer Snack and Appetizer Recipes..103
Pork Bites..103
Banana Chips..103
Lemony Apple Bites 104
Zucchini Balls 104
Basil and Cilantro Crackers 105
Balsamic Zucchini Slices 105
Turmeric Carrot Chips 106
Chives Radish Snack 106
Lentils Snack 107
Air Fried Corn 107
Coconut Shrimp Snack 108
Chicken Sticks 108
Cheesy Beef Meatballs..109
Pepper Rolls 109
Greek Cream Cheese Balls 110
Minty Shrimp Mix..110
Italian Mozzarella Sticks 111
Kale Crackers 111
Potato Chips 112
Crab Bites 112
Broccoli Bites..113
Sausage Bites..113
Lemony Endives Appetizer 114
Coriander Bites..114
Beef Dip 115
Lentils Spread 115
Chili Dip 116
Tomato Dip 116
Zucchini and Mint Spread 117
Squash Dip 117
Cheesy Sausage and Tomatoes Dip..118
Mushroom Salad 118
Minty Cauliflower Spread 119
Fast Mango Dip 119
Hot Dip 120
Spiced Tomato Party Mix..120
Tomatoes and Dates Salsa..121
Chili Tomato Salsa..121

Buttery Onion Dip..122
Cranberry Dip...122
Onion and Chili Dip 123
Easy Eggplant Spread...123
Broccoli Spread..124
Buttery Carrot Dip 124
Apple and Dates Dip 125
Simple Fennel and Tomato Spread 125
Creamy Leek Spread 126
Fast Parsley Dip...126
Scallions and Shallots Dip 127
Corn Dip 127
Air Fryer Fish and Seafood Recipes 128
Chinese Cod Fillets 128
Cod Fillets with Leeks 128
Rosemary Shrimp Kabobs 129
Simple Balsamic Cod Fillets 129
Chili Salmon Fillets 130
Shrimp and Veggie Mix 130
White Fish and Peas..131
Cod and Lime Sauce 131
Flavored Salmon Fillets..132
Herbed Tuna 132
Creamy Shrimp and Mushrooms 133
Maple Salmon 133
Salmon and Balsamic Orange Sauce 134
Pistachio Crusted Cod 134
Roasted Cod and Parsley 135
Salmon and Fennel..135
Salmon Fillets and Pineapple Mix 136
Easy Salmon Fillets and Bell Peppers 136
Coconut Cod Fillets 137
Salmon and Orange Vinaigrette 137
Sea Bass Paella 138
Easy Coconut Shrimp 138
Tiger Shrimp Mix 139
Hot Shrimp Mix...139
Butter Shrimp Mix 140
Salmon and Capers 140
Simple Snapper Mix 141
Simple Trout Mix 141
Cilantro Trout Fillets 142
Salmon and Jasmine Rice 142

Salmon and Carrots 143
Spicy Cod 143
Air Fried Salmon 144
Salmon Steaks Mix 144
Chinese Trout Bites 145
Simple Trout 145
Mussels Bowls 146
Mussels and Shrimp 146
Clams and Potatoes... 147
Parmesan Clams 147
Saffron Shrimp Mix... 148
Shrimp and Corn 148
Simple Shrimp 149
Shrimp and Tomatoes 149
Chili Tomato Shrimp 150
Pea Pods and Shrimp Mix... 150
Different Shrimp Mix 151
Shrimp and Spaghetti.. 151
Butter Flounder Fillets 152
Tarragon Shrimp 152
Shrimp, Crab and Sausage Mix... 153
Squid Mix 153
Squid and Peas 154
Garlicky Squid 154
Shrimp and Chestnut Mix... 155
Baby Shrimp Salad.. 155
Trout and Almond Butter Sauce 156
Baked Cod 156
Lime Salmon 157
Salmon and Blackberry Sauce 157
Shrimp and Zucchini Mix 158
Air Fryer Poultry Recipes 159
Turmeric Chicken Legs 159
Flavored Turkey Breast 159
Salsa Verde Chicken Breast 160
Creamy Chicken Thighs... 160
Chinese Chicken Thighs.. 161
Oregano Chicken Thighs 161
Herbed Chicken.. 162
Honey Duck Breasts 162
Duck and Sauce 163
Chicken Wings and Endives.. 163
Turkey and Parsley Pesto 164

Chicken Breasts and Veggies 164
Chicken and Green Coconut Sauce 165
Simple Chicken Thighs 165
Chicken Breasts Delight 166
Tomato Chicken Mix 166
Chicken and Veggies 167
Japanese Chicken Thighs 167
Air Fried Whole Chicken 168
Chicken Thighs and Rice 168
Glazed Chicken and Apples 169
Lemon Chicken and Asparagus... 169
Turkey with Fig Sauce 170
Simple Garlic and Lemon Chicken 170
Tarragon Chicken Breasts 171
Chicken and Pear Sauce 172
Honey Chicken and Dates 172
Chicken and Leeks 173
Chicken and Yogurt Mix 173
Air Fried Chicken Wings 174
Tomato Duck Breast 174
Turkey and Spring Onions Mix 175
Soy Sauce Chicken 175
Butter and Parmesan Chicken... 176
Duck Breast and Potatoes 176
Balsamic Chicken 177
Simple Lemongrass Chicken 177
Spiced Chicken 178
Turkey Chili 178
Mexican Turkey Mix 179
Chicken and Peppercorns Mix 179
Fast Turkey Meatballs 180
Rosemary Chicken Breasts... 180
Chicken and Smoked Pancetta 181
Turkey Wings and Orange Sauce 181
Cinnamon Chicken Mix 182
Hot Wings 182
Chicken and Baby Carrots Mix 183
Cajun Chicken and Okra 183
Chicken and Beans Chili 184
Chicken and Beer Mix 184
Chicken Curry 185
Marinara Chicken.. 185
Bleu Cheese Chicken Mix 186

Chicken and Potatoes 186
Chicken and Chickpeas Mix 187
Chicken and Squash 187
Indian Chicken Mix 188
Sesame Chicken Mix 188
Marjoram Chicken 189
Air Fryer Meat Recipes 190
Spiced Pork Chops 190
Chinese Pork and Broccoli Mix 190
French Beef Mix 191
Beef and Mushroom Mix 191
Oregano Pork Chops 192
Crusted Rack of Lamb 192
Coconut Pork Mix 193
Creamy Pork and Sprouts 193
Pork and Chives Mix 194
Beef and Wine Sauce 194
Lamb Chops and Dill 195
Mustard Pork Chops 195
Beef Roast and Grapes 196
Sage Pork Mix 196
Beef Roast 197
Tarragon Pork Loin 197
Beef and Celery Mix 198
Chinese Beef Mix 198
Pork and Bell Pepper Mix 199
Lamb and Beans 199
Pork Chops and Spinach Mix 200
Ground Beef Mix 200
Smoked Pork Roast 201
Pork and Cauliflower Mix 201
Pork and Bell Peppers 202
Beef and Peas 202
Fennel Pork Mix 203
Lamb Meatballs 203
Pork Meatloaf 204
Simple Pork Steaks 204
Sausage Mix 205
Hot Pork Mix 205
Beef, Arugula and Leeks 206
Garlicky Loin Roast 206
Pork and Peanuts Mix 207
Rubbed Steaks 207

Milky Lamb 208
Paprika Beef 208
Mustard Pork Chops 209
Beef and Chives Marinade 209
Cinnamon Beef 210
Basil Beef Roast 210
Simple Beef Curry 211
Creamy Beef 211
Jalapeno Beef Mix 212
Cumin Beef Mix 212
Lamb and Carrots Mix 213
Pork and Celery Mix 213
Pork and Shallots Mix 214
Beef Casserole 214
Beef and Tofu Mix 215
Marinated Beef 215
Pork and Cabbage 216
Great Pork Chops 216
Fast Lamb Ribs 217
Greek Lamb Chops 217
Curry Pork Mix 218
BBQ Lamb Chops 218
Beef and Plums Mix 219
French Lamb Mix 219
Air Fryer Vegetable Recipes 220
Spinach and Cream Cheese Mix 220
Balsamic Asparagus 220
Cheesy Asparagus 221
Simple Fennel Mix 221
Beets and Capers 222
Sesame Seed Beets Mix 222
Beets and Kale Mix 223
Beet and Tomato Salad 223
Cauliflower Mix 224
Broccoli and Tomatoes 224
Mustard Brussels Sprouts 225
Parmesan Broccoli 225
Red Cabbage and Carrots 226
Butter Carrots 226
Green Beans Mix 227
Spicy Kale Mix 227
Eggplant Mix 228
Hot Greek Potatoes 228

Coconut Mushroom Mix 229
Oregano Pearl Onions 229
Goat Cheese Brussels Sprouts 230
Tarragon Green Beans 230
Artichokes and Mayonnaise 231
Coconut Artichokes 232
Wrapped Asparagus 232
Cajun Asparagus 233
Squash Salad 233
Creamy Squash Mix 234
Orange Carrots 234
Tomato Salad 235
Tomato and Green Beans Salad 235
Bell Peppers and Kale 236
Garlic Parsnips 236
Broccoli and Pomegranate 237
Bacon Cauliflower 237
Butter Broccoli 238
New Potatoes Mix 238
Napa Cabbage Mix 239
Butter Cabbage Mix 239
Turmeric Kale Mix 240
Spicy Cabbage 240
Easy Celery Root Mix 241
Maple Glazed Corn 241
Dill Corn 242
Broccoli Casserole 242
Mustard Greens Mix 243
Balsamic Mustard Greens 243
Butter Endives 244
Endives and Bacon 244
Air Fryer Dessert Recipes 245
Avocado Cake... 245
Oreo Cheesecake 245
Cherry Cream Pudding.. 246
Amaretto Cream 246
Cinnamon Rolls 247
Simple Nutmeg Pumpkin Pie.. 247
Cinnamon Pears 248
Butter Donuts... 248
Cinnamon Apples 249
Lemon Cake 249
Yogurt Cake 250

Zucchini Bread...250

Cream of Tartar Bread..251

Orange Cake 251

Maple Apples..252

Pineapple and Carrot Cake..252

Rum Cheesecake 253

Strawberry Cream 253

Coffee Cream 254

Cream Cheese Cookies...254

Walnut Cookies 255

Creamy Blackberry Mix 255

Chocolate Brownies 256

Yogurt and Cream Cheese Cake..256

Creamy White Chocolate Cheesecake 257

Pumpkin Cake 257

Banana Bread 258

Pear Bread 258

Lemon Lava Cake 259

Pear Delight 259

Orange Stew...260

Baked Pears 260

Liqueur Chocolate Cream..261

Apricot Cake 261

Spiced Banana Pudding 262

Lime Tapioca Pudding 262

Strawberry Cake...263

Almond and Cocoa Cake 263

Creamy Pudding 264

Brioche Pudding...264

Apple and Cinnamon Sauce 265

Grape Stew 265

Creamy Rice Pudding 266

Honey Blackberry Pudding 266

Banana and Rice Pudding..267

Orange Marmalade 267

Strawberry Jam...268

Cranberry Jam 268

Sweet Plum Stew 269

Apple Jam...269

Conclusion 270

Recipe Index..271

Introduction

We all live in such a hectic and busy world that, by the end of the day, we barely have time for cooking. We tend to forget that cooking can be fun, and that home cooked meals are the best.

If you are one of those busy people who don't have the time (or maybe simply dislike) spending long hours in the kitchen cooking, the kitchen appliance you are going to discover next is exactly what you need.

We are talking about an air fryer. This modern and innovative cooking tool will make cooking fun again for you. It doesn't matter how busy you are. You only need a few minutes and the right ingredients, and you'll enjoy some of the best meals ever. You can forget about using all those pots and pans, and you certainly don't have to be an expert cook to use the air fryer. Just follow its directions, and you'll be making some incredible and rich dishes in no time.

The air fryer uses the circulation of hot air to cook the food. This is called *Rapid Air Technology*, and it means that your food will be done faster and in a healthy way. The air reaches up to 400 degrees F, and it allows you to cook perfectly crispy—but also tender and succulent—food in a few minutes.

But wait! There's more! The air fryer can successfully grill, cook, bake, steam, and even roast food.

The appliance first appeared in Europe and Australia in 2010, but it was not long before everyone was mad over it! Nowadays, millions of people all over the world have made this tool their best friend in the kitchen.

If you've decided to purchase such a magnificent kitchen appliance, make sure you get one with a lot of accessories that will make your job in the kitchen much easier. Get an air fryer that also has grilling pans, baking pans, or even a steak cage. This way you can make a great variety of delightful meals. Also, make sure you get an air fryer that fits your price range and that's easy to use.

Speaking of what you can make in an air fryer, we thought you could use a cooking guide that will help you get started. We searched and discovered that you can make some delicious and rich breakfasts, lunch dishes, side dishes, snacks, appetizers, seafood and fish meals, poultry, meat or vegetable dishes, and even some sweet desserts using the air fryer.

So, what are you waiting for? Get your new air fryer today, and start cooking the best meals for yourself and all your loved ones.

Enjoy, and have fun using your new air fryer!

Air Fryer Breakfast Recipes

Thyme Potato Breakfast Mix

Preparation time: 5 minutes
Cooking time: 25 minutes
Servings: 4

Ingredients:
- 1½ pounds hash browns
- 1 red onion, chopped
- 2 teaspoons vegetable oil
- 1 red bell pepper, chopped
- Salt and black pepper to taste
- 1 teaspoon thyme, chopped
- 2 eggs

Directions:
Heat up your air fryer at 350 degrees F. Then add the oil and heat it up. Add all other ingredients and cook for 25 minutes. Divide between plates and serve

Nutrition: calories 241, fat 4, fiber 2, carbs 12, protein 11

Chicken and Spinach Breakfast Casserole

Preparation time: 5 minutes
Cooking time: 25 minutes
Servings: 4

Ingredients:
- 1 pound chicken meat, ground
- 1 tablespoon olive oil
- ½ teaspoon sweet paprika
- 12 eggs, whisked
- 1 cup baby spinach
- Salt and black pepper to taste

Directions:
In a bowl, whisk the eggs with the salt, pepper, and paprika. Then add the spinach and chicken and mix well. Heat up your air fryer at 350 degrees F; add the oil and allow it to heat up. Add the chicken and spinach mix, cover, and cook for 25 minutes. Divide between plates and serve hot.

Nutrition: calories 270, fat 11, fiber 8, carbs 14, protein 7

Sausage Bake

Preparation time: 5 minutes
Cooking time: 20 minutes
Servings: 4

Ingredients:

- 4 bacon slices, cooked and crumbled
- A drizzle of olive oil
- 2 cups coconut milk
- 2½ cups cheddar cheese, shredded
- 1 pound breakfast sausage, chopped
- 2 eggs
- Salt and black pepper to taste
- 3 tablespoons cilantro, chopped

Directions:

In a bowl, mix the eggs with milk, cheese, salt, pepper, and the cilantro, and whisk well. Grease your air fryer with the drizzle of oil, and heat it up at 320 degrees F. Add the bacon, sausage, and the egg mixture, spread, and cook for 20 minutes. Serve hot and enjoy!

Nutrition: calories 244, fat 11, fiber 8, carbs 15, protein 9

Breakfast Chicken Burrito

Preparation time: 5 minutes
Cooking time: 10 minutes
Servings: 2

Ingredients:

- 4 chicken breast slices, cooked and shredded
- 1 green bell pepper, sliced
- 2 eggs, whisked
- 1 avocado, peeled, pitted and sliced
- 2 tablespoons mild salsa
- Salt and black pepper to taste
- 2 tablespoons cheddar cheese, grated
- 2 tortillas

Directions:

In a bowl, whisk the eggs with the salt and pepper, and pour them into a pan that fits your air fryer. Put the pan in the air fryer's basket, cook for 5 minutes at 400 degrees, and transfer the mix to a plate. Place the tortillas on a working surface, and between them divide the eggs, chicken, bell peppers, avocado, and the cheese; roll the burritos. Line your air fryer with tin foil, add the burritos, and cook them at 300 degrees F for 3-4 minutes. Serve for breakfast — or lunch, or dinner!

Nutrition: calories 329, fat 13, fiber 11, carbs 20, protein 8

Fruity Breakfast Casserole

Preparation time: 10 minutes
Cooking time: 20 minutes
Servings: 6

Ingredients:
- 2 cups old fashioned oats
- 1 teaspoon baking powder
- ⅓ cup sugar
- 1 teaspoon cinnamon powder
- 1 cup blueberries
- 1 banana, peeled and mashed
- 2 cups milk
- 2 eggs, whisked
- 2 tablespoons butter
- 1 teaspoon vanilla extract
- Cooking spray

Directions:
In a bowl, mix the sugar, baking powder, cinnamon, blueberries, banana, eggs, butter, and vanilla; whisk. Heat up your air fryer at 320 degrees F, and grease with cooking spray. Add the oats, the berries and banana mix; cover, and cook for 20 minutes. Divide into bowls and serve.

Nutrition: calories 260, fat 4, fiber 7, carbs 9, protein 10

Smoked Bacon and Bread Mix

Preparation time: 10 minutes
Cooking time: 30 minutes
Servings: 6

Ingredients:
- 1 pound white bread, cubed
- 1 pound smoked bacon, cooked and chopped
- ¼ cup avocado oil
- 1 red onion, chopped
- 30 ounces canned tomatoes, chopped
- ½ pound cheddar cheese, shredded
- 2 tablespoons chives, chopped
- ½ pound Monterey jack cheese, shredded
- 2 tablespoons chicken stock
- Salt and black pepper to taste
- 8 eggs, whisked

Directions:
Add the oil to your air fryer and heat it up at 350 degrees F. Add all other ingredients except the chives and cook for 30 minutes, shaking halfway. Divide between plates and serve with chives sprinkled on top.

Nutrition: calories 211, fat 8, fiber 7, carbs 14, protein 3

Cheesy Hash Brown Mix

Preparation time: 10 minutes
Cooking time: 20 minutes
Servings: 6

Ingredients:
- 1½ pounds hash browns
- 1 cup almond milk
- A drizzle of olive oil
- 6 bacon slices, chopped
- 8 ounces cream cheese, softened
- 1 yellow onion, chopped
- 1 cup cheddar cheese, shredded
- 6 spring onions, chopped
- Salt and black pepper to taste
- 6 eggs

Directions:
Heat up your air fryer with the oil at 350 degrees F. In a bowl, mix all other ingredients except the spring onions, and whisk well. Add this mixture to your air fryer, cover, and cook for 20 minutes. Divide between plates, sprinkle the spring onions on top, and serve.

Nutrition: calories 231, fat 9, fiber 9, carbs 8, protein 12

Roasted Peppers Frittata

Preparation time: 10 minutes
Cooking time: 20 minutes
Servings: 6

Ingredients:
- 6 ounces jarred roasted red bell peppers, chopped
- 12 eggs, whisked
- ½ cup parmesan cheese, grated
- 3 garlic cloves, minced
- 2 tablespoons parsley, chopped
- Salt and black pepper to taste
- 2 tablespoons chives, chopped
- 6 tablespoons ricotta cheese
- A drizzle of olive oil

Directions:
In a bowl, mix the bell peppers with the eggs, garlic, parsley, salt, pepper, chives, and ricotta; whisk well. Heat up your air fryer at 300 degrees F, add the oil, and spread. Add the egg mixture, spread, sprinkle the parmesan on top, and cook for 20 minutes. Divide between plates and serve.

Nutrition: calories 262, fat 6, fiber 9, carbs 18, protein 8

Blackberries and Cornflakes Mix

Preparation time: 5 minutes
Cooking time: 10 minutes
Servings: 4

Ingredients:
- 3 cups milk
- 1 tablespoon sugar
- 2 eggs, whisked
- ¼ teaspoon nutmeg, ground
- ¼ cup blackberries
- 4 tablespoons cream cheese, whipped
- 1½ cups corn flakes

Directions:
In a bowl, mix all ingredients and stir well. Heat up your air fryer at 350 degrees F, add the corn flakes mixture, spread, and cook for 10 minutes. Divide between plates, serve, and enjoy.

Nutrition: calories 180, fat 5, fiber 7, carbs 12, protein 5

Simple Scrambled Eggs

Preparation time: 5 minutes
Cooking time: 10 minutes
Servings: 4

Ingredients:
- 4 eggs, whisked
- A drizzle of olive oil
- Salt and black pepper to taste
- 1 red onion, chopped
- 2 teaspoons sweet paprika

Directions:
In a bowl, mix all ingredients and whisk. Heat up your air fryer with the oil at 240 degrees F, add the eggs mixture, stir again, and cook for 10 minutes. Serve right away.

Nutrition: calories 190, fat 7, fiber 7, carbs 12, protein 4

Creamy Mushroom Pie

Preparation time: 10 minutes
Cooking time: 10 minutes
Servings: 4

Ingredients:
- 1 tablespoon olive oil
- 9-inch pie dough
- 6 white mushrooms, chopped
- 2 tablespoons bacon, cooked and crumbled
- 3 eggs
- 1 red onion, chopped
- ½ cup heavy cream
- Salt and black pepper to taste
- ½ teaspoon thyme, dried
- ¼ cup cheddar cheese, grated

Directions:
Roll the dough on a working surface, then press it on the bottom of a pie pan that fits your air fryer and grease with the oil. In a bowl, mix all other ingredients except the cheese, stir well, and pour mixture into the pie pan. Sprinkle the cheese on top, put the pan in the air fryer, and cook at 400 degrees F for 10 minutes. Slice and serve.

Nutrition: calories 192, fat 6, fiber 6, carbs 14, protein 7

Carrots and Cauliflower Breakfast Mix

Preparation time: 10 minutes
Cooking time: 20 minutes
Servings: 4

Ingredients:
- 1 cauliflower head, stems removed, florets separated, and steamed
- 3 carrots, chopped and steamed
- 2 ounces cheddar cheese, grated
- 3 eggs
- 2 ounces milk
- 2 teaspoons cilantro, chopped
- Salt and black pepper to taste

Directions:
In a bowl, mix the eggs with the milk, parsley, salt, and pepper; whisk. Put the cauliflower and the carrots in your air fryer, add the egg mixture, and spread. Then sprinkle the cheese on top. Cook at 350 degrees F for 20 minutes, divide between plates, and serve.

Nutrition: calories 194, fat 4, fiber 7, carbs 11, protein 6

Pesto Breakfast Toast

Preparation time: 5 minutes
Cooking time: 8 minutes
Servings: 3

Ingredients:
- 6 bread slices
- 5 tablespoons butter, melted
- 3 garlic cloves, minced
- 6 teaspoons basil and tomato pesto
- 1 cup mozzarella cheese, grated

Directions:
Arrange bread slices on a working surface. In a bowl, mix the butter, pesto, and garlic, and spread on each bread slice. Place them in your air fryer's basket, sprinkle the cheese on top, and cook at 350 degrees F for 8 minutes. Serve right away.

Nutrition: calories 187, fat 6, fiber 6, carbs 13, protein 5

Sausage Omelet

Preparation time: 5 minutes
Cooking time: 11 minutes
Servings: 2

Ingredients:
- 1 sausage link, sliced
- 2 eggs, whisked
- 4 cherry tomatoes, halved
- 1 tablespoon cilantro, chopped
- 1 tablespoon olive oil
- 1 tablespoon cheddar cheese, grated
- Salt and black pepper to taste

Directions:
Put the tomatoes and sausage in the air fryer's basket and cook at 360 degrees F for 5 minutes. Take a pan that fits your air fryer, grease it with the oil, and then transfer the tomatoes and sausage to the pan. In a bowl, mix all remaining ingredients and stir. Pour this over the sausage and tomato mixture, spread, and place the pan in the air fryer; cook at 360 degrees F for 6 minutes more. Serve immediately and enjoy.

Nutrition: calories 270, fat 14, fiber 3, carbs 23, protein 16

Polenta Cakes

Preparation time: 10 minutes
Cooking time: 25 minutes
Servings: 4

Ingredients:
- 1 cup cornmeal
- 3 cups water
- Salt and black pepper to taste
- 1 tablespoon butter, softened
- ¼ cup potato starch
- A drizzle of vegetable oil
- Maple syrup for serving

Directions:
Put the water in a pot, heat up over medium heat, add the cornmeal, whisk, and cook for 10 minutes. Add the butter, whisk well again, then take off the heat and allow to cool down. Take spoonfuls of polenta and shape into balls; flatten them, dredge in potato starch, and place them on a lined baking sheet that fits your air fryer. Drizzle with oil. Place the baking sheet in the fryer and cook at 380 degrees F for 15 minutes, flipping them halfway. Serve with maple syrup drizzled on top.

Nutrition: calories 170, fat 2, fiber 2, carbs 12, protein 4

Vanilla Toast

Preparation time: 5 minutes
Cooking time: 5 minutes
Servings: 6

Ingredients:
- 1 stick butter, softened
- 12 bread slices
- ½ cup brown sugar
- 2 teaspoons vanilla extract

Directions:
In a bowl, mix the butter, sugar, and vanilla; stir. Spread mixture over bread slices, put them in your air fryer, and cook at 400 degrees F for 5 minutes. Serve immediately and enjoy.

Nutrition: calories 170, fat 6, fiber 5, carbs 11, protein 2

Chili and Parsley Soufflé

Preparation time: 5 minutes
Cooking time: 9 minutes
Servings: 3

Ingredients:

- 3 eggs
- 2 tablespoons heavy cream
- 1 red chili pepper, chopped
- 2 tablespoons parsley, finely chopped
- Salt and white pepper to taste

Directions:
In a bowl, mix all ingredients, whisk, and pour into 3 ramekins. Place ramekins in your air fryer's basket and cook at 400 degrees F for 9 minutes. Serve the soufflés immediately and enjoy!

Nutrition: calories 200, fat 6, fiber 1, carbs 11, protein 3

Air Fried Mushroom Mix

Preparation time: 5 minutes
Cooking time: 20 minutes
Servings: 4

Ingredients:

- 8 white mushrooms, sliced
- 1 garlic clove, minced
- 8 cherry tomatoes, halved
- 4 slices bacon, chopped
- 7 ounces spinach, torn
- A drizzle of olive oil
- 4 eggs
- Salt and black pepper to taste

Directions:
In a pan greased with oil and that fits your air fryer, mix all ingredients except for the spinach; stir. Put the pan in your air fryer and cook at 400 degrees F for 15 minutes. Add the spinach, toss, and cook for 5 minutes more. Divide between plates and serve.

Nutrition: calories 160, fat 2, fiber 5, carbs 12, protein 9

Parmesan Breakfast Muffins

Preparation time: 5 minutes
Cooking time: 15 minutes
Servings: 4

Ingredients:
- 2 eggs
- 2 tablespoons olive oil
- 3 ounces almond milk
- 1 tablespoon baking powder
- 4 ounces white flour
- A splash of Worcestershire sauce
- 2 ounces parmesan cheese, grated

Directions:
In a bowl, mix the eggs with 1 tablespoon of the oil, milk, baking powder, flour, Worcestershire sauce, and the parmesan; stir well. Grease a muffin pan that fits your air fryer with the remaining 1 tablespoon of oil, divide the cheesy mix evenly, and place the pan in the air fryer. Cook at 320 degrees F for 15 minutes. Enjoy.

Nutrition: calories 190, fat 12, fiber 2, carbs 11, protein 5

Tomato and Eggs Mix

Preparation time: 5 minutes
Cooking time: 30 minutes
Servings: 2

Ingredients:
- 2 eggs
- ½ cup cheddar cheese, shredded
- 2 tablespoons red onion, chopped
- A pinch of salt and black pepper
- ¼ cup milk
- ½ cup tomatoes, chopped

Directions:
In a bowl, mix all ingredients except for the cheese; stir well. Pour mixture into a pan that fits your air fryer, sprinkle the cheese on top, and place the pan in the fryer. Cook at 350 degrees F for 30 minutes. Divide the mix between plates, serve, and enjoy!

Nutrition: calories 210, fat 4, fiber 2, carbs 12, protein 9

Italian Eggplant Sandwich

Preparation time: 30 minutes
Cooking time: 25 minutes
Servings: 2

Ingredients:
- 1 eggplant, sliced
- 2 teaspoons parsley, chopped
- Salt and black pepper to taste
- ½ cup panko breadcrumbs
- ½ teaspoon garlic powder
- 2 tablespoons coconut milk
- ½ teaspoon Italian seasoning
- 4 bread slices
- 1 tablespoon avocado oil + a drizzle
- ½ cup mayonnaise
- ¾ cup tomato paste
- 2 tablespoons cheddar cheese, grated
- 2 cups mozzarella cheese, grated
- 2 tablespoons fresh basil, chopped

Directions:
Season eggplant slices with salt and pepper and set aside for 30 minutes. Then pat them dry them and brush with mayo and milk. In a bowl, combine the parsley, breadcrumbs, Italian seasoning, garlic powder, salt, and black pepper; stir. Next, dip the eggplant slices in this mix, and place them on a lined baking sheet; drizzle with oil. Place the baking sheet in your air fryer's basket and cook at 400 degrees F for 15 minutes, flipping the eggplant slices halfway. Brush the bread slices with the remaining 1 tablespoon of the oil. Then arrange 2 of them on a working surface, and add cheddar, mozzarella, baked eggplant slices, tomato paste, and basil; top with the other 2 bread slices. Grill sandwiches on your grill for 10 minutes, serve immediately, and enjoy.

Nutrition: calories 251, fat 11, fiber 4, carbs 8, protein 7

Corn Pudding

Preparation time: 10 minutes
Cooking time: 1 hour and 15 minutes
Servings: 6

Ingredients:

- 4 bacon slices, cooked and chopped
- 1 tablespoon olive oil
- 2 cups corn
- ½ cup green bell pepper, chopped
- 1 yellow onion, chopped
- ¼ cup celery, chopped
- 1 teaspoon thyme, chopped
- 2 teaspoons garlic, grated
- Salt and black pepper
- ½ cup heavy cream
- 1½ cups whole milk
- 3 eggs
- 3 cups bread, cubed
- 3 tablespoons parmesan cheese, grated
- 1 cup cheddar cheese, grated

Directions:

Heat up the oil in a pan over medium heat. Add the corn, celery, onion, bell pepper, salt, pepper, garlic, and thyme to the pan; stir, sauté for 15 minutes, and transfer to a bowl. To the same bowl, add the bacon, milk, cream, eggs, salt, pepper, bread, and the cheddar cheese. Stir well, then pour into a casserole dish that fits your air fryer. Place the dish in the fryer and cook at 350 degrees F for 30 minutes. Sprinkle the pudding with parmesan cheese, and cook for 30 minutes more. Slice, divide between plates, and serve.

Nutrition: calories 251, fat 6, fiber 9, carbs 14, protein 7

Breakfast Potatoes Mix

Preparation time: 5 minutes
Cooking time: 20 minutes
Servings: 4

Ingredients:
- 1½ pounds gold potatoes, cubed
- 2 tablespoons olive oil
- Salt and black pepper to taste
- 1 tablespoon sweet paprika
- 4 ounces Greek yogurt
- 1 tablespoon cilantro, chopped

Directions:
Put the potatoes in your air fryer, and then add the oil, salt, pepper, and paprika. Stir and cook at 360 degrees F for 20 minutes. Transfer the potatoes to a bowl, and add the yogurt and cilantro. Toss, serve, and enjoy.

Nutrition: calories 251, fat 7, fiber 4, carbs 14, protein 7

Breakfast Sausage Rolls

Preparation time: 10 minutes
Cooking time: 6 minutes
Servings: 4

Ingredients:
- 8 crescent roll dough pieces, separated
- 8 small sausages
- 8 cheddar cheese slices

Directions:
Unroll the crescent roll pieces on a working surface, and place one sausage and one slice of cheese on each. Wrap the sausage and cheese with each roll, and seal the edges. Place 4 wraps in your air fryer, cook at 380 degrees F for 3 minutes, and transfer to a plate. Repeat with the remaining 4 sausage rolls and serve.

Nutrition: calories 181, fat 11, fiber 1, carbs 14, protein 4

Breakfast Biscuits

Preparation time: 10 minutes
Cooking time: 8 minutes
Servings: 12

Ingredients:
- 2 cups white flour
- ¼ teaspoon baking soda
- ½ teaspoon baking powder
- 1 teaspoon sugar
- 5 tablespoons butter
- 1 cup buttermilk

Directions:
In a bowl, mix the flour, baking soda, baking powder, sugar, 4 tablespoons of the butter, and the buttermilk; stir until you obtain a dough. Transfer the dough to a floured working surface, roll, and cut 12 pieces with a cookie cutter. Melt the remaining 1 tablespoon of butter, brush the biscuits with it, and place them in your air fryer's cake pan. Cook at 400 degrees F for 8 minutes, serve, and enjoy.

Nutrition: calories 202, fat 11, fiber 9, carbs 14, protein 7

Chorizo Omelet

Preparation time: 5 minutes
Cooking time: 7 minutes
Servings: 4

Ingredients:
- 4 eggs, whisked
- ½ pound chorizo, chopped
- ½ cup corn
- 1 tablespoon vegetable oil
- 1 tablespoon cilantro, chopped
- 1 tablespoon feta cheese, crumbled
- Salt and black pepper to taste

Directions:
Heat up your air fryer at 350 degrees F, add the oil, and heat it up. Add the chorizo, stir, and cook for 1-2 minutes. In a bowl, mix all remaining ingredients; whisk, and then pour over the chorizo. Cook for 5 minutes, divide between plates, and serve.

Nutrition: calories 270, fat 6, fiber 9, carbs 12, protein 7

Oregano Artichoke Omelet

Preparation time: 5 minutes
Cooking time: 15 minutes
Servings: 6

Ingredients:
- 3 artichoke hearts, canned, drained and chopped
- 2 tablespoons avocado oil
- 6 eggs, whisked
- ½ teaspoon oregano, dried
- Salt and black pepper to taste

Directions:
In a bowl, mix all ingredients except the oil; stir well. Add the oil to your air fryer's pan, and heat it up at 320 degrees F. Add the egg mixture, cook for 15 minutes, divide between plates, and serve.

Nutrition: calories 216, fat 11, fiber 6, carbs 9, protein 4

Potato Frittata

Preparation time: 5 minutes
Cooking time: 20 minutes
Servings: 6

Ingredients:
- 8 eggs, whisked
- 1 tablespoon olive oil
- 1 pound small potatoes, chopped
- 2 red onions, chopped
- Salt and black pepper to taste
- 1 ounce parmesan cheese, grated
- ½ cup heavy cream

Directions:
In a bowl, mix all ingredients except the potatoes and oil; stir well. Heat up your air fryer's pan with the oil at 320 degrees F. Add the potatoes, stir, and cook for 5 minutes. Add the egg mixture, spread, and cook for 15 minutes more. Divide the frittata between plates and serve.

Nutrition: calories 271, fat 11, fiber 7, carbs 14, protein 6

Simple Cheese Toast

Preparation time: 5 minutes
Cooking time: 8 minutes
Servings: 2

Ingredients:
- 4 bread slices
- 4 teaspoons butter, softened
- 4 cheddar cheese slices

Directions:
Spread the butter on each slice of bread. Place 2 cheese slices each on 2 bread slices, then top with the other 2 bread slices; cut each in half. Arrange the sandwiches in your air fryer's basket and cook at 370 degrees F for 8 minutes. Serve hot, and enjoy!

Nutrition: calories 200, fat 3, fiber 5, carbs 12, protein 4

Green Beans Omelet

Preparation time: 5 minutes
Cooking time: 10 minutes
Servings: 4

Ingredients:
- 4 eggs, whisked
- 1 teaspoon soy sauce
- 1 tablespoon olive oil
- 4 garlic cloves, minced
- 3 ounces green beans, trimmed and halved
- Salt and black pepper to taste

Directions:
In a bowl, mix all ingredients except the beans and oil; whisk well. Heat up your air fryer at 320 degrees F, then add the oil and heat it up. Add the beans, stir, and sauté them for 3 minutes. Add the egg mixture over the beans, spread, and cook for 7-8 minutes more. Slice the omelet and serve immediately.

Nutrition: calories 212, fat 8, fiber 6, carbs 8, protein 6

Cod Tortilla

Preparation time: 10 minutes
Cooking time: 17 minutes
Servings: 4

Ingredients:
- 4 tortillas
- A drizzle of olive oil
- 1 green bell pepper, chopped
- 1 red onion, chopped
- 1 cup corn
- 4 cod fillets, skinless and boneless
- ½ cup salsa
- A handful of baby spinach
- 4 tablespoons parmesan cheese, grated

Directions:
Put the fish fillets in your air fryer's basket, cook at 350 degrees F for 6 minutes, and transfer to a plate. Heat up a pan with the oil over medium heat, add the bell peppers, onions, and corn, and stir. Sauté for 5 minutes and take off the heat. Arrange all the tortillas on a working surface, and divide the cod, salsa, sautéed veggies, spinach, and parmesan evenly between the 4 tortillas; then wrap / roll them. Place the tortillas in your air fryer's basket and cook at 350 degrees F for 6 minutes. Divide between plates, serve, and enjoy!

Nutrition: calories 230, fat 12, fiber 7, carbs 14, protein 5

Cheese and Ham Patties

Preparation time: 10 minutes
Cooking time: 10 minutes
Servings: 4

Ingredients:
- 1 puff pastry sheet
- 4 handfuls mozzarella cheese, grated
- 4 teaspoons mustard
- 8 ham slices, chopped

Directions:
Roll out puff pastry on a working surface and cut it in 12 squares. Divide cheese, ham, and mustard on half of them, top with the other halves, and seal the edges. Place all the patties in your air fryer's basket and cook at 370 degrees F for 10 minutes. Divide the patties between plates and serve.

Nutrition: calories 212, fat 12, fiber 7, carbs 14, protein 8

English Tuna Sandwiches

Preparation time: 5 minutes
Cooking time: 9 minutes
Servings: 4

Ingredients:
- 16 ounces canned tuna, drained
- ¼ cup mayonnaise
- 2 tablespoons mustard
- 1 tablespoon lime juice
- 2 spring onions, chopped
- 6 bread slices
- 3 tablespoons butter, melted
- 6 provolone cheese slices

Directions:
In a bowl, mix the tuna, mayo, lime juice, mustard, and spring onions; stir until combined. Spread the bread slices with the butter, place them in preheated air fryer, and bake them at 350 degrees F for 5 minutes. Spread tuna mix on half of the bread slices, and top with the cheese and the other bread slices. Place the sandwiches in your air fryer's basket and cook for 4 minutes more. Divide between plates and serve.

Nutrition: calories 212, fat 8, fiber 7, carbs 8, protein 6

Creamy Peas Omelet

Preparation time: 5 minutes
Cooking time: 10 minutes
Servings: 8

Ingredients:
- ½ pound baby peas
- 3 tablespoons avocado oil
- 1½ cups yogurt
- 8 eggs, whisked
- ½ cup mint, chopped
- Salt and black pepper to taste

Directions:
Heat up the oil in a pan that fits your air fryer over medium heat. Add the peas, stir, and cook for 3-4 minutes. In a bowl, mix the yogurt, salt, pepper, eggs, and mint; whisk. Pour yogurt mixture over the peas, toss, and cook at 350 degrees F for 7 minutes. Slice the omelet and serve right away; enjoy!

Nutrition: calories 212, fat 9, fiber 4, carbs 13, protein 7

Vanilla Oatmeal

Preparation time: 5 minutes
Cooking time: 17 minutes
Servings: 4

Ingredients:
- 1 cup milk
- 1 cup steel cut oats
- 2½ cups water
- 2 tablespoons brown sugar
- 2 teaspoons vanilla extract

Directions:
In a pan that fits your air fryer, mix all ingredients and stir well. Place the pan in your air fryer and cook at 360 degrees F for 17 minutes. Divide into bowls and serve. Enjoy!

Nutrition: calories 161, fat 7, fiber 6, carbs 9, protein 6

Pear Oatmeal

Preparation time: 5 minutes
Cooking time: 12 minutes
Servings: 4

Ingredients:
- 1 cup milk
- 1 tablespoon butter, softened
- ¼ cups brown sugar
- ½ teaspoon cinnamon powder
- 1 cup old fashioned oats
- ½ cup walnuts, chopped
- 2 cups pear, peeled and chopped

Directions:
In a heat-proof bowl that fits your air fryer, mix all ingredients and stir well. Place in your fryer and cook at 360 degrees F for 12 minutes. Divide into bowls and serve.

Nutrition: calories 210, fat 9, fiber 11, carbs 12, protein 5

Breakfast Rice Pudding

Preparation time: 5 minutes
Cooking time: 20 minutes
Servings: 4

Ingredients:
- 1 cup brown rice
- ½ cup coconut, shredded
- 3 cups almond milk
- ½ cup maple syrup
- ½ cup almonds, chopped

Directions:
Put the rice in a pan that fits your air fryer, and add all remaining ingredients; toss. Place pan in your air fryer and cook at 360 degrees F for 20 minutes. Divide into bowls and serve.

Nutrition: calories 201, fat 6, fiber 8, carbs 19, protein 6

Squash Breakfast Mix

Preparation time: 5 minutes
Cooking time: 10 minutes
Servings: 4

Ingredients:
- 1 red bell pepper, roughly chopped
- 1 cup white mushrooms, sliced
- 1 yellow squash, cubed
- 2 green onions, sliced
- 2 tablespoons butter, softened
- ½ cup feta cheese, crumbled

Directions:
In a bowl, mix all ingredients except the feta cheese. Transfer to your air fryer and cook at 350 degrees F for 10 minutes, shaking the fryer once. Divide the mixture between plates and serve with feta cheese sprinkled on top.

Nutrition: calories 202, fat 12, fiber 4, carbs 7, protein 2

Herbed Omelet

Preparation time: 5 minutes
Cooking time: 15 minutes
Servings: 4

Ingredients:
- 6 eggs, whisked
- 1 tablespoon parsley, chopped
- 1 tablespoon tarragon, chopped
- 2 tablespoons chives, chopped
- Salt and black pepper to taste
- 2 tablespoons parmesan cheese, grated
- 4 tablespoons heavy cream

Directions:
In a bowl, mix all ingredients—except for the parmesan—and whisk well. Pour this into a pan that fits your air fryer, place it in preheated fryer, and cook at 350 degrees F for 15 minutes. Divide the omelet between plates and serve with the parmesan sprinkled on top.

Nutrition: calories 251, fat 8, fiber 4, carbs 15, protein 4

Zucchini and Chicken Breakfast Tortillas

Preparation time: 5 minutes
Cooking time: 7 minutes
Servings: 4

Ingredients:
- 4 tortillas
- 4 tablespoons butter, softened
- 6 ounces rotisserie chicken, cooked and shredded
- 1 cup zucchini, shredded
- ⅓ cup mayonnaise
- 2 tablespoons mustard
- 1 cup parmesan cheese, grated

Directions:
Spread the butter on the tortillas, place them in your air fryer's basket, and heat them up at 400 degrees F for 3 minutes. In a bowl, mix the chicken, zucchini, mayo, and mustard; stir. Divide the mixture between the tortillas, sprinkle with cheese, roll them, and place in your air fryer's basket. Continue to cook at 400 degrees F for 4 minutes more. Serve right away, and enjoy!

Nutrition: calories 212, fat 8, fiber 8, carbs 9, protein 4

Kale Sandwich

Preparation time: 5 minutes
Cooking time: 6 minutes
Servings: 1

Ingredients:

- 1 teaspoon olive oil
- 2 cups kale, torn
- A pinch of salt and black pepper
- 2 tablespoons pumpkin seeds
- 1 small shallot, chopped
- 1½ tablespoons mayonnaise
- 1 avocado slice
- 1 English muffin, halved

Directions:

Heat up your air fryer with the oil at 360 degrees F. Add kale, salt, pepper, pumpkin seeds, and shallots; toss. Cover and cook for 6 minutes, shaking halfway. Spread the mayo on the English muffin halves, add the avocado slice on one half, then add the kale mix, and top with the other muffin half. Serve and enjoy.

Nutrition: calories 162, fat 4, fiber 7, carbs 9, protein 4

Breakfast Pancakes

Preparation time: 10 minutes
Cooking time: 20 minutes
Servings: 4

Ingredients:

- 1¾ cups white flour
- 2 tablespoons sugar
- 2 teaspoons baking powder
- ¼ teaspoon vanilla extract
- 2 teaspoons cinnamon powder
- 1¼ cups milk
- 1 egg, whisked
- 1 cup apple, peeled, cored and chopped
- Cooking spray

Directions:

In a bowl, mix all ingredients (except cooking spray) and stir until you obtain a smooth batter. Grease your air fryer's pan with the cooking spray, and pour in ¼ of the batter; spread it into the pan. Cover and cook at 360 degrees F for 5 minutes, flipping it halfway. Repeat steps 2 and 3 with ¼ of the batter 3 more times, and then serve the pancakes right away.

Nutrition: calories 172, fat 4, fiber 4, carbs 8, protein 3

Tofu and Quinoa Bowls

Preparation time: 10 minutes
Cooking time: 15 minutes
Servings: 4

Ingredients:
- 12 ounces firm tofu, cubed
- 3 tablespoons maple syrup
- ¼ cup soy sauce
- 2 tablespoons olive oil
- 2 tablespoons lime juice
- 1 pound fresh romanesco, torn
- 3 carrots, chopped
- 1 red bell pepper, chopped
- 8 ounces baby spinach, torn
- 2 cups red quinoa, cooked

Directions:
In your air fryer, mix the tofu with the oil, maple syrup, soy sauce, and lime juice; toss. Cook at 370 degrees F for 15 minutes, shaking halfway, and transfer to a bowl. Add romanesco, carrots, spinach, bell peppers, and quinoa; toss and then divide between bowls. Serve and enjoy.

Nutrition: calories 209, fat 7, fiber 6, carbs 8, protein 4

Black Bean Burritos

Preparation time: 10 minutes
Cooking time: 9 minutes
Servings: 2

Ingredients:
- 2 cups canned black beans, drained
- A drizzle of olive oil
- ½ red bell pepper, sliced
- 1 small avocado, peeled, pitted and sliced
- 2 tablespoons mild salsa
- Salt and black pepper to taste
- ⅛ cup mozzarella cheese, shredded
- 2 tortillas

Directions:
Grease your air fryer with the oil; then add the beans, bell peppers, salsa, salt, and pepper. Cover and cook at 400 degrees F for 6 minutes. Arrange the tortillas on a working surface, and divide the bean mixture, avocado, and cheese on each; roll the burritos. Put them in your air fryer, and cook at 300 degrees F for 3 minutes more. Divide between plates and serve.

Nutrition: calories 189, fat 3, fiber 7, carbs 12, protein 5

Veggie and Tofu Casserole

Preparation time: 10 minutes
Cooking time: 25 minutes
Servings: 2
Ingredients:

- 1 yellow onion, chopped
- 1 teaspoon garlic, minced
- 1 teaspoon olive oil
- 1 carrot, chopped
- 2 celery stalks, chopped
- ½ cup white mushrooms, chopped
- ½ cup red bell pepper, chopped
- Salt and black pepper to taste
- 1 teaspoon oregano, dried
- ½ teaspoon cumin, ground
- 7 ounces firm tofu, cubed
- 1 tablespoon lemon juice
- 2 tablespoons water
- ½ cup quinoa, already cooked
- 2 tablespoons cheddar cheese, grated

Directions:

Heat up a pan with the oil over medium heat. Add the garlic and onion, stir, and sauté for 3 minutes. Add bell peppers, celery, carrots, salt, pepper, mushrooms, oregano, and cumin; stir. Cook for 5-6 minutes more and remove from the heat. In your food processor, place the tofu, cheese, lemon juice, quinoa, and water; blend. Add the tofu mixture over the sautéed veggies and toss. Pour everything into your air fryer's pan and cook at 350 degrees F for 15 minutes. Divide between plates and serve.

Nutrition: calories 230, fat 11, fiber 7, carbs 14, protein 5

Yam Pudding

Preparation time: 5 minutes
Cooking time: 8 minutes
Servings: 4
Ingredients:

- 16 ounces canned candied yams, drained
- ½ teaspoon cinnamon powder
- ¼ teaspoon allspice, ground
- ½ cup coconut sugar
- 2 eggs, whisked
- 2 tablespoons heavy cream
- ½ cup maple syrup
- Cooking spray

Directions:

In a bowl, mix the yams, cinnamon, and all spice; mash with a fork. Grease your air fryer with cooking spray and heat it up to 400 degrees F. Then spread the yams mixture on the bottom. In another bowl, mix the eggs, cream, and maple syrup, then add to the air fryer; cover and cook for 8 minutes. Divide into bowls and serve.

Nutrition: calories 251, fat 11, fiber 7, carbs 9, protein 5

Breakfast Cauliflower Mix

Preparation time: 5 minutes
Cooking time: 20 minutes
Servings: 4

Ingredients:

- 1 big cauliflower head, stems discarded, florets separated and steamed
- 2 tablespoons olive oil
- Salt and black pepper to taste
- 1 tablespoon hot paprika
- 4 ounces sour cream

Directions:
In a pan that fits your air fryer, mix all ingredients and stir well. Put the pan in your air fryer and cook at 360 degrees F for 20 minutes. Divide into bowls and serve; enjoy!

Nutrition: calories 150, fat 3, fiber 2, carbs 10, protein 3

Easy Mushroom Fritters

Preparation time: 2 hours
Cooking time: 11 minutes
Servings: 8

Ingredients:

- 4 ounces mushrooms, chopped
- 1 red onion, chopped
- Salt and black pepper to taste
- ¼ teaspoon nutmeg, ground
- 2 tablespoons olive oil
- 1 tablespoon panko breadcrumbs
- 10 ounces milk

Directions:
Heat up a pan with 1 tablespoon of the oil over medium-high heat, add the onions and mushrooms, and stir / sauté for 3 minutes. Add the milk, salt, pepper, and nutmeg; stir. Remove the mixture from heat and set aside for 2 hours. In a bowl, mix the remaining 1 tablespoon of the oil with the panko and stir. Take 1 tablespoon of the mushroom mixture, roll in breadcrumbs, flatten with your palms, and put it in your air fryer's basket. Repeat step 5 with the rest of the mushroom mixture and breadcrumbs, and then cook the fritters at 400 degrees F for 8 minutes. Divide between plates and serve.

Nutrition: calories 202, fat 8, fiber 1, carbs 11, protein 6

Tofu and Bell Peppers Breakfast

Preparation time: 5 minutes
Cooking time: 10 minutes
Servings: 8

Ingredients:

- 1 yellow bell pepper, cut into strips
- 1 orange bell pepper, cut into strips
- 1 green bell pepper, cut into strips
- Salt and black pepper to taste
- 3 ounces firm tofu, crumbled
- 1 green onion, chopped
- 2 tablespoons parsley, chopped

Directions:
In a pan that fits your air fryer, place the bell pepper strips and mix. Then add all remaining ingredients, toss, and place the pan in the air fryer. Cook at 400 degrees F for 10 minutes. Divide between plates and serve.

Nutrition: calories 135, fat 2, fiber 2, carbs 8, protein 3

Stuffed Peppers

Preparation time: 5 minutes
Cooking time: 8 minutes
Servings: 8

Ingredients:

- 8 small bell peppers, tops cut off and seeds removed
- 1 tablespoon avocado oil
- Salt and black pepper to taste
- 3½ ounces feta cheese, cubed

Directions:
In a bowl, mix the cheese, salt, pepper, and the oil; toss. Stuff the peppers with the cheese. Place the peppers in your air fryer's basket and cook at 400 degrees F for 8 minutes. Divide the peppers between plates, serve, and enjoy!

Nutrition: calories 210, fat 2, fiber 1, carbs 6, protein 5

Peppers and Lettuce Salad

Preparation time: 5 minutes
Cooking time: 10 minutes
Servings: 4

Ingredients:

- 1 tablespoon lime juice
- 4 red bell peppers
- 1 lettuce head, torn
- Salt and black pepper to taste
- 3 tablespoons heavy cream
- 2 tablespoons olive oil
- 2 ounces rocket leaves

Directions:
Place the bell peppers in your air fryer's basket and cook at 400 degrees F for 10 minutes. Remove the peppers, peel, cut them into strips, and put them in a bowl. Add all remaining ingredients, toss, and serve.

Nutrition: calories 200, fat 5, fiber 3, carbs 7, protein 6

Breakfast Spinach Pie

Preparation time: 15 minutes
Cooking time: 19 minutes
Servings: 4

Ingredients:

- 7 ounces white flour
- 7 ounces spinach, torn
- 2 tablespoons olive oil
- 2 eggs, whisked
- 2 tablespoons milk
- 3 ounces mozzarella cheese, crumbled
- Salt and black pepper to taste
- 1 red onion, chopped

Directions:
In your food processor, mix the flour with 1 tablespoon of the oil, eggs, milk, salt, and pepper; pulse, then transfer to a bowl. Knead the mixture a bit, cover, and keep in the fridge for 10 minutes. Heat up a pan with the remaining 1 tablespoon of oil over medium heat, and then add all remaining ingredients. Stir, cook for 4 minutes, and remove from heat. Divide the dough into 4 pieces, roll each piece, and place in the bottom of a ramekin. Divide the spinach mixture between the ramekins, place them in your air fryer's basket, and cook at 360 degrees F for 15 minutes. Serve and enjoy!

Nutrition: calories 200, fat 12, fiber 2, carbs 13, protein 5

Eggplant and Zucchini Breakfast Mix

Preparation time: 10 minutes
Cooking time: 45 minutes
Servings: 4

Ingredients:

- 8 ounces eggplant, sliced
- 8 ounces zucchini, sliced
- 8 ounces bell peppers, chopped
- 2 garlic cloves, minced
- 5 tablespoons olive oil
- 2 yellow onions, chopped
- 8 ounces tomatoes, cut into quarters
- Salt and black pepper to taste

Directions:
Heat up a pan that fits your air fryer with half of the oil over medium heat. Add the eggplant, salt, and pepper. Stir, cook for 5 minutes, and then transfer to a bowl. Heat up the pan with 1 tablespoon of oil, add the zucchini and the bell peppers, cook for 4 minutes, and then add to the eggplant pieces. Heat up the pan with the remaining oil, add onions, stir, and sauté for 3 minutes. Add the tomatoes, garlic, and if desired, more salt and pepper; stir.Transfer the pan to your air fryer and cook at 300 degrees F for 30 minutes. Divide mixture between plates and serve right away.

Nutrition: calories 210, fat 1, fiber 3, carbs 14, protein 6

Herbed Tomatoes Breakfast Mix

Preparation time: 5 minutes
Cooking time: 20 minutes
Servings: 2

Ingredients:

- 1 pound cherry tomatoes, halved
- A drizzle of olive oil
- Salt and black pepper to taste
- 1 teaspoon cilantro, chopped
- 1 teaspoon basil, chopped
- 1 teaspoon oregano, chopped
- 1 teaspoon rosemary, chopped
- 1 cucumber, chopped
- 1 spring onion, chopped

Directions:
Grease the tomatoes with the oil, season with salt and pepper, and place them in your air fryer's basket. Cook the tomatoes at 320 degrees F for 20 minutes, and then transfer them to a bowl. Add all remaining ingredients, toss, and serve.

Nutrition: calories 140, fat 2, fiber 3, carbs 8, protein 4

Simple Pumpkin Oatmeal

Preparation time: 5 minutes
Cooking time: 20 minutes
Servings: 4

Ingredients:
- 1½ cups milk
- ½ cup pumpkin puree
- 1 teaspoon pumpkin pie spice
- 3 tablespoons sugar
- ½ cup steel cut oats

Directions:
In your air fryer's pan, mix all ingredients. Stir, cover, and cook at 360 degrees F for 20 minutes. Divide into bowls and serve.

Nutrition: calories 141, fat 4, fiber 7, carbs 8, protein 5

Apple Oatmeal

Preparation time: 5 minutes
Cooking time: 15 minutes
Servings: 6

Ingredients:
- 3 cups almond milk
- 2 apples, cored, peeled and chopped
- 1¼ cups steel cut oats
- ½ teaspoon cinnamon powder
- ¼ teaspoon nutmeg, ground
- ¼ teaspoon allspice, ground
- ¼ teaspoon ginger powder
- ¼ teaspoon cardamom, ground
- 2 teaspoons vanilla extract
- 2 teaspoons sugar
- Cooking spray

Directions:
Spray your air fryer with cooking spray, add all ingredients, and stir. Cover and cook at 360 degrees F for 15 minutes. Divide into bowls and serve.

Nutrition: calories 212, fat 5, fiber 7, carbs 14, protein 5

Carrot Oatmeal

Preparation time: 5 minutes
Cooking time: 15 minutes
Ingredients: 4

Ingredients:

- 2 cups almond milk
- ½ cup steel cut oats
- 1 cup carrots, shredded
- 1 teaspoon cardamom, ground
- 2 teaspoons sugar
- Cooking spray

Directions:
Spray your air fryer with cooking spray, add all ingredients, toss, and cover. Cook at 365 degrees F for 15 minutes. Divide into bowls and serve.

Nutrition: calories 172, fat 7, fiber 4, carbs 14, protein 5

Strawberry Oatmeal

Preparation time: 5 minutes
Cooking time: 10 minutes
Servings: 4

Ingredients:

- 1 cup strawberries, chopped
- 1 cup steel cut oats
- 1 cup almond milk
- 2 tablespoons sugar
- ½ teaspoon vanilla extract
- Cooking spray

Directions:
Spray your air fryer with cooking spray and then add all ingredients; toss and cover. Cook at 365 degrees F for 10 minutes. Divide into bowls and serve.

Nutrition: calories 172, fat 6, fiber 8, carbs 11, protein 5

Beans Oatmeal

Preparation time: 5 minutes
Cooking time: 15 minutes
Servings: 2

Ingredients:
- 1 cup steel cut oats
- 2 tablespoons canned kidney beans, drained
- 2 red bell peppers, chopped
- 4 tablespoons heavy cream
- Salt and black pepper to taste
- ¼ teaspoon cumin, ground

Directions:
Heat up your air fryer at 360 degrees F and add all ingredients; stir. Cover and cook for 15 minutes. Divide into bowls, serve, and enjoy!

Nutrition: calories 203, fat 4, fiber 6, carbs 12, protein 4

Apple Bran Granola

Preparation time: 5 minutes
Cooking time: 15 minutes
Servings: 4

Ingredients:
- ½ cup granola
- ½ cup bran flakes
- 2 green apples, cored, peeled and roughly chopped
- ¼ cup apple juice
- ⅛ cup maple syrup
- 2 tablespoons butter
- 1 teaspoon cinnamon powder

Directions:
In your air fryer, mix all ingredients. Toss, cover, and cook at 365 degrees F for 15 minutes. Divide into bowls and serve; enjoy!

Nutrition: calories 208, fat 6, fiber 9, carbs 14, protein 3

Air Fryer Lunch Recipes

Greek Sandwiches

Preparation time: 5 minutes
Cooking time: 6 minutes
Servings: 4

Ingredients:
- ⅓ cup barbecue sauce
- 2 tablespoons honey
- 8 bacon slices, cooked and cut into thirds
- 2 red bell peppers, sliced
- 3 pita pockets, halved
- 1¼ cups lettuce, torn
- 2 tomatoes, sliced

Directions:
In a bowl, mix the barbecue sauce with honey, whisk, and then brush the bacon and bell peppers with this mix. Place the bacon and bell peppers in your air fryer and cook at 350 degrees F for 6 minutes, shaking once. Stuff pita pockets with the bacon and bell peppers mix, and then add tomatoes and lettuce. Garnish with the rest of the barbecue sauce and honey, serve, and enjoy!

Nutrition: calories 206, fat 6, fiber 9, carbs 14, protein 5

Chicken and Mushroom Pie

Preparation time: 10 minutes
Cooking time: 10 minutes
Servings: 4

Ingredients:
- 1 large chicken breast, boneless, skinless and cubed
- 1 carrot, chopped
- 1 yellow onion, chopped
- 6 white mushrooms, chopped
- 1 teaspoon soy sauce
- Salt and black pepper to taste
- 1 teaspoon Italian seasoning
- ½ teaspoon garlic powder
- 1 teaspoon Worcestershire sauce
- 1 tablespoon white flour
- 1 tablespoon milk
- 2 puff pastry sheets
- 2 tablespoons olive oil

Directions:
Heat up a pan with half of the oil over medium-high heat, and then add the carrots and onions; stir and cook for 2 minutes. Add the chicken, mushrooms, salt, soy sauce, pepper, Italian seasoning, garlic powder, Worcestershire sauce, flour, and milk. Stir really well and remove from the heat. Place 1 puff pastry sheet on the bottom of your air fryer's pan, add the chicken mix, and top with the other puff pastry sheet. Brush the pastry with the rest of the oil, and then place the pan in the fryer; cook at 360 degrees F for 8 minutes. Slice, serve, and enjoy.

Nutrition: calories 270, fat 5, fiber 7, carbs 14, protein 5

Chicken Pizza Rolls

Preparation time: 10 minutes
Cooking time: 30 minutes
Servings: 4

Ingredients:

- 2 teaspoons olive oil
- 1 yellow onion, sliced
- 2 chicken breasts, skinless, boneless and sliced
- Salt and black pepper to taste
- 1 tablespoon Worcestershire sauce
- 14 ounces pizza dough
- 1½ cups parmesan cheese, grated
- ½ cup tomato sauce

Directions:
Preheat your air fryer at 400 degrees F, and add the onion and half of olive oil. Fry for 8 minutes, shaking the fryer halfway. Add the chicken, Worcestershire sauce, salt and pepper; toss and fry for 8 minutes more, stirring once, and then transfer to a bowl. Roll the pizza dough on a working surface and shape into a rectangle. Spread the cheese all over, then the chicken and onion mix, then the tomato sauce. Roll the dough, place it in your air fryer's basket, and brush the roll with the rest of the oil. Cook at 370 degrees F for 14 minutes, flipping the roll halfway. Slice your roll and serve.

Nutrition: calories 270, fat 8, fiber 17, carbs 16, protein 6

Chinese Pork Bites

Preparation time: 5 minutes
Cooking time: 12 minutes
Servings: 4

Ingredients:

- 2 eggs
- 2 pounds pork stew meat, cubed
- 1 cup cornstarch
- 1 teaspoon sesame oil
- Salt and black pepper to taste
- ¼ teaspoon Chinese five spice
- 3 tablespoons olive oil

Directions:
In a bowl, add the Chinese spice, salt, pepper, and cornstarch; mix well. In another bowl, mix the eggs and sesame oil; whisk. Dredge the pork cubes in the cornstarch mix, then dip them in the egg mix. Place the pork cubes in your air fryer, drizzle all over with the olive oil, and cook at 360 degrees F for 12 minutes. Divide into bowls and, if desired, serve with a side salad… enjoy!

Nutrition: calories 270, fat 8, fiber 12, carbs 16, protein 5

Old Bay Chicken Wings

Preparation time: 5 minutes
Cooking time: 45 minutes
Servings: 4

Ingredients:

- 3 pounds chicken wings
- ½ cup butter, melted
- 1 tablespoon Old Bay seasoning
- ¾ cup potato starch
- 1 teaspoon lemon juice

Directions:
In a bowl, mix the chicken wings with the starch and Old Bay seasoning, toss, and then place the pieces in your air fryer's basket. Cook at 360 degrees F for 35 minutes, shaking the fryer from time to time. Increase temperature to 400 degrees F, and cook chicken wings for 10 minutes more. Divide the wings between plates and serve with the melted butter mixed with the lemon juice drizzled all over.

Nutrition: calories 261, fat 6, fiber 8, carbs 18, protein 13

Dijon Hot Dogs

Preparation time: 5 minutes
Cooking time: 8 minutes
Servings: 2

Ingredients:

- 2 hot dog buns
- 2 hot dogs
- 1 tablespoon Dijon mustard
- 2 tablespoons parmesan cheese, grated

Directions:
Put hot dogs in preheated air fryer and cook them at 390 degrees F for 5 minutes. Place the hot dogs into the buns, spread the mustard all over, and sprinkle with the parmesan. Air fry the hot dogs at 390 degrees F for 3 minutes more. Serve and enjoy!

Nutrition: calories 251, fat 7, fiber 8, carbs 16, protein 7

Lentils Lunch Cakes

Preparation time: 10 minutes
Cooking time: 10 minutes
Servings: 2

Ingredients:

- 1 cup canned yellow lentils, drained
- 1 hot chili pepper, chopped
- 1 teaspoon ginger, grated
- ½ teaspoon turmeric powder
- 1 teaspoon garam masala
- 1 teaspoon baking powder
- Salt and black pepper to taste
- 2 teaspoons olive oil
- ⅓ cup water
- ½ cup cilantro, chopped
- 1½ cups baby spinach, chopped
- 4 garlic cloves, minced
- ¾ cup yellow onion, chopped

Directions:

In your blender, add all ingredients and blend well. From the mixture, shape 2 medium cakes. Place the lentils cakes in your preheated air fryer at 400 degrees F and cook for 10 minutes. Place lentils cakes on plates, serve, and enjoy.

Nutrition: calories 182, fat 2, fiber 8, carbs 16, protein 4

Beef Meatballs and Sauce

Preparation time: 10 minutes
Cooking time: 15 minutes
Servings: 4

Ingredients:

- 1 pound lean ground beef
- 1 red onion, chopped
- 2 garlic cloves, minced
- 1 egg yolk
- ¼ cup panko breadcrumbs
- Salt and black pepper to taste
- 1 tablespoon olive oil
- 16 ounces tomato sauce

Directions:

In a bowl, mix all ingredients except for the tomato sauce and olive oil. Stir well and then shape into medium-sized meatballs. Grease the meatballs with oil, place them in your air fryer, and cook at 400 degrees F for 10 minutes. Heat up a pan over medium heat; add the tomato sauce and heat it up for 2 minutes. Add the meatballs, toss a bit, and cook for 3 minutes more. Divide the meatballs between plates and serve.

Nutrition: calories 270, fat 8, fiber 9, carbs 16, protein 4

Beef Meatball Sandwiches

Preparation time: 10 minutes
Cooking time: 22 minutes
Servings: 4

Ingredients:

- 3 baguettes, sliced halfway
- 14 ounces beef, minced
- 7 ounces tomato sauce
- 1 yellow onion, chopped
- 1 egg, whisked
- 1 tablespoon breadcrumbs
- 2 tablespoons parmesan cheese, grated
- 1 tablespoon oregano, chopped
- 1 tablespoon olive oil
- Salt and black pepper to taste
- 1 teaspoon fresh basil, chopped

Directions:
In a bowl, mix all ingredients except the tomato sauce, oil, and baguettes; stir and then shape into medium-sized meatballs. Heat up your air fryer with the oil at 375 degrees F, add the meatballs, and cook them for 12 minutes, flipping them halfway. Add the tomato sauce, and cook for 10 minutes more. Divide the meatballs and sauce on half of the baguette halves, top with the other baguette halves, and serve.

Nutrition: calories 280, fat 9, fiber 6, carbs 16, protein 15

Cod Fillets and Kale Salad

Preparation time: 10 minutes
Cooking time: 10 minutes
Servings: 2

Ingredients:

- 2 black cod fillets, boneless
- 2 tablespoons olive oil + 1 teaspoon
- Salt and black pepper to taste
- 1 fennel bulb, thinly sliced
- 1 cup grapes, halved
- 3 cups kale leaves, shredded
- ½ cup pecans
- 2 teaspoons balsamic vinegar

Directions:
Put the fish in your air fryer's basket, and add salt and pepper. Drizzle 1 teaspoon of the olive oil over the fish, and cook at 400 degrees F for 10 minutes. Divide fish between plates. In a bowl, mix the fennel, grapes, kale, pecans, vinegar, and 2 tablespoons of oil; toss. Divide the salad next to the fish, serve, and enjoy.

Nutrition: calories 240, fat 4, fiber 2, carbs 15, protein 12

Simple Lunch Turkey

Preparation time: 10 minutes
Cooking time: 1 hour
Servings: 6

Ingredients:
- 1 whole turkey breast
- 2 teaspoons olive oil
- ½ teaspoon sweet paprika
- 1 teaspoon thyme, dried
-
- Salt and black pepper to taste
- 1 tablespoon butter, melted
- 2 tablespoons mustard
- ¼ cup maple syrup

Directions:
Brush the turkey breast with the oil, and then season with salt, pepper, paprika, and thyme; rub seasoning into turkey breast. Place the turkey in your air fryer and cook at 350 degrees F for 25 minutes. Flip the turkey breast and cook for 12 minutes more. Flip again and cook another 12 minutes. In a bowl, mix the butter, mustard, and maple syrup; whisk. Brush the turkey breast with the maple syrup mix and cook for another 5 minutes. Transfer the meat to a cutting board, slice, and, if desired, serve with a side salad.
Nutrition: calories 230, fat 13, fiber 3, carbs 16, protein 11

Cod Meatballs

Preparation time: 10 minutes
Cooking time: 12 minutes
Servings: 4

Ingredients:
- 3 tablespoons fresh cilantro, minced
- 1 pound cod, skinless and chopped
- 1 yellow onion, chopped
- 1 egg
- Salt and black pepper to taste
- 2 garlic cloves, minced
- ½ teaspoon sweet paprika
- ¼ cup panko breadcrumbs
- ½ teaspoon oregano, ground
- A drizzle of olive oil

Directions:
In your food processor, mix all ingredients except the oil; blend, and then shape medium-sized meatballs out of this mix. Place the meatballs in your air fryer's basket, grease them with oil, and cook at 320 degrees F for 12 minutes, shaking halfway. Divide the meatballs between plates and, if desired, serve with a side salad.
Nutrition: calories 230, fat 9, fiber 3, carbs 10, protein 15

Beef and Potato Stew

Preparation time: 10 minutes
Cooking time: 25 minutes
Servings: 4

Ingredients:

- 2 pounds beef stew meat, cubed
- 1 carrot, sliced
- 4 gold potatoes, cubed
- Salt and black pepper to taste
- 1 quart beef stock
- ½ teaspoon smoked paprika
- A handful of cilantro, chopped
- 4 tablespoons Worcestershire sauce

Directions:

In a pan that fits your air fryer, mix all the ingredients except the cilantro and,; toss. Place in your air fryer and cook at 375 degrees F for 25 minutes. Divide into bowls, sprinkle the cilantro on top and serve right away.

Nutrition: calories 250, fat 8, fiber 1, carbs 20, protein 17

Shrimp Pasta

Preparation time: 10 minutes
Cooking time: 15 minutes
Servings: 4

Ingredients:

- 5 ounces spaghetti, cooked
- 8 ounces shrimp, peeled and deveined
- Salt and black pepper to taste
- 5 garlic cloves, minced
- 1 teaspoon chili powder
- 1 tablespoon butter, melted
- 2 tablespoons olive oil

Directions:

Put 1 tablespoon of the oil, along with the butter, in your air fryer. Preheat the air fryer at 350 degrees F, add the shrimp, and cook for 10 minutes. Add all other ingredients, including the remaining 1 tablespoon of oil, toss, and cook for 5 minutes more. Divide between plates, serve, and enjoy.

Nutrition: calories 270, fat 7, fiber 4, carbs 15, protein 6

Cheese Ravioli

Preparation time: 5 minutes
Cooking time: 5 minutes
Servings: 6

Ingredients:
- 15 ounces cheese ravioli
- 10 ounces marinara sauce
- 1 teaspoon butter, melted
- 1 cup buttermilk
- 2 cups breadcrumbs
- ¼ cup cheddar cheese, grated

Directions:
Put the buttermilk in one bowl, and the breadcrumbs in another. Dip each ravioli in buttermilk, then in breadcrumbs. Put the ravioli in your air fryer's basket, brush them with the melted butter, and cook at 400 degrees F for 5 minutes. Divide the ravioli between plates, sprinkle the cheddar cheese on top, and serve.

Nutrition: calories 260, fat 12, fiber 4, carbs 14, protein 11

Cod Curry

Preparation time: 10 minutes
Cooking time: 15 minutes
Servings: 4

Ingredients:
- 4 cod fillets, skinless, boneless and cubed
- 1½ cups milk, heated up
- 2 teaspoons curry paste
- 2 tablespoons cilantro, chopped
- 2 teaspoons ginger, grated
- Salt and black pepper to taste

Directions:
In a bowl, mix the milk, curry paste, ginger, salt, and pepper; whisk. Put the fish in a pan that fits your air fryer, and then add the milk and curry mix; toss gently. Place the pan in the fryer and cook at 400 degrees F for 15 minutes, shaking halfway. Divide the curry into bowls, sprinkle the cilantro on top, and serve.

Nutrition: calories 260, fat 8, fiber 3, carbs 13, protein 9

Chicken Lunch Casserole

Preparation time: 15 minutes
Cooking time: 25 minutes
Servings: 6

Ingredients:
- 2 tablespoons butter, melted
- 1 cup yogurt
- 12 ounces cream cheese, softened
- 2 cups chicken meat, cooked and cubed
- 2 teaspoons curry powder
- 4 scallions, chopped
- 6 ounces Monterey jack cheese, grated
- ¼ cup cilantro, chopped
- ½ cup almonds, sliced
- Salt and black pepper to taste
- ½ cup chutney

Directions:
In a baking dish that fits your air fryer, add all ingredients except the Monterey jack cheese; mix well. Sprinkle the Monterey jack cheese all over chicken mixture, put the dish in your air fryer, and cook at 350 degrees F for 25 minutes. Divide between plates and serve.

Nutrition: calories 280, fat 10, fiber 2, carbs 24, protein 15

Creamy Potato Lunch

Preparation time: 10 minutes
Cooking time: 17 minutes
Servings: 4

Ingredients:
- 4 gold potatoes, cut into medium wedges
- Salt and black pepper to taste
- 2 eggs
- ¼ cup sour cream
- 1 teaspoon olive oil
- 1½ teaspoons sweet paprika
- 1 teaspoon garlic powder
- ½ teaspoon Cajun seasoning

Directions:
In a bowl, mix the eggs with the sour cream, paprika, garlic powder, Cajun seasoning, salt, and pepper; whisk well. Take a pan that fits your air fryer and grease with the oil. Arrange the potatoes on the bottom of the pan, and spread the sour cream mix all over. Place the pan in the fryer and cook at 370 degrees F for 17 minutes. Divide between plates and serve.

Nutrition: calories 290, fat 8, fiber 2, carbs 15, protein 7

Chinese Beef and Cabbage Bowls

Preparation time: 10 minutes
Cooking time: 10 minutes
Servings: 4

Ingredients:

- ½ pound sirloin steak, cut into strips
- 1 tablespoon olive oil
- 1 teaspoon soy sauce
- 2 cups green cabbage, shredded
- 1 yellow bell pepper, chopped
- 2 green onions, chopped
- 2 garlic cloves, minced
- Salt and black pepper to taste

Directions:

In a pan that fits your air fryer, mix the cabbage, salt, pepper, and oil; toss. Put the pan in your air fryer and cook at 370 degrees F for 4 minutes. Add the steak, green onions, bell peppers, soy sauce, and garlic; then toss, cover, and cook for another 6 minutes. Divide into bowls and serve.

Nutrition: calories 262, fat 9, fiber 8, carbs 14, protein 11

Veggie Pudding

Preparation time: 10 minutes
Cooking time: 30 minutes
Servings: 6

Ingredients:

- 1 tablespoon butter, softened
- 2 cups corn
- 1 yellow onion, chopped
- ¼ cup celery, chopped
- 2 red bell peppers, chopped
- 1 teaspoon thyme, chopped
- 4 tablespoons cheddar cheese, grated
- 2 teaspoons garlic, minced
- Salt and black pepper to taste
- ½ cup heavy cream
- 1½ cups milk
- 3 eggs, whisked
- 3 cups bread, cubed

Directions:

Use the butter to grease a baking dish that fits your air fryer. Add all other ingredients—except the cheddar cheese—and toss. Sprinkle the cheese all over, place the dish in the fryer, and cook at 360 degrees F for 30 minutes. Divide between plates, serve, and enjoy.

Nutrition: calories 286, fat 10, fiber 2, carbs 16, protein 11

Coconut Zucchini Mix

Preparation time: 5 minutes
Cooking time: 16 minutes
Servings: 8

Ingredients:
- 1 cup veggie stock
- 2 tablespoons olive oil
- 8 zucchinis, cut in medium wedges
- 2 yellow onions, chopped
- 1 cup coconut cream
- Salt and black pepper to taste
- 1 tablespoon soy sauce
- ¼ teaspoon thyme, dried
- ¼ teaspoon rosemary, dried
- ½ teaspoon basil, chopped

Directions:
Take a pan that fits your air fryer and grease it with the oil. Add all other ingredients to the pan, and toss. Place the pan in the fryer and cook at 360 degrees F for 16 minutes. Divide the mix between plates, serve, and enjoy.

Nutrition: calories 181, fat 4, fiber 4, carbs 10, protein 5

Simple Chicken, Kale and Mushroom Mix

Preparation time: 5 minutes
Cooking time: 20 minutes
Servings: 6

Ingredients:
- 1 bunch kale, torn
- Salt and black pepper to taste
- 2 tablespoons chicken stock
- ¼ cup tomato sauce
- 1 cup chicken breast, skinless, boneless, cooked and shredded
- 1½ cups shiitake mushrooms, roughly sliced

Directions:
In a pan that fits your air fryer, mix all ingredients and then toss. Place the pan in the fryer and cook at 350 degrees F for 20 minutes. Divide between plates and serve.

Nutrition: calories 210, fat 7, fiber 2, carbs 14, protein 5

Chicken and Beans Casserole

Preparation time: 10 minutes
Cooking time: 20 minutes
Servings: 6

Ingredients:
- 3 cups chicken breast, skinless, boneless, cooked and shredded
- 24 ounces canned black beans, drained and rinsed
- ½ cup cilantro, chopped
- 6 kale leaves, chopped
- ½ cup green onions, chopped
- 2 cups salsa
- A drizzle of olive oil
- 2 teaspoons chili powder
- 2 teaspoons cumin, ground
- 3 cups mozzarella cheese, shredded
- 1 tablespoon garlic powder

Directions:
Take a baking dish that fits your air fryer and grease it with the oil. Add all other ingredients—except the cheese—to the baking dish; then sprinkle the cheese all over. Place the dish in the air fryer and cook at 350 degrees F for 20 minutes. Divide between plates, serve, and enjoy!

Nutrition: calories 285, fat 12, fiber 6, carbs 22, protein 15

Cod and Warm Tomato Mix

Preparation time: 10 minutes
Cooking time: 12 minutes
Servings: 2

Ingredients:
- 4 tablespoons butter, softened
- 1 fennel bulb, sliced
- 2 tablespoons dill, chopped
- 8 cherry tomatoes, halved
- 2 cod fillets, boneless
- Salt and black pepper to taste
- ¼ cup vermouth, dry

Directions:
Divide the butter onto 2 parchment paper pieces. Place the fennel, tomatoes, dill, salt, pepper, and the vermouth in a bowl and toss a bit; then divide between the 2 parchment papers as well. Top this mix with the cod fillets and fold the packets. Place the packets in your preheated air fryer and cook at 400 degrees F for 12 minutes. Unwrap the packets, place on plates, serve, and enjoy!

Nutrition: calories 200, fat 9, fiber 2, carbs 9, protein 12

Chicken and Cauliflower Bake

Preparation time: 5 minutes
Cooking time: 25 minutes
Servings: 4

Ingredients:
- 2 chicken breasts, skinless, boneless and cubed
- 1 tablespoon olive oil
- 1 cup cauliflower florets
- 1 cup tomato sauce
- 1 teaspoon sweet paprika
- Salt and black pepper to taste

Directions:
In a baking dish that fits your air fryer, mix all ingredients. Place the dish in the fryer and bake at 370 degrees F for 25 minutes. Divide between plates and serve.

Nutrition: calories 270, fat 8, fiber 12, carbs 17, protein 12

Japanese Pork Mix

Preparation time: 10 minutes
Cooking time: 15 minutes
Servings: 2

Ingredients:
- ¼ pound pork tenderloin, cubed
- 2 ginger slices, minced
- 3 garlic cloves, minced
- ¼ cup soy sauce
- ¼ cup mirin
- ⅛ cup sake
- ½ teaspoon olive oil
- ⅛ cup water
- 2 tablespoons sugar
- 1 tablespoon cornstarch mixed with 2 tablespoons water

Directions:
In pan that fits your air fryer, mix all ingredients and toss. Place the pan in the fryer and cook at 370 degrees F for 15 minutes. Divide into bowls and serve.

Nutrition: calories 290, fat 7, fiber 9, carbs 17, protein 9

Sea Bass Stew

Preparation time: 10 minutes
Cooking time: 20 minutes
Servings: 4

Ingredients:

- 5 ounces white rice
- 2 ounces peas
- 1 red bell pepper, chopped
- 14 ounces white wine
- 3 ounces water

- 1½ pounds sea bass fillets, skinless, boneless and cubed
- 4 shrimp
- Salt and black pepper to taste
- 1 tablespoon olive oil

Directions:

In your air fryer's pan, mix all ingredients and toss. Place the pan in your air fryer and cook at 400 degrees F for 20 minutes, stirring halfway. Divide into bowls, serve, and enjoy.

Nutrition: calories 280, fat 12, fiber 2, carbs 16, protein 11

Bourbon Lunch Burger

Preparation time: 10 minutes
Cooking time: 30 minutes
Servings: 2

Ingredients:

- 2 tablespoons brown sugar
- 1 tablespoon bourbon
- 3 maple bacon strips, halved
- 1 pound lean ground beef
- 1 tablespoon onion, chopped
- 2 tablespoons barbecue sauce
- A pinch of salt and black pepper
- A pinch of salt and black pepper
- 2 Colby jack cheese slices
- 2 Kaiser rolls

For the sauce:

- 2 tablespoons mayonnaise
- 2 tablespoons barbecue sauce
- ¼ teaspoon sweet paprika

Directions:

In a bowl, mix the brown sugar with the bourbon and whisk. Place the bacon strips in your air fryer's basket, brush them with the bourbon mix, and cook at 390 degrees F for 4 minutes on each side. Meanwhile, in a bowl, mix the beef with 2 tablespoons of barbecue sauce, salt, pepper, and onions; stir, and then shape 2 burgers out of this mix. Place the burgers in your air fryer's basket and cook them at 370 degrees F for 20 minutes, flipping them halfway. Top each burger with a Colby jack cheese slice and leave them in the fryer for 1-2 minutes more. In a bowl, mix all sauce ingredients and stir well. Spread this sauce on the inside of the Kaiser rolls, place the burgers on the rolls, top with the bourbon bacon, and serve.

Nutrition: calories 251, fat 14, fiber 8, carbs 16, protein 8

Air Fryer Lamb

Preparation time: 10 minutes
Cooking time: 30 minutes
Servings: 4

Ingredients:
- 1 tablespoon olive oil
- 1 garlic clove, minced
- 2 tablespoons macadamia nuts
- 1 tablespoon breadcrumbs
- 1 tablespoon rosemary, chopped
- 1 egg, whisked
- 1½ pounds rack of lamb
- Salt and black pepper to taste

Directions:
In a bowl, mix the oil and garlic; whisk. Brush the rack of lamb with this mix, and season with salt and pepper. In a bowl (can use same as for oil and garlic), mix the egg with salt and pepper. In another bowl, mix the breadcrumbs and rosemary; stir. Dip the lamb in the egg and then in the breadcrumbs, place it in your air fryer's basket, and cook at 400 degrees F for 30 minutes. Serve right away, and enjoy!

Nutrition: calories 251, fat 8, fiber 6, carbs 16, protein 9

Lunch Broccoli Mix

Preparation time: 5 minutes
Cooking time: 20 minutes
Servings: 4

Ingredients:
- 2 broccoli heads, florets separated
- 2 teaspoons sweet paprika
- Juice of ½ lemon
- 1 tablespoon olive oil
- Salt and black pepper to taste
- 1 tablespoon sesame seeds
- 3 garlic cloves, minced
- ½ cup bacon, cooked and crumbled

Directions:
In your air fryer's pan, mix all ingredients except the bacon, toss, cover, and cook at 360 degrees F for 15 minutes. Add the bacon and cook for 5 more minutes. Divide between plates and serve.

Nutrition: calories 251, fat 7, fiber 4, carbs 9, protein 5

Lunch Tomato and Okra Stew

Preparation time: 5 minutes
Cooking time: 20 minutes
Servings: 5

Ingredients:

- 1 cup okra, sliced
- 1 red bell pepper, chopped
- 2 garlic cloves, minced
- 3 celery ribs, chopped
- 1 yellow onion, chopped
- 20 ounces canned tomatoes, roughly cubed
- ½ cup veggie stock
- Salt and black pepper to taste
- ½ teaspoon sweet paprika

Directions:
In your air fryer, mix all ingredients, cover, and cook at 360 degrees F for 20 minutes. Divide into bowls and serve; enjoy!

Nutrition: calories 251, fat 9, fiber 5, carbs 14, protein 4

Veggie Stew

Preparation time: 10 minutes
Cooking time: 20 minutes
Servings: 6

Ingredients:

- 2 tomatoes, roughly chopped
- 2 yellow onions, roughly chopped
- 4 zucchinis, halved lengthwise and sliced
- 1 eggplant, cubed
- 1 teaspoon oregano, dried
- 1 teaspoon sugar
- 2 green bell peppers, cut into strips
- 2 garlic cloves, minced
- 1 teaspoon basil, dried
- Salt and black pepper to taste
- 7 ounces tomato paste
- 2 tablespoons olive oil
- 2 tablespoons cilantro, chopped

Directions:
In a pan that fits your air fryer, combine all ingredients—except the cilantro—and toss well. Place the pan in the air fryer and cook the stew at 360 degrees F for 20 minutes. Divide the stew into bowls, sprinkle the cilantro on top, and serve.

Nutrition: calories 200, fat 4, fiber 5, carbs 16, protein 6

Black Beans Lunch Mix

Preparation time: 10 minutes
Cooking time: 25 minutes
Servings: 6

Ingredients:

- 30 ounces canned black beans, drained
- 1 cup veggie stock
- 1 tablespoon olive oil
- 1 yellow onion, chopped
- 1 jalapeno, chopped
- 1 red bell pepper, chopped
- 2 garlic cloves, minced
- 1 teaspoon ginger, grated
- ½ teaspoon cumin, ground
- ½ teaspoon oregano, dried
- Salt and black pepper to taste
- ½ teaspoon allspice, ground
- 3 cups brown rice, cooked

Directions:

In a pan that fits your air fryer, mix all ingredients except the rice; toss. Place the pan in your air fryer and cook at 360 degrees F for 25 minutes. Add the rice and toss again. Divide into bowls, serve, and enjoy.

Nutrition: calories 200, fat 8, fiber 4, carbs 8, protein 3

Beans and Quinoa Stew

Preparation time: 10 minutes
Cooking time: 15 minutes
Servings: 4

Ingredients:

- 30 ounces canned black beans, drained
- 1 cup quinoa
- 30 ounces canned tomatoes, chopped
- 2 sweet potatoes, cubed
- 1 yellow onion, chopped
- 1 green bell pepper, chopped
- 1 tablespoon chili powder
- 2 teaspoons cumin, ground
- ¼ teaspoon sweet paprika
- Salt and black pepper to taste
- 2 tablespoons cocoa powder

Directions:

Place all ingredients in a pan that fits your air fryer, and stir well. Then put the pan in the air fryer and cook at 400 degrees F for 15 minutes. Divide into bowls and serve right away.

Nutrition: calories 200, fat 8, fiber 4, carbs 9, protein 4

Green Beans Lunch Stew

Preparation time: 5 minutes
Cooking time: 15 minutes
Servings: 4

Ingredients:
- 1 pound green beans, halved
- 4 carrots, sliced
- 1 yellow onion, chopped
- 1 tablespoon thyme, chopped
- 3 tablespoons tomato paste
- Salt and black pepper to taste
- 4 garlic cloves, minced

Directions:
In a pan that fits your air fryer, place all the ingredients and toss until combined. Place the pan in the air fryer and cook at 365 degrees F for 15 minutes. Divide the stew into bowls and serve.

Nutrition: calories 200, fat 8, fiber 2, carbs 8, protein 6

Chickpeas Stew

Preparation time: 5 minutes
Cooking time: 15 minutes
Servings: 4

Ingredients:
- 15 ounces canned chickpeas, drained
- 1 red onion, chopped
- 2 garlic cloves, minced
- 1 tablespoon olive oil
- 2 teaspoons sweet paprika
- Salt and black pepper to taste
- 28 ounces canned tomatoes, chopped

Directions:
Place all ingredients into a pan that fits your air fryer, and stir / mix well. Then put the pan in the air fryer and cook at 370 degrees F for 15 minutes. Divide the stew into bowls and serve.

Nutrition: calories 200, fat 8, fiber 3, carbs 15, protein 5

Lentils Lunch Curry

Preparation time: 5 minutes
Cooking time: 15 minutes
Servings: 6

Ingredients:
- 2 cups canned lentils, drained
- 1 tablespoon garlic, minced
- 10 ounces baby spinach
- 15 ounces canned tomatoes, drained and chopped
- 1 teaspoon ginger, grated
- 1 red onion, chopped
- ½ teaspoon cumin, ground
- 2 teaspoons sugar
- ½ teaspoon coriander, ground
- 1 tablespoon lemon juice
- 2 tablespoons curry paste
- 2 tablespoons cilantro, chopped
- Salt and black pepper to taste

Directions:
In a pan that fits your air fryer, mix all the ingredients except the cilantro and lemon juice; stir. Place the pan in the air fryer and cook at 370 degrees F for 15 minutes. Add the cilantro and the lemon juice, and toss. Divide into bowls, serve, and enjoy!

Nutrition: calories 251, fat 6, fiber 8, carbs 16, protein 7

Delicious Eggplant Stew

Preparation time: 5 minutes
Cooking time: 15 minutes
Servings: 4

Ingredients:
- 1 red onion, chopped
- 25 ounces canned tomatoes, chopped
- 2 teaspoons cumin, ground
- 1 teaspoon sweet paprika
- Salt and black pepper to taste
- 3 eggplants, cubed
- 2 red bell peppers, cubed
- 1 tablespoon cilantro, chopped
- Juice of ½ lime

Directions:
In a pan that fits your air fryer, add all ingredients except the lime juice and cilantro and mix. Place the pan in the fryer and cook at 370 degrees F for 15 minutes. Then add the lime juice and cilantro, and stir. Divide the stew between bowls and serve.

Nutrition: calories 251, fat 7, fiber 6, carbs 14, protein 9

Simple Okra Lunch Salad

Preparation time: 5 minutes
Cooking time: 15 minutes
Servings: 4

Ingredients:
- 15 ounces okra, sliced
- 2 cups corn
- 1 red bell pepper, chopped
- 1 red onion, chopped
- 2 garlic cloves, minced
- 1 teaspoon sweet paprika
- 1 teaspoon thyme, dried
- 1 teaspoon oregano, dried
- 1 teaspoon rosemary, dried
- Salt and black pepper to taste
- 12 ounces canned tomatoes, chopped

Directions:
Place all ingredients in a pan that fits your air fryer; toss well. Place the pan in the fryer and cook at 370 degrees F for 15 minutes. Divide the salad into bowls and serve cold.

Nutrition: calories 181, fat 7, fiber 4, carbs 9, protein 6

Lunch Green Beans Casserole

Preparation time: 5 minutes
Cooking time: 20 minutes
Servings: 4

Ingredients:
- 1 teaspoon olive oil
- 3 cups green beans, trimmed and halved
- 2 red chilies, chopped
- ½ teaspoon black mustard seeds
- ½ cup yellow onion, chopped
- ¼ teaspoon fenugreek seeds
- ½ teaspoon turmeric powder
- Salt and black pepper to taste
- 2 tomatoes, chopped
- 3 garlic cloves, minced
- 2 teaspoons tamarind paste
- 2 teaspoons coriander powder
- 1 tablespoon cilantro, chopped

Directions:
Use the oil to grease a heat-proof dish that fits your air fryer, then add all the ingredients and toss. Place the dish in the fryer and cook at 370 degrees F for 20 minutes. Divide between plates, serve, and enjoy.

Nutrition: calories 251, fat 7, fiber 7, carbs 14, protein 6

Italian Chicken Mix

Preparation time: 10 minutes
Cooking time: 20 minutes
Servings: 4

Ingredients:
- 1 cup chicken stock
- Salt and black pepper to taste
- 8 chicken drumsticks, bone-in
- 1 teaspoon garlic powder
- 1 yellow onion, chopped
- 28 ounces canned tomatoes, chopped
- 1 teaspoon oregano, dried
- ½ cup black olives, pitted and sliced

Directions:
Add all the ingredients to a baking dish that fits your air fryer and toss. Place the dish in your air fryer and cook at 380 degrees F for 20 minutes. Divide the mix into bowls and serve.

Nutrition: calories 261, fat 7, fiber 4, carbs 9, protein 15

Honey Chicken Thighs

Preparation time: 10 minutes
Cooking time: 25 minutes
Servings: 4

Ingredients:
- 1½ pounds chicken thighs, skinless and boneless
- Salt and black pepper to taste
- ¾ cup honey
- ½ cup chicken stock
- 2 teaspoons sweet paprika
- ½ teaspoon basil, dried

Directions:
In a bowl, make a mixture with all the ingredients except the chicken thighs; whisk well. Add the chicken thighs to this mix and toss until the wings are coated. Put the chicken in your air fryer's basket and cook at 380 degrees F for 25 minutes. Divide between plates, serve, and enjoy.

Nutrition: calories 200, fat 7, fiber 6, carbs 16, protein 14

Lunch Baby Carrots Mix

Preparation time: 5 minutes
Cooking time: 15 minutes
Servings: 4

Ingredients:
- 16 ounces baby carrots
- Salt and black pepper to taste
- 2 tablespoons butter, melted
- 4 ounces chicken stock
- 2 tablespoons dill, chopped

Directions:
In a pan that fits your air fryer, mix all the ingredients and toss. Place the pan in the fryer and cook at 380 degrees F for 15 minutes. Divide between bowls and serve.

Nutrition: calories 100, fat 3, fiber 3, carbs 8, protein 8

Quinoa and Spinach Pesto Mix

Preparation time: 5 minutes
Cooking time: 15 minutes
Servings: 4

Ingredients:
- 1 cup quinoa, cooked
- 3 tablespoons chicken stock
- ¾ cup jarred spinach pesto
- 1 green apple, chopped
- ¼ cup celery, chopped
- Salt and black pepper to taste

Directions:
Mix all the ingredients in a pan that fits your air fryer; toss. Place the pan in your fryer and cook at 370 degrees F for 15 minutes. Divide into bowls and serve right away.

Nutrition: calories 200, fat 6, fiber 9, carbs 11, protein 6

Greek Quinoa Salad

Preparation time: 10 minutes
Cooking time: 15 minutes
Servings: 6

Ingredients:
- 1½ cups quinoa, cooked
- 1 tablespoon olive oil
- Salt and black pepper to taste
- 1 tablespoon balsamic vinegar
- 1 cup cherry tomatoes, halved
- 2 green onions, chopped
- 2 ounces feta cheese, crumbled
- ½ cup Kalamata olives, pitted and chopped
- A handful of basil leaves, chopped
- A handful of parsley leaves, chopped

Directions:
Add all the ingredients—except the feta cheese—to a pan that fits your air fryer and toss. Sprinkle the cheese on top, and then place the pan in the air fryer and cook at 370 degrees F for 15 minutes. Divide into bowls and serve.

Nutrition: calories 251, fat 8, fiber 4, carbs 14, protein 7

Quinoa and Spinach Salad

Preparation time: 10 minutes
Cooking time: 15 minutes
Servings: 4

Ingredients:
- ½ cups quinoa, cooked
- 1 red bell pepper, chopped
- 3 celery stalks, chopped
- Salt and black pepper to taste
- 4 cups spinach, torn
- 2 tomatoes, chopped
- ½ cup chicken stock
- ½ cup black olives, pitted and chopped
- ½ cup feta cheese, crumbled
- ⅓ cup basil pesto
- ¼ cup almonds, sliced

Directions:
In a pan that fits your air fryer, combine the quinoa, bell peppers, celery, salt, pepper, spinach, tomatoes, chicken stock, olives, and basil pesto. Sprinkle the almonds and the cheese on top, and then place the pan in the air fryer and cook at 380 degrees F for 15 minutes. Divide between plates and serve.

Nutrition: calories 251, fat 8, fiber 5, carbs 20, protein 6

Chicken and Cabbage Curry

Preparation time: 10 minutes
Cooking time: 30 minutes
Servings: 3

Ingredients:
- 1½ pounds chicken thighs, boneless
- 1 green cabbage, shredded
- 1 tablespoon olive oil
- Salt and black pepper to taste
- 2 chili peppers, chopped
- 1 yellow onion, chopped
- 4 garlic cloves, minced
- 3 tablespoons curry paste
- ½ cup white wine
- 10 ounces coconut milk
- 1 tablespoon soy sauce

Directions:
Use the oil to grease a baking dish and then add all ingredients; toss. Place the pan in the fryer and cook at 380 degrees F for 30 minutes. Divide between bowls and serve.

Nutrition: calories 251, fat 11, fiber 4, carbs 17, protein 5

Potatoes and Calamari Stew

Preparation time: 10 minutes
Cooking time: 16 minutes
Servings: 4

Ingredients:
- 10 ounces calamari, cut into strips
- 1 cup red wine
- 1 cup water
- 2 tablespoons olive oil
- 2 teaspoons pepper sauce
- 1 tablespoon hot sauce
- 1 tablespoon sweet paprika
- 1 tablespoon tomato sauce
- Salt and black pepper to taste
- ½ bunch cilantro, chopped
- 2 garlic cloves, minced
- 1 yellow onion, chopped
- 4 potatoes, cut into quarters.

Directions:
Place all the ingredients in a pan that fits the air fryer and toss. Put the pan in the fryer and cook at 400 degrees F for 16 minutes. Divide the stew between bowls and serve.

Nutrition: calories 251, fat 8, fiber 2, carbs 9, protein 15

Salsa Chicken Mix

Preparation time: 10 minutes
Cooking time: 17 minutes
Servings: 4

Ingredients:

- 4 chicken breasts, skinless, boneless and cubed
- 2 tablespoons olive oil
- 1 onion, chopped
- 3 garlic cloves, minced
- 16 ounces jarred chunky salsa
- 20 ounces canned tomatoes, peeled and chopped
- Salt and black pepper to taste
- 2 tablespoons parsley, dried
- 1 teaspoon garlic powder
- 1 tablespoon chili powder
- 12 ounces canned black beans, drained

Directions:
Place all ingredients into a pan that fits your air fryer and toss. Put the pan in the fryer and cook at 380 degrees F for 17 minutes. Divide into bowls, serve, and enjoy.

Nutrition: calories 251, fat 7, fiber 8, carbs 17, protein 20

Corn Stew

Preparation time: 5 minutes
Cooking time: 15 minutes
Servings: 4

Ingredients:

- 2 leeks, chopped
- 2 tablespoons butter, melted
- 2 tomatoes, cubed
- 2 garlic cloves, minced
- 4 cups corn
- ¼ cup chicken stock
- 1 teaspoon olive oil
- 4 tarragon sprigs, chopped
- Salt and black pepper to taste
- 1 tablespoon chives, chopped

Directions:
Grease a pan with the oil, and then add all the ingredients and toss. Place the pan in the fryer and cook at 370 degrees F for 15 minutes. Divide the stew between bowls and serve.

Nutrition: calories 265, fat 6, fiber 4, carbs 16, protein 11

Butternut Squash Stew

Preparation time: 10 minutes
Cooking time: 15 minutes
Servings: 5

Ingredients:
- 1½ pounds butternut squash, cubed
- ½ cup green onions, chopped
- 3 tablespoons butter, melted
- ½ cup carrots, chopped
- ½ cup celery, chopped
- 1 garlic clove, minced
- ½ teaspoon Italian seasoning
- 15 ounces canned tomatoes, chopped
- Salt and black pepper to taste
- ⅛ teaspoon red pepper flakes, dried
- 1 cup quinoa, cooked
- 1½ cups heavy cream
- 1 cup chicken meat, already cooked and shredded

Directions:
Place all the ingredients in a pan that fits your air fryer and toss. Put the pan into the fryer and cook at 400 degrees F for 15 minutes. Divide the stew between bowls, serve, and enjoy.

Nutrition: calories 200, fat 4, fiber 4, carbs 15, protein 8

Air Fryer Side Dish Recipes

Creamy Potatoes

Preparation time: 5 minutes
Cooking time: 20 minutes
Servings: 4

Ingredients:

- 2 gold potatoes, cut into medium pieces
- 1 tablespoon olive oil
- Salt and black pepper to taste
- 3 tablespoons sour cream

Directions:
In a baking dish that fits your air fryer, mix all the ingredients and toss. Place the dish in the air fryer and cook at 370 degrees F for 20 minutes. Divide between plates and serve as a side dish.

Nutrition: calories 201, fat 8, fiber 9, carbs 18, protein 5

Sweet Potato Side Salad

Preparation time: 5 minutes
Cooking time: 20 minutes
Servings: 2

Ingredients:

- 2 sweet potatoes, peeled and cut into wedges
- Salt and black pepper to taste
- 2 tablespoons avocado oil
- ½ teaspoon curry powder
- ¼ teaspoon coriander, ground
- 4 tablespoons mayonnaise
- ½ teaspoon cumin, ground
- A pinch of ginger powder
- A pinch of cinnamon powder

Directions:
In your air fryer's basket, mix the sweet potato wedges with salt, pepper, coriander, curry powder, and the oil; toss well. Cook at 370 degrees F for 20 minutes, flipping them once. Transfer the potatoes to a bowl, then add the mayonnaise, cumin, ginger and the cinnamon. Toss and serve as a side salad.

Nutrition: calories 190, fat 5, fiber 8, carbs 14, protein 5

Mayo Brussels Sprouts

Preparation time: 5 minutes
Cooking time: 15 minutes
Servings: 4

Ingredients:

- 1 pound Brussels sprouts, trimmed and halved
- Salt and black pepper to taste
- 6 teaspoons olive oil
- ½ cup mayonnaise
- 2 tablespoons garlic, minced

Directions:

In your air fryer, mix the sprouts, salt, pepper, and oil; toss well. Cook the sprouts at 390 degrees F for 15 minutes. Transfer them to a bowl; then add the mayo and the garlic and toss. Divide between plates and serve as a side dish.

Nutrition: calories 202, fat 6, fiber 8, carbs 12, protein 8

Green Beans and Shallots

Preparation time: 5 minutes
Cooking time: 25 minutes
Servings: 4

Ingredients:

- 1½ pounds green beans, trimmed
- Salt and black pepper to taste
- ½ pound shallots, chopped
- ¼ cup walnuts, chopped
- 2 tablespoons olive oil

Directions:

In your air fryer, mix all ingredients and toss. Cook at 350 degrees F for 25 minutes. Divide between plates and serve as a side dish.

Nutrition: calories 182, fat 3, fiber 6, carbs 11, protein 5

Italian Mushroom Mix

Preparation time: 5 minutes
Cooking time: 15 minutes
Servings: 4

Ingredients:
- 1 pound button mushrooms, halved
- 2 tablespoons parmesan cheese, grated
- 1 teaspoon Italian seasoning
- A pinch of salt and black pepper
- 3 tablespoons butter, melted

Directions:
In a pan that fits your air fryer, mix all the ingredients and toss. Place the pan in the air fryer and cook at 360 degrees F for 15 minutes. Divide the mix between plates and serve.

Nutrition: calories 194, fat 4, fiber 4, carbs 14, protein 7

Simple Eggplant Mix

Preparation time: 10 minutes
Cooking time: 10 minutes
Servings: 4

Ingredients:
- 8 baby eggplants, cubed
- Salt and black pepper to taste
- 1 green bell pepper, chopped
- 1 tablespoon tomato sauce
- 1 bunch coriander, chopped
- ½ teaspoon garlic powder
- 1 tablespoon olive oil
- 1 yellow onion, chopped

Directions:
In a pan that fits your air fryer, combine all the ingredients and toss. Place the pan in the fryer and cook at 370 degrees F for 10 minutes. Divide between plates and serve as a side dish.

Nutrition: calories 210, fat 5, fiber 7, carbs 12, protein 5

Creamy Tomatoes

Preparation time: 5 minutes
Cooking time: 6 minutes
Servings: 4

Ingredients:
- 1 pound cherry tomatoes, halved
- Salt and black pepper to taste
- A drizzle of olive oil
- 1 cup heavy cream
- ½ tablespoon Creole seasoning

Directions:
In a pan that fits your air fryer, combine all the ingredients and toss. Place the pan in the fryer and cook at 400 degrees F for 6 minutes. Divide between plates and serve.

Nutrition: calories 174, fat 5, fiber 7, carbs 11, protein 4

Brussels Sprouts Side Dish Delight

Preparation time: 10 minutes
Cooking time: 25 minutes
Servings: 8

Ingredients:
- 3 pounds Brussels sprouts, halved
- 1 teaspoon olive oil
- 1 pound bacon, chopped
- Salt and black pepper to taste
- 4 tablespoons butter, melted
- 3 shallots, chopped
- 1 cup milk
- 2 cups heavy cream
- ¼ teaspoon nutmeg, ground
- 3 tablespoons prepared horseradish

Directions:
Preheat your air fryer at 370 degrees F, and add oil, bacon, salt, pepper, and Brussels sprouts; toss. Then add butter, shallots, heavy cream, milk, nutmeg, and horseradish; toss again and cook for 25 minutes. Divide between plates and serve as a side dish. Enjoy!

Nutrition: calories 214, fat 5, fiber 8, carbs 12, protein 5

Simple Zucchini Fries

Preparation time: 10 minutes
Cooking time: 12 minutes
Servings: 4

Ingredients:
- 2 small zucchinis, cut into fries
- 2 teaspoons olive oil
- Salt and black pepper to taste
- 2 eggs, whisked
- 1 cup breadcrumbs
- ½ cup white flour

Directions:
In a bowl, mix the flour, salt, and pepper; stir. Put the breadcrumbs in another bowl and whisk the eggs in a third bowl. Dredge the zucchini fries in the flour, then in the eggs, and then in the breadcrumbs. Use the oil to grease your air fryer and heat to 400 degrees F. Add the zucchini fries and cook for 12 minutes; serve as a side dish.

Nutrition: calories 182, fat 6, fiber 3, carbs 11, protein 5

Mixed Peppers Side Dish

Preparation time: 5 minutes
Cooking time: 20 minutes
Servings: 4

Ingredients:
- 1 tablespoon smoked paprika
- 1 tablespoon olive oil
- 4 red bell peppers, cut into medium strips
- 4 green bell peppers, cut in medium strips
- 1 red onion, chopped
- Salt and black pepper to taste

Directions:
In your air fryer, mix all ingredients, toss, and cook at 360 degrees F for 20 minutes. Divide the peppers between plates and serve as a side dish.

Nutrition: calories 172, fat 5, fiber 4, carbs 7, protein 4

French Carrots Mix

Preparation time: 5 minutes
Cooking time: 20 minutes
Servings: 4

Ingredients:

- 1 pound baby carrots, trimmed
- 2 teaspoons olive oil
- 1 teaspoon herbs de Provence
- 2 tablespoons lime juice

Directions:
In a bowl, mix all ingredients well and then transfer to your air fryer's basket. Cook at 320 degrees F for 20 minutes. Divide between plates and serve as a side dish.

Nutrition: calories 132, fat 4, fiber 3, carbs 11, protein 4

Maple Parsnips Mix

Preparation time: 5 minutes
Cooking time: 40 minutes
Servings: 6

Ingredients:

- 2 pounds parsnips, roughly cubed
- 2 tablespoons maple syrup
- 1 tablespoon cilantro, chopped
- 1 tablespoon olive oil

Directions:
Preheat your air fryer at 360 degrees F, then add the oil and heat it up. Add the other ingredients, toss, and cook for 40 minutes. Divide between plates and serve as a side dish.

Nutrition: calories 174, fat 5, fiber 3, carbs 11, protein 4

Simple Air Fried Beets

Preparation time: 5 minutes
Cooking time: 35 minutes
Servings: 6

Ingredients:
- 3 pounds small beets, trimmed and halved
- 4 tablespoons maple syrup
- 1 tablespoon olive oil

Directions:
Heat up your air fryer at 360 degrees F, then add the oil and heat it up. Add the beets and maple syrup, toss, and cook for 35 minutes. Divide the beets between plates and serve as a side dish.

Nutrition: calories 171, fat 4, fiber 2, carbs 13, protein 3

Cauliflower and Mushroom Risotto

Preparation time: 10 minutes
Cooking time: 40 minutes
Servings: 6

Ingredients:
- 2 tablespoons olive oil
- 4 tablespoons soy sauce
- 3 garlic cloves, minced
- 1 tablespoon ginger, grated
- Juice of 1 lime
- 1 cauliflower head, riced
- 10 ounces water chestnuts, drained
- 15 ounces mushrooms, chopped
- 1 egg, whisked

Directions:
In your air fryer, mix the cauliflower rice, oil, soy sauce, garlic, ginger, lime juice, chestnuts, and mushrooms. Stir, cover, and cook at 350 degrees F for 20 minutes. Add the egg, toss, and cook at 360 degrees F for 20 minutes more. Divide between plates and serve.

Nutrition: calories 182, fat 3, fiber 2, carbs 8, protein 4

Moroccan Eggplant Side Dish

Preparation time: 5 minutes
Cooking time: 20 minutes
Servings: 6

Ingredients:

- 1½ pounds eggplant, cubed
- 1 tablespoon olive oil
- 1 teaspoon onion powder
- 1 teaspoon sumac
- 2 teaspoons za'atar
- Juice of 1 lime

Directions:

Place all ingredients in your air fryer and mix well. Cook at 370 degrees F for 20 minutes. Divide between plates and serve as a side dish.

Nutrition: calories 182, fat 4, fiber 7, carbs 12, protein 4

Air Fried Cauliflower Mix

Preparation time: 5 minutes
Cooking time: 20 minutes
Servings: 4

Ingredients:

- 1 tablespoon olive oil
- 1 cauliflower head, florets separated
- 3 garlic cloves, minced
- Juice of 1 lime
- 1 tablespoon black sesame seeds

Directions:

Heat up your air fryer at 350 degrees F, then add the oil and heat it up. Add the cauliflower, garlic, and lime juice; toss and then cook for 20 minutes. Divide between plates, sprinkle the sesame seeds on top, and serve as a side dish.

Nutrition: calories 182, fat 4, fiber 3, carbs 11, protein 4

Simple Rosemary Potatoes

Preparation time: 10 minutes
Cooking time: 30 minutes
Servings: 4

Ingredients:

- 4 potatoes, thinly sliced
- Salt and black pepper to taste
- 1 tablespoon olive oil
- 2 teaspoons rosemary, chopped

Directions:

Place all the ingredients in a bowl, mix well, and then transfer to your air fryer's basket. Cook at 370 degrees F for 30 minutes. Divide between plates and serve as a side dish.

Nutrition: calories 190, fat 4, fiber 4, carbs 14, protein 4

Parsnips and Carrots Fries

Preparation time: 5 minutes
Cooking time: 15 minutes
Servings: 4

Ingredients:

- 4 parsnips, cut into medium sticks
- 4 carrots, cut into medium sticks
- Salt and black pepper to taste
- 2 tablespoons thyme, chopped
- 2 tablespoons olive oil
- ½ teaspoon onion powder

Directions:

In a bowl, mix all ingredients and toss. Transfer the fries to your air fryer's basket and cook at 350 degrees F for 15 minutes. Divide between plates and serve as a side dish.

Nutrition: calories 160, fat 3, fiber 4, carbs 7, protein 3

Easy Mushroom Mix

Preparation time: 5 minutes
Cooking time: 15 minutes
Servings: 6

Ingredients:
- 15 ounces mushrooms, roughly sliced
- 1 red onion, chopped
- Salt and black pepper to taste
- ½ teaspoon nutmeg, ground
- 2 tablespoons olive oil
- 6 ounces canned tomatoes, chopped

Directions:
Place all ingredients in a pan that fits your air fryer and mix well. Put the pan in the fryer and cook at 380 degrees F for 15 minutes. Divide the mix between plates and serve as a side dish.

Nutrition: calories 202, fat 6, fiber 1, carbs 16, protein 4

Yellow Squash and Zucchini Mix

Preparation time: 10 minutes
Cooking time: 35 minutes
Servings: 4

Ingredients:
- 5 teaspoons olive oil
- 1 pound zucchinis, sliced
- 1 yellow squash, halved, deseeded, and cut in chunks
- Salt and white pepper to taste
- 1 tablespoon cilantro, chopped

Directions:
In a bowl, mix all the ingredients, toss well, and transfer them to your air fryer's basket. Cook for 35 minutes at 400 degrees. Divide everything between plates and serve as a side dish.

Nutrition: calories 200, fat 4, fiber 1, carbs 15, protein 4

Cheesy Mushroom Salad

Preparation time: 5 minutes
Cooking time: 15 minutes
Servings: 3

Ingredients:
- 10 large mushrooms, halved
- 1 tablespoon mixed herbs, dried
- 1 tablespoon cheddar cheese, grated
- 1 tablespoon mozzarella cheese, grated
- A drizzle of olive oil
- 2 teaspoons parsley flakes
- Salt and black pepper to taste

Directions:
Use the oil to grease a pan that fits your air fryer. Add all other ingredients and toss. Place the pan in the fryer and cook at 380 degrees F for 15 minutes. Divide between plates and serve as a side dish.

Nutrition: calories 161, fat 7, fiber 1, carbs 12, protein 6

Lime Corn

Preparation time: 5 minutes
Cooking time: 15 minutes
Servings: 2

Ingredients:
- 2 ears of corn, shucked and silk removed
- Salt and black pepper to taste
- 2 teaspoons olive oil
- Juice of 2 limes
- 2 teaspoons smoked paprika

Directions:
In a bowl, mix the salt with the pepper, oil, lime juice, and paprika and stir well. Rub the corn with this mix and put it in your air fryer's basket. Cook at 400 degrees F for 15 minutes. Divide between plates and serve.

Nutrition: calories 180, fat 7, fiber 2, carbs 12, protein 6

Garlic Potatoes

Preparation time: 5 minutes
Cooking time: 40 minutes
Servings: 4

Ingredients:

- 4 large potatoes, pricked with a fork
- Salt and black pepper to taste
- 2 tablespoons olive oil
- 1 tablespoon garlic, minced

Directions:
Place all of the ingredients in a bowl and mix well, ensuring the potatoes are coated. Put the potatoes in your air fryer's basket and cook at 400 degrees F for 40 minutes. Peel the potatoes (if desired), cut up, divide between plates, and serve as a side dish.

Nutrition: calories 173, fat 3, fiber 2, carbs 16, protein 4

Creamy Cabbage Mix

Preparation time: 10 minutes
Cooking time: 20 minutes
Servings: 2

Ingredients:

- 1 green cabbage head, shredded
- 1 yellow onion, chopped
- Salt and black pepper to taste
- 4 bacon slices, chopped
- 1 cup whipped cream

Directions:
In a pan that fits your air fryer, mix all the ingredients and stir. Place the pan in the fryer and cook at 400 degrees F for 20 minutes. Divide between plates and serve as a side dish.

Nutrition: calories 208, fat 10, fiber 4, carbs 12, protein 4

Wild Rice Mix

Preparation time: 5 minutes
Cooking time: 30 minutes
Servings: 8

Ingredients:

- 1 shallot, chopped
- 1 teaspoon garlic, minced
- 1 teaspoon olive oil
- 1½ cups wild rice
- 4 cups chicken stock
- Salt and black pepper to taste
- 1 tablespoon parsley, chopped
- ½ cup hazelnuts, toasted and chopped

Directions:
Heat up the oil in a pan that fits your air fryer over medium heat. Add the garlic and the shallots, stir, and cook for 2-3 minutes. Add the rice, stock, salt, and pepper, and stir completely. Place the pan in the air fryer and cook at 380 degrees F for 25 minutes. Add the parsley and the hazelnuts, stir, divide between plates, and serve as a side dish.

Nutrition: calories 200, fat 4, fiber 6, carbs 16, protein 4

Parsley Quinoa

Preparation time: 5 minutes
Cooking time: 18 minutes
Servings: 4

Ingredients:

- 2 cups quinoa
- 2 garlic cloves, minced
- 2 tablespoons olive oil
- Salt and black pepper to taste
- 2 teaspoons turmeric powder
- 3 cups veggie stock
- A handful of parsley, chopped

Directions:
Heat the oil up in a pan that fits your air fryer over medium heat. Add the garlic, stir, and cook for 2 minutes. Add the quinoa, salt, pepper, turmeric, and the stock; cover and cook at 360 degrees F for 16 minutes. Add the parsley, stir, and then divide between plates and serve as a side dish.

Nutrition: calories 171, fat 4, fiber 8, carbs 16, protein 7

Creamy Risotto

Preparation time: 10 minutes
Cooking time: 20 minutes
Servings: 4

Ingredients:

- 2 cups risotto rice
- 4 cups chicken stock, heated up
- 2 garlic cloves, minced
- 1 tablespoon olive oil
- 1 yellow onion, chopped
- 8 ounces mushrooms, sliced
-

- 4 ounces heavy cream
- 2 tablespoons parmesan cheese, grated
- 1 tablespoon cilantro, chopped

Directions:
Add all ingredients—except the cilantro—to a pan that fits your air fryer. Place the pan in the fryer and cook at 360 degrees F for 20 minutes. Add the cilantro, stir, divide between plates, and serve.

Nutrition: calories 261, fat 5, fiber 8, carbs 15, protein 5

Spiced Pumpkin Rice

Preparation time: 5 minutes
Cooking time: 25 minutes
Servings: 4

Ingredients:

- 2 tablespoons olive oil
- 1 small yellow onion, chopped
- 2 garlic cloves, minced
- 12 ounces risotto rice
- 4 cups chicken stock
- 6 ounces pumpkin puree

- ½ teaspoon nutmeg, ground
- ½ teaspoon ginger, grated
- ½ teaspoon cinnamon powder
- ½ teaspoon allspice
- 4 ounces heavy cream

Directions:
In a pan that fits your air fryer, heat up the oil over medium heat. Add the onion and the garlic, stir, and cook for 2 minutes. Add the nutmeg, ginger, cinnamon, and allspice; stir and cook for 1 more minute. Add the rice, stock, pumpkin puree, and the cream; stir. Place the pan in the fryer and cook at 360 degrees F for 20 minutes. Divide between plates and serve as a side dish.

Nutrition: calories 251, fat 6, fiber 8, carbs 16, protein 6

Mashed Sweet Potatoes

Preparation time: 10 minutes
Cooking time: 12 minutes
Servings: 8

Ingredients:
- 2 garlic cloves
- 3 pounds sweet potatoes, baked, peeled, and chopped
- Salt and black pepper to taste
- ½ teaspoon parsley, dried
- ¼ teaspoon sage, dried
- ½ teaspoon rosemary, dried
- ¼ cup milk
- ½ cup parmesan cheese, grated
- 2 tablespoons butter

Directions:
In a pan that fits your air fryer, combine the sweet potatoes, garlic, salt, pepper, parsley, sage, and rosemary; mix well. Place the pan in the fryer and cook at 360 degrees F for 12 minutes. Mash the potatoes, adding the milk, parmesan, and butter; stir well. Divide between plates and serve as a side dish.

Nutrition: calories 251, fat 6, fiber 5, carbs 16, protein 6

Saffron Rice

Preparation time: 5 minutes
Cooking time: 20 minutes
Servings: 6

Ingredients:
- 2 tablespoons olive oil
- ½ teaspoon saffron powder
- ½ cup onion, chopped
- 2 tablespoons milk, hot
- 1½ cups Arborio rice
- Salt and black pepper to taste
- 3½ cups chicken stock
- 1 tablespoon honey
- ⅓ cup almonds, chopped

Directions:
Add all of the ingredients to a pan that fits your air fryer. Place the pan in the fryer and cook at 360 degrees F for 20 minutes. Divide between plates and serve as a side dish.

Nutrition: calories 251, fat 4, fiber 3, carbs 13, protein 6

Mint and Cherries Rice

Preparation time: 10 minutes
Cooking time: 22 minutes
Servings: 6

Ingredients:

- 1 tablespoon apple cider vinegar
- 1 cup white rice
- 1 teaspoon lemon juice
- Salt and black pepper to taste
- 3 cups water, hot
- 1 teaspoon olive oil
- ¼ cup green onions, chopped
- 10 mint leaves, chopped
- 2 cups cherries, pitted and halved

Directions:
In a pan that fits your air fryer, add all of the ingredients and mix well. Place the pan in the fryer and cook at 370 degrees F for 22 minutes. Divide between plates and serve as a side dish.

Nutrition: calories 200, fat 5, fiber 5, carbs 9, protein 5

Broccoli Risotto

Preparation time: 10 minutes
Cooking time: 20 minutes
Servings: 4

Ingredients:

- 2 tablespoons olive oil
- Salt and black pepper to taste
- 1 broccoli head, florets separated and roughly chopped
- ½ cup parmesan cheese, grated
- 2 garlic cloves, minced
- 1 cup white rice
- 1 yellow onion, chopped
- 3 cups chicken stock, heated up
- 2 tablespoons parsley, chopped
- 1 tablespoon butter

Directions:
In a pan that fits your air fryer, mix the oil with the broccoli, salt, pepper, garlic, onions, rice, and stock; stir well. Place the pan in the air fryer and cook at 370 degrees F for 20 minutes. Add the parsley, butter, and the parmesan, and stir. Divide between plates and serve as a side dish.

Nutrition: calories 200, fat 6, fiber 5, carbs 15, protein 5

Artichoke Rice

Preparation time: 5 minutes
Cooking time: 20 minutes
Servings: 4

Ingredients:
- 1 tablespoon olive oil
- 1 cup Arborio rice
- 2 garlic cloves, minced
- 3 cups chicken stock
- 15 ounces canned artichoke hearts, chopped
- 8 ounces cream cheese
- 1 tablespoon parmesan cheese, grated
- 1½ tablespoons thyme, chopped
- Salt and black pepper to taste

Directions:
In a pan that fits your air fryer, add all the ingredients except the parmesan cheese; stir well. Place the pan in the air fryer and cook at 370 degrees F for 20 minutes. Add the parmesan, stir, divide between plates, and serve as a side dish.

Nutrition: calories 215, fat 4, fiber 6, carbs 14, protein 4

Air Fried Beans Mix

Preparation time: 10 minutes
Cooking time: 15 minutes
Servings: 4

Ingredients:
- 1 cup canned garbanzo beans, drained
- 1 cup canned cranberry beans, drained
- 1½ cups green beans, blanched
- 4 cups water
- 1 garlic clove, minced
- 2 celery stalks, chopped
- 1 bunch cilantro, chopped
- 1 small red onion, chopped
- 1 tablespoon sugar
- 5 tablespoons apple cider vinegar
- 4 tablespoons olive oil
- Salt and black pepper to taste

Directions:
In a pan that fits your air fryer, mix all ingredients except the cilantro; stir well. Place the pan in the air fryer and cook at 380 degrees F for 15 minutes. Add the cilantro, stir, divide between plates, and serve as a side dish.

Nutrition: calories 231, fat 4, fiber 6, carbs 14, protein 6

Black Beans Mix

Preparation time: 5 minutes
Cooking time: 15 minutes
Servings: 6

Ingredients:
- 1 cup canned black beans, drained
- 1 cup water
- Salt and black pepper to taste
- 1 spring onion, chopped
- 2 garlic cloves, minced
- ½ teaspoon cumin seeds

Directions:
Add all ingredients to a pan that fits your air fryer; mix well. Place the pan in the fryer and cook at 370 degrees F for 15 minutes. Divide between plates and serve as a side dish.

Nutrition: calories 265, fat 6, fiber 7, carbs 14, protein 6

Pineapple Rice

Preparation time: 5 minutes
Cooking time: 20 minutes
Servings: 6

Ingredients:
- 2 cups rice
- 4 cups chicken stock, heated up
- 1 pineapple, peeled and chopped
- Salt and black pepper to taste
- 2 teaspoons olive oil

Directions:
In a pan that fits your air fryer, place all the ingredients and toss. Insert the pan into your preheated air fryer and cook at 370 degrees F for 20 minutes. Divide between plates and serve as a side dish.

Nutrition: calories 200, fat 4, fiber 5, carbs 11, protein 4

Beans Mix

Preparation time: 10 minutes
Cooking time: 25 minutes
Servings: 6

Ingredients:

- 1 pound canned red kidney beans, drained
- Salt and black pepper to taste
- 1 teaspoon olive oil
- 1 yellow onion, chopped
- 1 celery stalk, chopped
- 4 garlic cloves, chopped
- 1 green bell pepper, chopped
- 1 teaspoon thyme, dried
- 2 green onions, minced
- 2 tablespoons tomato sauce
- 2 tablespoons parsley, minced

Directions:
Place all the ingredients—except the parsley—into a pan that fits your air fryer, and stir. Put the pan into your air fryer and cook at 370 degrees F for 25 minutes. Add the parsley, stir, divide between plates, and serve.

Nutrition: calories 161, fat 4, fiber 6, carbs 15, protein 6

Mashed Cauliflower

Preparation time: 5 minutes
Cooking time: 10 minutes
Servings: 4

Ingredients:

- 1 cauliflower, florets separated and steamed
- Salt and black pepper to taste
- ½ cup veggie stock, heated up
- ½ teaspoon turmeric powder
- 1 tablespoon butter
- 3 spring onions, chopped

Directions:
In a pan that fits your air fryer, mix the cauliflower with the stock, salt, pepper, and turmeric; then stir well. Place the pan in the fryer and cook at 360 degrees F for 10 minutes. Mash the cauliflower mixture using a potato masher, adding the butter and the spring onions. Stir, divide between plates, and serve.

Nutrition: calories 140, fat 2, fiber 6, carbs 15, protein 4

Parsnips Mash

Preparation time: 10 minutes
Cooking time: 15 minutes
Servings: 4

Ingredients:
- 4 parsnips, peeled and chopped
- Salt and black pepper to taste
- 1 yellow onion, chopped
- ¼ cup sour cream
- ½ cup chicken stock, heated up

Directions:
In a pan that fits your air fryer, place all ingredients except the sour cream; stir well. Place the pan in the air fryer and cook at 370 degrees F for 15 minutes. Mash the parsnip mixture, adding the sour cream; stir well again. Divide between plates and serve as a side dish.

Nutrition: calories 151, fat 3, fiber 6, carbs 11, protein 4

Carrot Puree

Preparation time: 10 minutes
Cooking time: 15 minutes
Servings: 4

Ingredients:
- 1½ pounds carrots, peeled and chopped
- 1 tablespoon butter, softened
- Salt and black pepper to taste
- 1 cup chicken stock, heated up
- 1 tablespoon honey
- 1 teaspoon brown sugar

Directions:
In a pan that fits your air fryer, mix the carrots with the stock, salt, pepper, and sugar; stir well. Put the pan into the fryer and cook at 370 degrees F for 15 minutes. Transfer the carrot mixture to a blender, add the butter and the honey, and pulse well. Divide between plates and serve.

Nutrition: calories 100, fat 3, fiber 3, carbs 7, protein 6

Butternut Puree

Preparation time: 5 minutes
Cooking time: 20 minutes
Servings: 4

Ingredients:

- 1 cup veggie stock
- 1 butternut squash, peeled and cut into medium chunks
- 2 tablespoons butter, melted
- 1 yellow onion, thinly sliced
- ½ teaspoon apple pie spice
- Salt and black pepper to taste

Directions:
In a pan that fits your air fryer, mix the stock, squash, onion, spice, salt, and pepper; stir well. Place the pan in the fryer and cook at 370 degrees F for 20 minutes. Transfer the squash mixture to a blender, add the butter, and pulse well. Divide between plates and serve as a side dish.

Nutrition: calories 200, fat 6, fiber 7, carbs 15, protein 5

Parmesan Asparagus Mix

Preparation time: 5 minutes
Cooking time: 10 minutes
Servings: 4

Ingredients:

- 3 garlic cloves, minced
- 1 bunch asparagus, trimmed
- 3 tablespoons butter, melted
- 3 tablespoons parmesan cheese, grated

Directions:
Mix the melted butter with the garlic, and then brush the asparagus with the mixture. Put the asparagus in the air fryer's basket, sprinkle the parmesan on top, and cook at 380 degrees F for 10 minutes. Divide the asparagus between plates and serve.

Nutrition: calories 141, fat 4, fiber 4, carbs 8, protein 3

Simple Air Fried Fennel

Preparation time: 5 minutes
Cooking time: 12 minutes
Servings: 3

Ingredients:
- 2 big fennel bulbs, sliced
- 2 tablespoons butter, melted
- A pinch of ground nutmeg
- Salt and black pepper to taste

Directions:
Place all of the ingredients into a bowl and toss. Transfer the fennel mixture to your air fryer's basket and cook at 370 degrees F for 12 minutes. Divide between plates and serve as a side dish.

Nutrition: calories 151, fat 3, fiber 6, carbs 8, protein 3

Minty Peas

Preparation time: 5 minutes
Cooking time: 12 minutes
Servings: 4

Ingredients:
- 1 pound fresh peas
- 1 green onion, sliced
- 1 tablespoon mint, chopped
- ¼ cup veggie stock
- 1 tablespoon butter, melted
- Salt and black pepper to taste

Directions:
Place all of the ingredients into a pan that fits your air fryer and mix well. Put the pan in the air fryer and cook at 370 degrees F for 12 minutes. Divide between plates and serve.

Nutrition: calories 151, fat 2, fiber 6, carbs 9, protein 5

Lemony Artichokes

Preparation time: 10 minutes
Cooking time: 25 minutes
Servings: 4

Ingredients:

- 2 medium artichokes, trimmed
- Juice of ½ lemon
- A drizzle of olive oil
- Salt to taste

Directions:
Brush the artichokes with the oil, season with salt, and put them in your air fryer's basket. Cook at 370 degrees F for 20 minutes. Divide between plates, drizzle lemon juice all over, and serve.

Nutrition: calories 151, fat 3, fiber 7, carbs 8, protein 4

Citrus Cauliflower Mix

Preparation time: 5 minutes
Cooking time: 14 minutes
Servings: 4

Ingredients:

- 2 small cauliflower heads, florets separated
- Juice of 1 orange
- A pinch of hot pepper flakes
- Salt and black pepper to taste
- 4 tablespoons olive oil

Directions:
Brush the cauliflower with the oil, then season with salt, pepper, and the pepper flakes. Transfer the cauliflower to your air fryer's basket and cook at 380 degrees F for 14 minutes. Divide between plates, drizzle orange juice all over, and serve.

Nutrition: calories 151, fat 7, fiber 4, carbs 9, protein 4

Garlicky Beets

Preparation time: 5 minutes
Cooking time: 20 minutes
Servings: 4

Ingredients:
- 3 beets, trimmed, peeled, and cut into wedges
- 1 tablespoon olive oil
- Salt and black pepper to taste
- 4 garlic cloves, minced
- 1 teaspoon lemon juice

Directions:
Place all the ingredients in a bowl and mix well. Transfer the beets to your air fryer's basket and cook at 400 degrees F for 20 minutes. Divide between plates and serve as a side dish.

Nutrition: calories 121, fat 3, fiber 5, carbs 12, protein 4

Fava Beans Mix

Preparation time: 10 minutes
Cooking time: 15 minutes
Servings: 4

Ingredients:
- 3 pounds fava beans, shelled
- 1 teaspoon olive oil
- Salt and black pepper to taste
- 4 ounces bacon, cooked and crumbled
- ½ cup white wine
- 1 tablespoon parsley, chopped

Directions:
Place all of the ingredients into a pan that fits your air fryer and mix well. Put the pan in the air fryer and cook at 380 degrees F for 15 minutes. Divide between plates and serve as a side dish.

Nutrition: calories 141, fat 3, fiber 2, carbs 12, protein 3

Simple Cabbage Mix

Preparation time: 10 minutes
Cooking time: 15 minutes
Servings: 4

Ingredients:
- 4 garlic cloves, minced
- ½ cup red onion, chopped
- 1 tablespoon olive oil
- 6 cups red cabbage, shredded
- 1 tablespoon balsamic vinegar
- 3 tablespoons applesauce
- Salt and black pepper to taste

Directions:
Heat the oil up in a pan that fits your air fryer over medium-high heat. Add the onions and the garlic, stir, and cook for 1-2 minutes. Add the cabbage, vinegar, applesauce, salt, and pepper, and toss. Place the pan in the air fryer and cook at 380 degrees F for 12 minutes. Divide the cabbage mix between plates and serve as a side dish.

Nutrition: calories 151, fat 4, fiber 4, carbs 12, protein 3

Bell Pepper and Lettuce Side Salad

Preparation time: 5 minutes
Cooking time: 15 minutes
Servings: 4

Ingredients:
- 1 tablespoon lemon juice
- 1 red bell pepper
- 1 lettuce head, torn
- Salt and black pepper to taste
- 3 tablespoons yogurt
- 2 tablespoons olive oil

Directions:
In your air fryer, place the bell pepper along with the oil, salt, and pepper; air fry at 400 degrees F for 15 minutes. Cool the bell pepper down, peel, cut it into strips and put it in a bowl. Add lettuce, lemon juice, yogurt, salt, and pepper. Toss well, and serve as a side dish.

Nutrition: calories 150, fat 1, fiber 3, carbs 3, protein 2

Cheesy Spinach

Preparation time: 5 minutes
Cooking time: 10 minutes
Servings: 4

Ingredients:
- 14 ounces spinach
- 1 tablespoon olive oil
- 2 eggs, whisked
- 2 tablespoons milk
- 3 ounces cottage cheese
- Salt and black pepper to taste
- 1 yellow onion, chopped

Directions:
In a pan that fits your air fryer, heat up the oil over medium heat, add the onions, stir, and sauté for 2 minutes. Add all other ingredients and toss. Place the pan in the air fryer and cook at 380 degrees F for 8 minutes. Divide the spinach between plates and serve as a side dish.

Nutrition: calories 180, fat 4, fiber 2, carbs 13, protein 4

Roasted Rhubarb

Preparation time: 10 minutes
Cooking time: 15 minutes
Servings: 4

Ingredients:
- 1 pound rhubarb, cut in chunks
- 2 teaspoons olive oil
- 2 tablespoons orange zest
- ½ cup walnuts, chopped
- ½ teaspoon sugar

Directions:
In your air fryer, mix all the listed ingredients, and toss. Cook at 380 degrees F for 15 minutes. Divide the rhubarb between plates and serve as a side dish.

Nutrition: calories 180, fat 4, fiber 8, carbs 12, protein 4

Herbed Potatoes Mix

Preparation time: 10 minutes
Cooking time: 30 minutes
Servings: 4

Ingredients:
- 3 large potatoes, peeled and cut into chunks
- 1 teaspoon parsley, chopped
- 1 teaspoon chives, chopped
- 1 teaspoon oregano, chopped
- 1 tablespoon garlic, minced
- Salt and black pepper to taste
- 2 tablespoons olive oil

Directions:
Mix all of the ingredients in your air fryer, and stir well. Cook at 370 degrees F for 30 minutes. Divide between plates and serve as a side dish.

Nutrition: calories 160, fat 2, fiber 3, carbs 13, protein 4

Cranberry Beans Side Salad

Preparation time: 10 minutes
Cooking time: 15 minutes
Servings: 6

Ingredients:
- 6 garlic cloves, minced
- 2½ cups canned cranberry beans, drained
- 1 yellow onion, chopped
- 2 celery ribs, chopped
- ½ teaspoon smoked paprika
- ½ teaspoon red pepper flakes
- 3 teaspoons basil, chopped
- Salt and black pepper to taste
- 25 ounces canned tomatoes, drained and chopped
- 10 ounces kale, tor

Directions:
In a pan that fits your air fryer, add all of the ingredients and mix. Place the pan in the fryer and cook at 370 degrees F for 15 minutes. Divide between plates and serve as a side salad.

Nutrition: calories 190, fat 4, fiber 4, carbs 9, protein 6

Endives and Rice Mix

Preparation time: 5 minutes
Cooking time: 20 minutes
Servings: 4

Ingredients:
- 2 scallions, chopped
- 3 garlic cloves, minced
- 1 tablespoon olive oil
- Salt and black pepper to taste
- ½ cup white rice
- 1 cup veggie stock
- 1 teaspoon chili sauce
- 4 endives, trimmed and shredded

Directions:
Take the oil and grease a pan that fits your air fryer. Add all other ingredients and toss. Place the pan in the air fryer and cook at 365 degrees F for 20 minutes. Divide everything between plates and serve as a side dish.

Nutrition: calories 200, fat 7, fiber 4, carbs 9, protein 5

Turmeric Cabbage Mix

Preparation time: 5 minutes
Cooking time: 12 minutes
Servings: 4

Ingredients:
- 1 tablespoon olive oil
- 1 big green cabbage head, shredded
- ½ cup yellow onion, chopped
- 2 teaspoons turmeric powder
- Salt and black pepper to taste
- 4 tablespoons tomato sauce

Directions:
Take the oil and grease a pan that fits your air fryer. Add all of the other ingredients and toss. Place the pan in the fryer and cook at 365 degrees F for 12 minutes. Divide between plates and serve as a side dish.

Nutrition: calories 188, fat 3, fiber 4, carbs 9, protein 7

Tomato Endives Mix

Preparation time: 5 minutes
Cooking time: 10 minutes
Servings: 4

Ingredients:

- 8 endives, trimmed
- Juice of 1 lime
- 1 tablespoon tomato sauce
- 2 tablespoons cilantro, chopped
- 1 teaspoon sugar
- Salt and black pepper to taste
- 3 tablespoons avocado oil

Directions:

1. In a bowl, mix all of the ingredients well, then transfer to your air fryer's basket.
2. Cook at 370 degrees F for 10 minutes.
3. Divide between plates and serve as a side dish.

Nutrition: calories 199, fat 6, fiber 6, carbs 9, protein 6

Mung Beans Mix

Preparation time: 10 minutes
Cooking time: 16 minutes
Servings: 3

Ingredients:

- 1 cup mung beans
- ½ teaspoon olive oil
- 1 teaspoon coriander, ground
- ½ teaspoon turmeric powder
- 1 cup veggie stock
- ½ cup red onion, chopped
- ½ teaspoon cumin seeds
- 3 tomatoes, chopped
- ½ teaspoon garam masala
- Salt and black pepper to taste
- 1 tablespoon lemon juice
- 4 garlic cloves, minced

Directions:
Place all of the ingredients into a pan that fits your air fryer and toss. Place the pan in the fryer and cook at 365 degrees F for 16 minutes. Divide the mix between plates and serve as a side dish.

Nutrition: calories 199, fat 6, fiber 4, carbs 12, protein 6

Brown Lentils Mix

Preparation time: 10 minutes
Cooking time: 15 minutes
Servings: 4

Ingredients:

- 1 cup canned brown lentils, drained
- 1 teaspoon olive oil
- 2 tomatoes, chopped
- 4 garlic cloves, minced
- 1 teaspoon ginger, grated
- ½ teaspoon turmeric powder
- ¼ teaspoon cinnamon powder
- ¼ teaspoon cardamom powder
- Salt and black pepper to taste
- 8 ounces baby spinach

Directions:
In a pan that fits your air fryer, add all of the listed ingredients and toss. Place the pan the fryer and cook at 370 degrees F for 15 minutes. Divide the lentils between plates and serve as a side dish.

Nutrition: calories 188, fat 4, fiber 8, carbs 15, protein 7

Indian Red Potatoes

Preparation time: 10 minutes
Cooking time: 20 minutes
Servings: 5

Ingredients:

- 2 pounds red potatoes, cubed
- ½ teaspoon mustard seeds
- 1 teaspoon garlic, minced
- ¼ cup veggie stock
- ½ cup mint
- ½ cup cilantro
- 1 teaspoon ginger, grated
- 2 teaspoons lime juice
- Salt and black pepper to taste

Directions:
In a blender, add the stock, mint, cilantro, ginger, lime juice, salt, and pepper; pulse well. Then place this mint mix into a pan that fits your air fryer, along with the remaining ingredients, and toss. Place the pan in the fryer and cook at 370 degrees F for 20 minutes. Divide the potatoes between plates and serve as a side dish.

Nutrition: calories 199, fat 4, fiber 7, carbs 12, protein 6

Air Fryer Snack and Appetizer Recipes

Pork Bites

Preparation time: 10 minutes
Cooking time: 15 minutes
Servings: 4

Ingredients:
- 2 teaspoons garlic powder
- 2 eggs
- Salt and black pepper to taste
- ¾ cup panko breadcrumbs
- ¾ cup coconut, shredded
- A drizzle of olive oil
- 1 pound ground pork

Directions:
In a bowl, mix coconut with panko and stir well. In another bowl, mix the pork, salt, pepper, eggs, and garlic powder, and then shape medium meatballs out of this mix. Dredge the meatballs in the coconut mix, place them in your air fryer's basket, introduce in the air fryer, and cook at 350 degrees F for 15 minutes. Serve and enjoy!

Nutrition: calories 192, fat 4, fiber 2, carbs 14, protein 6

Banana Chips

Preparation time: 5 minutes
Cooking time: 5 minutes
Servings: 8

Ingredients:
- ¼ cup peanut butter, soft
- 1 banana, peeled and sliced into 16 pieces
- 1 tablespoon vegetable oil

Directions:
Put the banana slices in your air fryer's basket and drizzle the oil over them. Cook at 360 degrees F for 5 minutes. Transfer to bowls and serve them dipped in peanut butter.

Nutrition: calories 100, fat 4, fiber 1, carbs 10, protein 4

Lemony Apple Bites

Preparation time: 5 minutes
Cooking time: 5 minutes
Servings: 4

Ingredients:
- 3 big apples, cored, peeled and cubed
- 2 teaspoons lemon juice
- ½ cup caramel sauce

Directions:
In your air fryer, mix all the ingredients; toss well. Cook at 340 degrees F for 5 minutes. Divide into cups and serve as a snack.

Nutrition: calories 180, fat 4, fiber 3, carbs 10, protein 3

Zucchini Balls

Preparation time: 10 minutes
Cooking time: 12 minutes
Servings: 8

Ingredients:
- Cooking spray
- ½ cup dill, chopped
- 1 egg
- ½ cup white flour
- Salt and black pepper to taste
- 2 garlic cloves, minced
- 3 zucchinis, grated

Directions:
In a bowl, mix all the ingredients and stir. Shape the mix into medium balls and place them into your air fryer's basket. Cook at 375 degrees F for 12 minutes, flipping them halfway. Serve them as a snack right away.

Nutrition: calories 120, fat 1, fiber 2, carbs 5, protein 3

Basil and Cilantro Crackers

Preparation time: 10 minutes
Cooking time: 16 minutes
Servings: 6

Ingredients:
- ½ teaspoon baking powder
- Salt and black pepper to taste
- 1¼ cups flour
- 1 garlic clove, minced
- 2 tablespoons basil, minced
- 2 tablespoons cilantro, minced
- 4 tablespoons butter, melted

Directions:
Add all of the ingredients to a bowl and stir until you obtain a dough. Spread this on a lined baking sheet that fits your air fryer. Place the baking sheet in the fryer at 325 degrees F and cook for 16 minutes. Cool down, cut, and serve.

Nutrition: calories 171, fat 9, fiber 1, carbs 8, protein 4

Balsamic Zucchini Slices

Preparation time: 5 minutes
Cooking time: 50 minutes
Servings: 6

Ingredients:
- 3 zucchinis, thinly sliced
- Salt and black pepper to taste
- 2 tablespoons avocado oil
- 2 tablespoons balsamic vinegar

Directions:
Add all of the ingredients to a bowl and mix. Put the zucchini mixture in your air fryer's basket and cook at 220 degrees F for 50 minutes. Serve as a snack and enjoy!

Nutrition: calories 40, fat 3, fiber 7, carbs 3, protein 7

Turmeric Carrot Chips

Preparation time: 5 minutes
Cooking time: 25 minutes
Servings: 4

Ingredients:
- 4 carrots, thinly sliced
- Salt and black pepper to taste
- ½ teaspoon turmeric powder
- ½ teaspoon chaat masala
- 1 teaspoon olive oil

Directions:
Place all ingredients in a bowl and toss well. Put the mixture in your air fryer's basket and cook at 370 degrees F for 25 minutes, shaking the fryer from time to time. Serve as a snack.

Nutrition: calories 161, fat 1, fiber 2, carbs 5, protein 3

Chives Radish Snack

Preparation time: 5 minutes
Cooking time: 10 minutes
Servings: 4

Ingredients:
- 16 radishes, sliced
- A drizzle of olive oil
- Salt and black pepper to taste
- 1 tablespoon chives, chopped

Directions:
In a bowl, mix the radishes, salt, pepper, and oil; toss well. Place the radishes in your air fryer's basket and cook at 350 degrees F for 10 minutes. Divide into bowls and serve with chives sprinkled on top.

Nutrition: calories 100, fat 1, fiber 2, carbs 4, protein 1

Lentils Snack

Preparation time: 5 minutes
Cooking time: 12 minutes
Servings: 4

Ingredients:
- 15 ounces canned lentils, drained
- ½ teaspoon cumin, ground
- 1 tablespoon olive oil
- 1 teaspoon sweet paprika
- Salt and black pepper to taste

Directions:
Place all ingredients in a bowl and mix well. Transfer the mixture to your air fryer and cook at 400 degrees F for 12 minutes. Divide into bowls and serve as a snack (or a side, or appetizer!).

Nutrition: calories 151, fat 1, fiber 6, carbs 10, protein 6

Air Fried Corn

Preparation time: 5 minutes
Cooking time: 10 minutes
Servings: 4

Ingredients:
- 2 tablespoons corn kernels
- 2½ tablespoons butter

Directions:
In a pan that fits your air fryer, mix the corn with the butter. Place the pan in the fryer and cook at 400 degrees F for 10 minutes. Serve as a snack and enjoy!

Nutrition: calories 70, fat 2, fiber 2, carbs 7, protein 3

Coconut Shrimp Snack

Preparation time: 10 minutes
Cooking time: 12minutes
Servings: 4

Ingredients:

- 12 large shrimp, deveined and peeled
- 2 eggs, whisked
- 2 cups coconut, shredded
- 1 cup white flour
- Salt and black pepper to taste

Directions:
Put the coconut in one bowl, the flour in a second one, and the eggs in a third. Season the shrimp with the salt and pepper, then dredge them in the flour, then the eggs, and then the coconut. Place the shrimp in your air fryer's basket and cook at 360 degrees F for 12 minutes, flipping them halfway. Divide the shrimp into bowls and serve as a snack (or an appetizer, or even an entrée!).

Nutrition: calories 150, fat 4, fiber 3, carbs 13, protein 4

Chicken Sticks

Preparation time: 10 minutes
Cooking time: 16 minutes
Servings: 4

Ingredients:

- ¾ cup white flour
- 1 pound chicken breast, skinless, boneless and cut in medium sticks
- 1 cup breadcrumbs
- 1 egg, whisked
- Salt and black pepper to taste
- ½ tablespoon olive oil

Directions:
Combine the flour, salt, and pepper in a bowl. Put the egg in another bowl and the breadcrumbs in a third one. Dredge the chicken pieces in the flour, then the egg, and then the breadcrumbs. Place the chicken pieces in your air fryer's basket, drizzle the oil over them, and cook at 400 degrees F for 16 minutes, flipping them halfway. Serve right away and enjoy.

Nutrition: calories 181, fat 4, fiber 7, carbs 15, protein 18

Cheesy Beef Meatballs

Preparation time: 10 minutes
Cooking time: 8 minutes
Servings: 8

Ingredients:

- 4 ounces beef meat, minced
- Salt and black pepper to taste
- 1 tablespoon breadcrumbs
- 2 tablespoons feta cheese, crumbled
- ½ tablespoon lemon peel, grated
- 1 tablespoon oregano, chopped

Directions:
Place all of the ingredients in a bowl and stir well. Shape medium meatballs out of this mix. Place the meatballs in your air fryer's basket and cook at 400 degrees F for 8 minutes. Serve as an appetizer, or even as an entrée.

Nutrition: calories 194, fat 9, fiber 2, carbs 11, protein 15

Pepper Rolls

Preparation time: 10 minutes
Cooking time: 10 minutes
Servings: 8

Ingredients:

- 1 yellow bell pepper, deseeded and halved
- 1 orange bell pepper, deseeded and halved
- Salt and black pepper to taste
- 4 ounces feta cheese, crumbled
- 1 green onion, chopped
- 2 tablespoons oregano, chopped

Directions:
Place the bell pepper halves in your air fryer's basket and cook at 400 degrees F for 10 minutes. Transfer the bell peppers to a cutting board, cool down, peel, and arrange them on a working surface. In a bowl, mix the cheese, salt, pepper, cilantro, and green onions; stir well. Spread the cheese mixture on each pepper half, roll the peppers, and secure them with toothpicks. Serve as an appetizer, or even as a great side.

Nutrition: calories 150, fat 1, fiber 2, carbs 7, protein 5

Greek Cream Cheese Balls

Preparation time: 5 minutes
Cooking time: 5 minutes
Servings: 6

Ingredients:
- 8 black olives, pitted and minced
- Salt and black pepper to taste
- 2 tablespoons basil pesto
- 14 pepperoni slices, chopped
- 4 ounces cream cheese
- 1 tablespoon basil, chopped

Directions:
In a bowl, place all of the ingredients and stir. Shape the mixture into medium balls and then place them in your lined air fryer's basket. Cook at 360 degrees F for 5 minutes. Serve as a snack.

Nutrition: calories 140, fat 1, fiber 4, carbs 8, protein 3

Minty Shrimp Mix

Preparation time: 5 minutes
Cooking time: 8 minutes
Servings: 12

Ingredients:
- 2 tablespoons olive oil
- 10 ounces shrimp, peeled and deveined
-
- 1 tablespoon mint, chopped
- ⅓ cup red wine

Directions:
In your air fryer, mix / toss all the ingredients. Cook at 390 degrees F for 8 minutes. Divide into bowls and serve as an appetizer.

Nutrition: calories 194, fat 4, fiber 2, carbs 12, protein 7

Italian Mozzarella Sticks

Preparation time: 10 minutes
Cooking time: 8 minutes
Servings: 12

Ingredients:
- 2 eggs, whisked
- Salt and black pepper to taste
- 8 mozzarella cheese strings, halved
- 1 cup parmesan cheese, grated
- 1 tablespoon Italian seasoning
- A drizzle of olive oil

Directions:
In a bowl, mix the parmesan, salt, pepper, and Italian seasoning; stir. Put the whisked eggs in another bowl. Dip the mozzarella sticks in the egg mixture, then in the parmesan mix. Dip the sticks one more time in egg and parmesan and place them in your air fryer's basket. Drizzle the oil over them, and cook at 390 degrees F for 8 minutes, flipping them halfway. Serve as an appetizer.

Nutrition: calories 200, fat 5, fiber 3, carbs 13, protein 4

Kale Crackers

Preparation time: 10 minutes
Cooking time: 20 minutes
Servings: 6

Ingredients:
- 4 cups flax seed, soaked overnight, drained and ground
- 4 bunches kale, chopped
- 1 bunch basil, chopped
- 4 garlic cloves, minced
- ⅓ cup avocado oil

Directions:
Place all ingredients in your food processor and pulse well. Spread the mixture in your air fryer's pan and cut into medium crackers. Cook in the air fryer cook at 380 degrees F for 20 minutes. Cool and serve as a snack.

Nutrition: calories 153, fat 1, fiber 2, carbs 11, protein 5

Potato Chips

Preparation time: 5 minutes
Cooking time: 12 minutes
Servings: 4

Ingredients:
- 4 potatoes, thinly sliced
- Salt and black pepper to taste
- 1 tablespoon olive oil
- Sour cream for serving

Directions:
Brush the potato slices with the oil and place them in your air fryer's basket. Cook at 400 degrees F for 12 minutes, flipping them halfway. Serve as a snack along with the sour cream.

Nutrition: calories 143, fat 4, fiber 1.5, carbs 10, protein 5

Crab Bites

Preparation time: 5 minutes
Cooking time: 12 minutes
Servings: 6

Ingredients:
- 10 crabsticks, cut into medium bites
- 2 teaspoons olive oil
- Salt and black pepper to taste

Directions:
Mix all the ingredients in your air fryer. Cook at 350 degrees F for 12 minutes. Divide into bowls and serve.

Nutrition: calories 100, fat 3, fiber 3, carbs 12, protein 5

Broccoli Bites

Preparation time: 5 minutes
Cooking time: 15 minutes
Servings: 6

Ingredients:

- 1 broccoli head, florets separated
- Salt and black pepper to taste
- 1 teaspoon olive oil
- 2 teaspoons garlic powder
- 1 teaspoon butter, melted

Directions:
Spread the broccoli florets on a lined baking sheet that fits your air fryer; then add all other ingredients and toss. Cook at 450 degrees F for 15 minutes. Divide into bowls and serve as a snack (or as a side).

Nutrition: calories 138, fat 2, fiber 2, carbs 11, protein 2

Sausage Bites

Preparation time: 10 minutes
Cooking time: 15 minutes
Servings: 9

Ingredients:

- 5 ounces ground sausage meat
- Salt and black pepper to taste
- ½ teaspoon garlic, minced
- 1 yellow onion, chopped
- 3 tablespoons breadcrumbs

Directions:
Mix all of the ingredients in a bowl; stir well. Shape medium balls out of this mix, place them in your air fryer, and cook at 360 degrees F for 15 minutes. Serve as an appetizer, or, would be a great breakfast food!

Nutrition: calories 200, fat 7, fiber 1, carbs 13, protein 9

Lemony Endives Appetizer

Preparation time: 10 minutes
Cooking time: 10 minutes
Servings: 4

Ingredients:
- 6 endives, halved lengthwise
- Salt and black pepper to taste
- ½ cup yogurt
-

- 1 teaspoon garlic powder
- 3 tablespoons lemon juice

Directions:
In a bowl, mix all ingredients *except* the endives; whisk. Now add the endives, toss, and set them aside for 10 minutes. Place the endives in your air fryer's basket and cook at 360 degrees F for 10 minutes. Serve as an appetizer.

Nutrition: calories 179, fat 6, fiber 12, carbs 11, protein 4

Coriander Bites

Preparation time: 10 minutes
Cooking time: 20 minutes
Servings: 4

Ingredients:
- 12 ounces tofu, cubed
- 1 teaspoon sweet paprika
- 2 teaspoons olive oil

- 1 tablespoon coriander paste
- 2 tablespoons soy sauce
- 2 tablespoons fish sauce

Directions:
In a bowl, mix the tofu, paprika, 1 teaspoon of the oil, coriander paste, soy sauce, and fish sauce; toss and set aside for 10 minutes. Transfer the coriander tofu bites to your air fryer's basket, drizzle the remaining teaspoon of the oil over them, and cook at 350 degrees F for 20 minutes, shaking halfway. Serve as a snack.

Nutrition: calories 100, fat 4, fiber 1, carbs 11, protein 1

Beef Dip

Preparation time: 10 minutes
Cooking time: 30 minutes
Servings: 6

Ingredients:

- 2 pounds ground beef, browned
- 2 carrots, chopped
- 4 garlic cloves, minced
- 2 celery ribs, chopped
- 28 ounces canned tomatoes, crushed
- ¼ cup beef stock
- 1 yellow onion, chopped
- 1 tablespoon olive oil
- A pinch of basil, dried
- A pinch of oregano, dried
- A splash of red wine
- Salt and black pepper to taste

Directions:
Place all the ingredients in a pan that fits your air fryer and whisk. Put the pan in the fryer and cook at 380 degrees F for 30 minutes. Divide into bowls and serve as a snack or appetizer.

Nutrition: calories 251, fat 14, fiber 5, carbs 23, protein 17

Lentils Spread

Preparation time: 5 minutes
Cooking time: 20 minutes
Servings: 4

Ingredients:

- 30 ounces canned tomatoes, crushed
- 3 garlic cloves, minced
- 2 cups canned red lentils, drained
- Salt and black pepper to taste
- 1 cup chicken stock

Directions:
Add all of the ingredients to a pan that fits your air fryer and stir. Place the pan into the fryer and cook at 370 degrees F for 20 minutes. Blend the mix with an immersion blender. Divide into bowls and serve as a snack or an appetizer.

Nutrition: calories 171, fat 6, fiber 4, carbs 12, protein 5

Chili Dip

Preparation time: 10 minutes
Cooking time: 12 minutes
Servings: 4

Ingredients:
- 6 ancho chilies, dried, seedless and chopped
- 2 garlic cloves, minced
- Salt and black pepper to taste
- 1 cup water
- 1½ teaspoons sugar
- ½ teaspoon oregano, dried
- 2 tablespoons apple cider vinegar

Directions:
Mix all the ingredients together in a pan that fits your air fryer; stir well. Place the pan in the air fryer and cook at 380 degrees F for 12 minutes. Transfer the mixture to a blender and pulse. Divide into bowls and serve as a dip.

Nutrition: calories 72, fat 1, fiber 0, carbs 2, protein 3

Tomato Dip

Preparation time: 5 minutes
Cooking time: 10 minutes
Servings: 4

Ingredients:
- 1 tablespoon olive oil
- 1 cup tomato puree
- 1 yellow onion, chopped
- 4 tablespoons white vinegar
- 4 tablespoons honey
- Salt and black pepper to taste
- 2 garlic cloves, minced
- 1 teaspoon liquid smoke
- 1 teaspoon Tabasco sauce
- ⅛ teaspoon cumin powder

Directions:
Place all the ingredients in a pan that fits your air fryer and mix well. Put the pan into the fryer and cook at 370 degrees F for 10 minutes. Whisk well, divide into bowls, and serve as a dip.

Nutrition: calories 72, fat 1, fiber 3, carbs 7, protein 4

Zucchini and Mint Spread

Preparation time: 10 minutes
Cooking time: 12 minutes
Servings: 4

Ingredients:
- 1 yellow onion, chopped
- 1 tablespoon olive oil
- 1½ pounds zucchini, chopped
- Salt and white pepper to taste
- ½ cup veggie stock
- 1 bunch mint, chopped
- 2 garlic cloves, minced

Directions:
Over medium heat, heat up the oil in a pan that fits your air fryer. Add the onions and garlic, stir, and cook for 1-2 minutes. Add the remaining ingredients; stir well. Place the pan in the air fryer and cook at 380 degrees F for 10 minutes. Blend using an immersion blender, and serve as an appetizer or party spread.

Nutrition: calories 87, fat 6, fiber 2, carbs 5, protein 2

Squash Dip

Preparation time: 10 minutes
Cooking time: 25 minutes
Servings: 6

Ingredients:
- 1 yellow onion, chopped
- 2 tablespoons olive oil
- 8 carrots, chopped
- 2 butternut squash, chopped
- 8 garlic cloves, minced
- 1 cup veggie stock
- ¼ cup lemon juice
- 1 bunch basil, chopped
- Salt and black pepper to taste

Directions:
In a pan that fits your air fryer, mix all the ingredients except the lemon juice. Place the pan in the fryer and cook at 380 degrees F for 25 minutes. Transfer the entire mixture to a blender, add the lemon juice, and pulse well. Divide into bowls and serve as a party dip or an appetizer.

Nutrition: calories 141, fat 4, fiber 3, carbs 11, protein 4

Cheesy Sausage and Tomatoes Dip

Preparation time: 5 minutes
Cooking time: 10 minutes
Servings: 4

Ingredients:
- 2 cups processed cheese, cut into chunks
- 1 cup Italian sausage, cooked and chopped
- 5 ounces canned tomatoes, chopped
- 4 tablespoons chicken stock

Directions:
Place all the ingredients into a pan that fits your air fryer and mix well. Put the pan into the fryer and cook at 378 degrees F for 10 minutes. Stir well and serve as a party dip or appetizer; enjoy!

Nutrition: calories 151, fat 8, fiber 4, carbs 16, protein 5

Mushroom Salad

Preparation time: 10 minutes
Cooking time: 25 minutes
Servings: 6

Ingredients:
- 1 yellow onion, chopped
- ¼ cup olive oil
- Salt and black pepper to taste
- 1 tablespoon thyme, chopped
- 3 garlic cloves, minced
- 1 cup chicken stock
- 10 ounces shiitake mushrooms, chopped
- 10 ounces cremini mushrooms, chopped
- 10 ounces Portobello mushrooms, chopped
- ¼ cup coconut cream
- 1 ounce parmesan cheese, grated
- 1 tablespoon parsley, minced

Directions:
In a pan that fits your air fryer, heat up the oil over medium heat. Add the onions, garlic, thyme, salt, and pepper; stir and cook for 3-4 minutes. Add the stock and the mushrooms; stir and cook for 1-2 minutes more. Place the pan in the air fryer and cook at 350 degrees F for 20 minutes. Add the cream, parmesan, and parsley, and stir well. Divide into bowls and serve as an appetizer.

Nutrition: calories 200, fat 5, fiber 6, carbs 15, protein 5

Minty Cauliflower Spread

Preparation time: 5 minutes
Cooking time: 15 minutes
Servings: 6

Ingredients:

- 2 tablespoons butter, melted
- 8 garlic cloves, minced
- 3 cups veggie stock
- 6 cups cauliflower florets
- A handful of mint, chopped
- Salt and black pepper to taste

Directions:

Place all the ingredients into a pan that fits your air fryer; mix well. Put the pan into the air fryer and cook at 370 degrees F for 15 minutes. Blend using an immersion blender, divide into bowls, and serve.

Nutrition: calories 161, fat 5, fiber 9, carbs 14, protein 6

Fast Mango Dip

Preparation time: 5 minutes
Cooking time: 20 minutes
Servings: 4

Ingredients:

- 1 shallot, chopped
- 1 tablespoon avocado oil
- 2 tablespoons ginger, minced
- ½ teaspoon cinnamon powder
- 2 mangos, chopped
- 2 red hot chilies, chopped
- 1¼ cups sugar
- 1¼ cups apple cider vinegar

Directions:

In a pan that fits your air fryer, mix all the ingredients well. Place the pan in the fryer and cook at 350 degrees F for 20 minutes. Transfer the contents to a blender and pulse. Divide into bowls and serve as a party dip.

Nutrition: calories 100, fat 1, fiber 0, carbs 6, protein 2

Hot Dip

Preparation time: 5 minutes
Cooking time: 5 minutes
Servings: 6

Ingredients:
- 12 ounces hot peppers, chopped
- Salt and black pepper to taste
- 1¼ cups apple cider vinegar

Directions:
Add the ingredients to a pan that fits your air fryer and mix. Place the pan in the fryer and cook at 380 degrees F for 5 minutes. Blend using an immersion blender, divide into bowls, and serve.

Nutrition: calories 20, fat 0, fiber 2, carbs 3, protein 1

Spiced Tomato Party Mix

Preparation time: 5 minutes
Cooking time: 13 minutes
Servings: 6

Ingredients:
- 3 pounds tomatoes, roughly cubed
- 1 cup balsamic vinegar
- 1 tablespoon ginger, grated
- 3 garlic cloves, minced
- 2 onions, chopped
- ¼ cup raisins
- ¾ teaspoon cinnamon powder
- ½ teaspoon coriander, ground
- ¼ teaspoon nutmeg powder
- 1 teaspoon sweet paprika
- 1 teaspoon chili powder

Directions:
Add all the ingredients to a pan that fits your air fryer and toss. Place the pan in the air fryer and cook at 360 degrees F for 13 minutes. Remove, place in a bowl, and chill. Serve cold as an appetizer or snack.

Nutrition: calories 151, fat 8, fiber 4, carbs 11, protein 5

Tomatoes and Dates Salsa

Preparation time: 5 minutes
Cooking time: 15 minutes
Servings: 12

Ingredients:

- 1½ pounds tomatoes, peeled and cubed
- 1 apple, cored and cubed
- 1 yellow onion, chopped
- 6 ounces sultanas, chopped
- 3 ounces dates, roughly chopped
- Salt and black pepper to taste
- 1 tablespoon balsamic vinegar
- 1 teaspoon whole spice
- ½ tablespoon brown sugar

Directions:
In a pan that fits your air fryer, add and toss all the ingredients. Place the pan in the fryer and cook at 370 degrees F for 15 minutes. Remove the salsa, place in a bowl, and chill. Serve the salsa cold as a snack or appetizer.

Nutrition: calories 131, fat 7, fiber 4, carbs 9, protein 3

Chili Tomato Salsa

Preparation time: 5 minutes
Cooking time: 10 minutes
Servings: 12

Ingredients:

- 1½ pounds green tomatoes, cubed
- 1 white onion, chopped
- ¼ cup currants
- 4 red chili peppers, chopped
- 2 tablespoons ginger, grated
- 1 tablespoon brown sugar
- 1 tablespoon balsamic vinegar

Directions:
Mix all the ingredients in a pan that fits your air fryer and toss. Place the pan in the fryer and cook at 370 degrees F for 10 minutes. Put the salsa into a bowl and chill. Serve cold as a party salsa or as an appetizer.

Nutrition: calories 100, fat 1, fiber 3, carbs 7, protein 4

Buttery Onion Dip

Preparation time: 10 minutes
Cooking time: 30 minutes
Servings: 8

Ingredients:

- 6 tablespoons butter, softened
- 2½ pounds red onions, chopped
- Salt and black pepper to taste
- ½ teaspoon baking soda

Directions:
Place the butter into a pan that fits your air fryer and heat over medium heat. Add the onions and the baking soda, stir, and sauté for 5 minutes. Transfer the pan to your air fryer and cook at 370 degrees F for 25 minutes. Serve warm as a party dip.

Nutrition: calories 151, fat 2, fiber 4, carbs 9, protein 4

Cranberry Dip

Preparation time: 10 minutes
Cooking time: 30 minutes
Servings: 10

Ingredients:

- 4 garlic cloves, minced
- 2 red onions, chopped
- 4 red chili peppers, seeded and chopped
- 17 ounces cranberries
- 4 ounces sugar
- 1 teaspoon olive oil
- Black pepper to taste
- 2 tablespoons balsamic vinegar

Directions:
In a pan that fits your air fryer, place all the ingredients and mix well. Place the pan in the air fryer and cook at 370 degrees F for 30 minutes. Blend using an immersion blender and cool. Serve cold as a party dip or appetizer.

Nutrition: calories 121, fat 1, fiber 3, carbs 7, protein 3

Onion and Chili Dip

Preparation time: 5 minutes
Cooking time: 20 minutes
Servings: 6

Ingredients:

- 5 ounces red chilies, seeded and chopped
- 4 ounces red onion, chopped
- 3 tablespoons sugar
- 12 garlic cloves, minced
- 2 ounces distilled vinegar
- 2 ounces water

Directions:

Place all the ingredients into a pan that fits your air fryer and mix well. Put the pan into the air fryer and cook at 370 degrees F for 20 minutes. Blend using an immersion blender, divide into bowls, and serve as a party dip.

Nutrition: calories 100, fat 1, fiber 2, carbs 7, protein 4

Easy Eggplant Spread

Preparation time: 10 minutes
Cooking time: 25 minutes
Servings: 6

Ingredients:

- 15 ounces canned tomatoes, chopped
- 5 garlic cloves, minced
- 3 ounces canned tomato paste
- 1 sweet onion, chopped
- 3 small eggplants, chopped
- ½ cup olive oil
- ½ teaspoon turmeric powder
- 1 cup beef stock
- 1 tablespoon apple cider vinegar
- Salt and black pepper to taste
- ¼ cup parsley, chopped

Directions:

In a pan that fits your air fryer, place all the ingredients except the parsley; stir well. Put the pan in the fryer and cook at 380 degrees F for 25 minutes. Blend a bit using an immersion blender, add the parsley, and stir. Put into a bowl, chill, and serve cold.

Nutrition: calories 151, fat 8, fiber 6, carbs 11, protein 5

Broccoli Spread

Preparation time: 10 minutes
Cooking time: 15 minutes
Servings: 4

Ingredients:
- 1½ cups veggie stock
- 3 cups broccoli florets
- 2 garlic cloves, minced
- Salt and black pepper to taste
- ⅓ cup coconut milk
- 1 tablespoon white wine vinegar
- 1 tablespoon olive oil

Directions:
In a pan that fits your air fryer, mix all the ingredients *except* the coconut milk. Place the pan in the fryer and cook at 390 degrees F for 15 minutes. Add the coconut milk and blend using an immersion blender. Put the spread into a bowl and chill. Serve cold as an appetizer.

Nutrition: calories 151, fat 4, fiber 7, carbs 12, protein 5

Buttery Carrot Dip

Preparation time: 10 minutes
Cooking time: 15 minutes
Servings: 6

Ingredients:
- 4 tablespoons butter, melted
- 2 cups carrots, grated
- Salt and black pepper to taste
- A pinch of cayenne pepper
- 1 tablespoon chives

Directions:
Add all ingredients to a pan that fits your air fryer and mix. Place the pan in the fryer and cook at 380 degrees F for 15 minutes. Blend a bit using an immersion blender, and then divide into bowls. Serve as a dip.

Nutrition: calories 151, fat 4, fiber 5, carbs 13, protein 5

Apple and Dates Dip

Preparation time: 5 minutes
Cooking time: 19 minutes
Servings: 6

Ingredients:
- 2 cups apples, cored, peeled and grated
- ¼ cup apple juice
- 2 cups dates, dried
- 1 tablespoon lemon juice

Directions:
In a pan that fits your air fryer, mix all the ingredients. Place the pan in the fryer and cook at 380 degrees F for 19 minutes. Blend a bit using an immersion blender, then place in a bowl and chill. Serve cold as a dip.

Nutrition: calories 100, fat 1, fiber 3, carbs 9, protein 3

Simple Fennel and Tomato Spread

Preparation time: 10 minutes
Cooking time: 16 minutes
Servings: 6

Ingredients:
- 1 fennel bulb, chopped
- 2 pints grape tomatoes, chopped
- ¼ cup dry white wine
- 3 tablespoons olive oil
- Salt and black pepper to taste

Directions:
In a pan that fits your air fryer, mix all the ingredients. Place the pan in the fryer and cook at 390 degrees F for 16 minutes. Stir well, divide into bowls, and serve as a dip.

Nutrition: calories 100, fat 2, fiber 2, carbs 11, protein 4

Creamy Leek Spread

Preparation time: 5 minutes
Cooking time: 15 minutes
Servings: 6

Ingredients:

- 3 leeks, roughly chopped
- 2 tablespoons butter, melted
- ½ cup whipping cream
- 3 tablespoons lemon juice
- Salt and pepper to taste

Directions:

In a pan that fits your air fryer, mix the leeks, butter, lemon juice, salt, and pepper; stir well. Put the pan into the fryer and cook at 380 degrees F for 15 minutes. Transfer the mixture to a blender, add the cream, and pulse. Divide into bowls and serve cold.

Nutrition: calories 161, fat 8, fiber 2, carbs 14, protein 6

Fast Parsley Dip

Preparation time: 5 minutes
Cooking time: 8 minutes
Servings: 6

Ingredients:

- ¼ cup chicken stock
- 1 yellow onion, chopped
- 2 tablespoons butter, melted
- 3 tablespoons whole milk
- 6 tablespoons parsley, chopped
- ¼ cup heavy cream
- Salt and white pepper to taste

Directions:

Place all of the ingredients—*except* the cream—into a pan that fits your air fryer; mix well. Put the pan into the fryer and cook at 370 degrees F for 8 minutes. Transfer to a blender, add the cream, and pulse. Put the mixture into a bowl and chill. Serve cold.

Nutrition: calories 100, fat 2, fiber 5, carbs 11, protein 3

Scallions and Shallots Dip

Preparation time: 5 minutes
Cooking time: 15 minutes
Servings: 6

Ingredients:

- 3 garlic cloves, minced
- 1 tablespoon olive oil
- 2 red chilies, minced
- 3 shallots, minced
- 3 scallions, chopped
- 1 tomato, chopped
- Salt and black pepper to taste
- 2 tablespoons cilantro, chopped
- 3½ tablespoons veggie stock

Directions:
In a pan that fits your air fryer, add all the ingredients and toss. Place the pan in the fryer and cook at 390 degrees F for 15 minutes. Blend a bit using an immersion blender, then put in a bowl and chill. Serve cold as a snack or appetizer; enjoy!

Nutrition: calories 131, fat 5, fiber 4, carbs 14, protein 3

Corn Dip

Preparation time: 5 minutes
Cooking time: 18 minutes
Servings: 4

Ingredients:

- 1 yellow onion, chopped
- 1 tablespoon olive oil
- 1 cup chicken stock
- 2 tablespoons white wine
- 2 cups corn kernels
- Salt and black pepper to taste
- 2 teaspoons butter, melted
- 1 teaspoon thyme, chopped

Directions:
Put a pan that fits your air fryer over medium heat and add the oil and the butter; heat up. Add the onion; stir, and sauté for 3 minutes. Add the corn, stock, wine, salt, pepper, and thyme; stir. Place the pan in the fryer and cook at 390 degrees F for 15 minutes. Blend a bit using an immersion blender, divide into bowls, and serve as a party dip or appetizer.

Nutrition: calories 151, fat 2, fiber 5, carbs 14, protein 4

Air Fryer Fish and Seafood Recipes

Chinese Cod Fillets

Preparation time: 10 minutes
Cooking time: 15 minutes
Servings: 4

Ingredients:
- 4 cod fillets, boneless
- Salt and black pepper to taste
- 1 cup water
- 4 tablespoons light soy sauce
- 1 tablespoon sugar
- 3 tablespoons olive oil + a drizzle
- 4 ginger slices
- 3 spring onions, chopped
- 2 tablespoons coriander, chopped

Directions:
Season the fish with salt and pepper, then drizzle some oil over it and rub well. Put the fish in your air fryer and cook at 360 degrees F for 12 minutes. Put the water in a pot and heat up over medium heat; add the soy sauce and sugar, stir, bring to a simmer, and remove from the heat. Heat up a pan with the olive oil over medium heat; add the ginger and green onions, stir, cook for 2-3 minutes, and remove from the heat. Divide the fish between plates and top with ginger, coriander, and green onions. Drizzle the soy sauce mixture all over, serve, and enjoy!

Nutrition: calories 270, fat 12, fiber 8, carbs 16, protein 14

Cod Fillets with Leeks

Preparation time: 10 minutes
Cooking time: 15 minutes
Servings: 2

Ingredients:
- 2 black cod fillets, boneless
- 1 tablespoon olive oil
- Salt and black pepper to taste
- 2 leeks, sliced
- ½ cup pecans, chopped

Directions:
In a bowl, mix the cod with the oil, salt, pepper, and the leeks; toss / coat well. Transfer the cod to your air fryer and cook at 360 degrees F for 15 minutes. Divide the fish and leeks between plates, sprinkle the pecans on top, and serve immediately.

Nutrition: calories 280, fat 4, fiber 2, carbs 12, protein 15

Rosemary Shrimp Kabobs

Preparation time: 5 minutes
Cooking time: 7 minutes
Servings: 2

Ingredients:

- 8 shrimps, peeled and deveined
- 4 garlic cloves, minced
- Salt and black pepper to taste
- 8 red bell pepper slices
- 1 tablespoon rosemary, chopped
- 1 tablespoon olive oil

Directions:

Place all ingredients in a bowl and toss them well. Thread 2 shrimp and 2 bell pepper slices on a skewer, and then repeat with 2 more shrimp and bell pepper slices. Thread another 2 shrimp and 2 bell pepper slices on the other skewer and then repeat with the last 2 shrimp and 2 bell pepper slices. Put the kabobs in your air fryer's basket, cook at 360 degrees F for 7 minutes and serve immediately with a side salad.

Nutrition: calories 200, fat 4, fiber 12, carbs 15, protein 6

Simple Balsamic Cod Fillets

Preparation time: 5 minutes
Cooking time: 12 minutes
Servings: 2

Ingredients:

- 2 cod fillets, boneless
- 2 tablespoons lemon juice
- Salt and black pepper to taste
- ½ teaspoon garlic powder
- ⅓ cup water
- ⅓ cup balsamic vinegar
- 3 shallots, chopped
- 2 tablespoons olive oil

Directions:

In a bowl, toss the cod with the salt, pepper, lemon juice, garlic powder, water, vinegar, and oil; coat well. Transfer the fish to your fryer's basket and cook at 360 degrees F for 12 minutes, flipping them halfway. Divide the fish between plates, sprinkle the shallots on top, and serve.

Nutrition: calories 271, fat 12, fiber 10, carbs 16, protein 20

Chili Salmon Fillets

Preparation time: 5 minutes
Cooking time: 8 minutes
Servings: 2

Ingredients:
- 2 salmon fillets, boneless
- Salt and black pepper to taste
- 3 red chili peppers, chopped
- 2 tablespoons lemon juice
- 2 tablespoon olive oil
- 2 tablespoon garlic, minced

Directions:
In a bowl, combine the ingredients, toss, and coat fish well. Transfer everything to your air fryer and cook at 365 degrees F for 8 minutes, flipping the fish halfway. Divide between plates and serve right away.

Nutrition: calories 280, fat 4, fiber 8, carbs 15, protein 20

Shrimp and Veggie Mix

Preparation time: 10 minutes
Cooking time: 20 minutes
Servings: 4

Ingredients:
- ½ cup red onion, chopped
- 1 cup red bell pepper, chopped
- 1 cup celery, chopped
- 1 pound shrimp, peeled and deveined
- 1 teaspoon Worcestershire sauce
- Salt and black pepper to taste
- 1 tablespoon butter, melted
- 1 teaspoon sweet paprika

Directions:
Add all the ingredients to a bowl and mix well. Transfer everything to your air fryer and cook 320 degrees F for 20 minutes, shaking halfway. Divide between plates and serve.

Nutrition: calories 220, fat 14, fiber 9, carbs 17, protein 20

White Fish and Peas

Preparation time: 10 minutes
Cooking time: 12 minutes
Servings: 4

Ingredients:

- 4 white fish fillets, boneless
- 2 tablespoons cilantro, chopped
- 2 cups peas, cooked and drained
- 4 tablespoons veggie stock
- ½ teaspoon basil, dried
- ½ teaspoon sweet paprika
- 2 garlic cloves, minced
- Salt and pepper to taste

Directions:
In a bowl, mix the fish with all ingredients *except* the peas; toss to coat the fish well. Transfer everything to your air fryer and cook at 360 degrees F for 12 minutes. Add the peas, toss, and divide everything between plates. Serve and enjoy.

Nutrition: calories 241, fat 8, fiber 12, carbs 15, protein 18

Cod and Lime Sauce

Preparation time: 5 minutes
Cooking time: 12 minutes
Servings: 4

Ingredients:

- 4 cod fillets, boneless
- Salt and black pepper to taste
- 3 teaspoons lime zest
- 2 teaspoons lime juice
- 3 tablespoons chives, chopped
- 6 tablespoons butter, melted
- 2 tablespoons olive oil

Directions:
Season the fish with the salt and pepper, rub it with the oil, and then put it in your air fryer. Cook at 360 degrees F for 10 minutes, flipping once. Heat up a pan with the butter over medium heat, and then add the chives, salt, pepper, lime juice, and zest, whisk; cook for 1-2 minutes. Divide the fish between plates, drizzle the lime sauce all over, and serve immediately.

Nutrition: calories 280, fat 12, fiber 9, carbs 17, protein 15

Flavored Salmon Fillets

Preparation time: 5 minutes
Cooking time: 12 minutes
Servings: 4

Ingredients:
- 4 salmon fillets, boneless
- 1 tablespoon olive oil
- Salt and black pepper to taste
- 1 teaspoon cumin, ground
- 1 teaspoon sweet paprika
- ½ teaspoon chili powder
- 1 teaspoon garlic powder
- Juice of 1 lime

Directions:
In a bowl, mix the salmon with the other ingredients, rub / coat well, and transfer to your air fryer. Cook at 350 degrees F for 6 minutes on each side. Divide the fish between plates and serve right away with a side salad.

Nutrition: calories 280, fat 14, fiber 4, carbs 18, protein 20

Herbed Tuna

Preparation time: 10 minutes
Cooking time: 8 minutes
Servings: 4

Ingredients:
- ½ cup cilantro, chopped
- ⅓ cup olive oil
- 1 small red onion, chopped
- 3 tablespoons balsamic vinegar
- 2 tablespoons parsley, chopped
- 2 tablespoons basil, chopped
- 1 jalapeno pepper, chopped
- 4 sushi tuna steaks
- Salt and black pepper to taste
- 1 teaspoon red pepper flakes
- 1 teaspoon thyme, chopped
- 3 garlic cloves, minced

Directions:
Place all ingredients *except* the fish into a bowl and stir well. Add the fish and toss, coating it well. Transfer everything to your air fryer and cook at 360 degrees F for 4 minutes on each side. Divide the fish between plates and serve.

Nutrition: calories 306, fat 8, fiber 1, carbs 14, protein 16

Creamy Shrimp and Mushrooms

Preparation time: 5 minutes
Cooking time: 10 minutes
Servings: 2

Ingredients:

- 1 tablespoon butter, melted
- A drizzle of olive oil
- 1 pound shrimp, peeled and deveined
- ¼ cup heavy cream
- 8 ounces mushrooms, roughly sliced
- A pinch of red pepper flakes
- Salt and black pepper to taste
- 2 garlic cloves, minced
- ½ cup beef stock
- 1 tablespoon parsley, chopped
- 1 tablespoon chives, chopped

Directions:

Season the shrimp with salt and pepper and grease with the oil. Place the shrimp in your air fryer, cook at 360 degrees F for 7 minutes, and divide between plates. Heat up a pan with the butter over medium heat, add the mushrooms, stir, and cook for 3-4 minutes. Add all remaining ingredients; stir and then cook for a few minutes more. Drizzle the butter / garlic mixture over the shrimp and serve.

Nutrition: calories 305, fat 13, fiber 4, carbs 14, protein 11

Maple Salmon

Preparation time: 5 minutes
Cooking time: 10 minutes
Servings: 2

Ingredients:

- 2 salmon fillets, boneless
- Salt and black pepper to taste
- 2 tablespoons mustard
- 1 tablespoon olive oil
- 1 tablespoon maple syrup

Directions:

In a bowl, mix the mustard with the oil and the maple syrup; whisk well and brush the salmon with this mix. Place the salmon in your air fryer and cook it at 370 degrees F for 5 minutes on each side. Serve immediately with a side salad.

Nutrition: calories 290, fat 7, fiber 14, carbs 18, protein 17

Salmon and Balsamic Orange Sauce

Preparation time: 5 minutes
Cooking time: 15 minutes
Servings: 4

Ingredients:
- 4 salmon fillets, boneless and cubed
- 2 lemons, sliced
- ¼ cup balsamic vinegar
- ¼ cup orange juice
- A pinch of salt and black pepper

Directions:
In a pan that fits your air fryer, mix all ingredients *except* the fish; whisk. Heat the mixture up over medium-high heat for 5 minutes and add the salmon. Toss gently, and place the pan in the air fryer and cook at 360 degrees F for 10 minutes. Divide between plates and serve right away with a side salad.

Nutrition: calories 227, fat 9, fiber 12, carbs 14, protein 11

Pistachio Crusted Cod

Preparation time: 10 minutes
Cooking time: 10 minutes
Servings: 4

Ingredients:
- 1 cup pistachios, chopped
- 4 cod fillets, boneless
- ¼ cup lime juice
- 2 tablespoons honey
- 1 teaspoon parsley, chopped
- Salt and black pepper to taste
- 1 tablespoon mustard

Directions:
Place all the ingredients *except* the fish into a bowl; whisk. Spread the mixture over the fish fillets, put them in your air fryer, and cook at 350 degrees F for 10 minutes. Divide the fish between plates and serve immediately with a side salad.

Nutrition: calories 270, fat 17, fiber 12, carbs 20, protein 12

Roasted Cod and Parsley

Preparation time: 10 minutes
Cooking time: 10 minutes
Servings: 4

Ingredients:
- 3 tablespoons parsley, chopped
- 4 medium cod filets, boneless
- ¼ cup butter, melted
- 2 garlic cloves, minced
- 2 tablespoons lemon juice
- 1 shallot, chopped
- Salt and black pepper to taste

Directions:
In a bowl, mix all ingredients *except* the fish; whisk well. Spread this mixture over the cod fillets. Put them in your air fryer and cook at 390 degrees F for 10 minutes. Divide the fish between plates and serve.

Nutrition: calories 280, fat 4, fiber 7, carbs 12, protein 15

Salmon and Fennel

Preparation time: 10 minutes
Cooking time: 20 minutes
Servings: 4

Ingredients:
- 2 red onions, chopped
- 2 tablespoons olive oil
- 2 small fennel bulbs, trimmed and sliced
- ¼ cup almonds, toasted and sliced
- Salt and black pepper to taste
- 4 salmon fillets, boneless
- 5 teaspoons fennel seeds, toasted

Directions:
Season the fish with salt and pepper, grease it with 1 tablespoon of the oil, and place in your air fryer's basket. Cook at 350 degrees F for 5-6 minutes on each side and divide between plates. Heat up a pan with the remaining tablespoon of oil over medium-high heat; add the onions, stir, and sauté for 2 minutes. Add the fennel bulbs and seeds, almonds, salt, and pepper, and cook for 2-3 minutes more. Spread the mixture over the fish and serve right away; enjoy!

Nutrition: calories 284, fat 7, fiber 10, carbs 17, protein 16

Salmon Fillets and Pineapple Mix

Preparation time: 5 minutes
Cooking time: 10 minutes
Servings: 2

Ingredients:

- 20 ounces canned pineapple pieces
- ½ teaspoon ginger, grated
- A drizzle of olive oil
- 2 teaspoons garlic powder
- 1 tablespoon balsamic vinegar
- 2 medium salmon fillets, boneless
- Salt and black pepper to taste

Directions:
Grease a pan that fits your air fryer with the oil and add the fish inside. Add the remaining ingredients and place the pan in the air fryer. Cook at 350 degrees F for 10 minutes. Divide between plates and serve.

Nutrition: calories 236, fat 8, fiber 12, carbs 17, protein 16

Easy Salmon Fillets and Bell Peppers

Preparation time: 5 minutes
Cooking time: 15 minutes
Servings: 6

Ingredients:

- 1 cup green olives, pitted
- 3 red bell peppers, cut into medium pieces
- ½ teaspoon smoked paprika
- Salt and black pepper to taste
- 3 tablespoons olive oil
- 6 medium salmon fillets, skinless and boneless
- 2 tablespoons cilantro, chopped

Directions:
In a baking dish that fits your air fryer, mix all the ingredients and toss gently. Place the baking dish in your air fryer and cook at 360 degrees F for 15 minutes. Divide the fillets between plates and serve.

Nutrition: calories 281, fat 8, fiber 14, carbs 17, protein 16

Coconut Cod Fillets

Preparation time: 5 minutes
Cooking time: 10 minutes
Servings: 4

Ingredients:

- 4 medium cod fillets, boneless
- Salt and black pepper to taste
- ½ cup coconut milk
- A drizzle of olive oil
- 1 teaspoon ginger, grated
- ½ cup parsley, chopped
- 2 garlic cloves, chopped
- ½ jalapeno, chopped

Directions:

Place all ingredients *except* the fish in your blender; pulse well. In a baking dish that fits your air fryer, place the fish along with the coconut milk mixture and toss gently. Place the dish in your air fryer and cook at 380 degrees F for 10 minutes. Divide between plates and serve hot.

Nutrition: calories 250, fat 5, fiber 6, carbs 15, protein 18

Salmon and Orange Vinaigrette

Preparation time: 5 minutes
Cooking time: 10 minutes
Servings: 2

Ingredients:

- 2 salmon fillets, boneless
- Zest of ½ orange
- Juice of ½ orange
- A pinch of salt and black pepper
- 2 tablespoons mustard
- 2 teaspoons honey
- 2 tablespoons olive oil
- 1 tablespoon dill, chopped
- 2 tablespoons parsley, chopped

Directions:

In a bowl, mix the orange zest with the orange juice, salt, pepper, mustard, honey, oil, dill, and parsley, and whisk well. Add the salmon to this mix, toss, and transfer the fish to your air fryer. Cook at 350 degrees F for 10 minutes, flipping halfway. Divide the fish between plates, drizzle the orange vinaigrette all over, and serve.

Nutrition: calories 272, fat 8, fiber 12, carbs 15, protein 16

Sea Bass Paella

Preparation time: 10 minutes
Cooking time: 25 minutes
Servings: 4

Ingredients:

- 5 ounces wild rice
- 2 ounces peas
- 1 red bell pepper, deseeded and chopped
- 14 ounces dry white wine
- 3½ ounces chicken stock
- 1 pound sea bass fillets, cubed
- 6 scallops
- 8 shrimp, peeled and deveined
- Salt and black pepper to taste
- A drizzle of olive oil

Directions:
In a heatproof dish that fits your air fryer, place all the ingredients and toss. Place the dish in your air fryer and cook at 380 degrees F and cook for 25 minutes, stirring halfway. Divide between plates and serve.

Nutrition: calories 290, fat 12, fiber 2, carbs 16, protein 19

Easy Coconut Shrimp

Preparation time: 5 minutes
Cooking time: 10 minutes
Servings: 4

Ingredients:

- 12 large shrimp, deveined and peeled
- 1 cup coconut cream
- 1 tablespoon cornstarch
- 1 tablespoon parsley, chopped
- Salt and black pepper to taste

Directions:
Add all ingredients to a pan that fits your air fryer and toss. Place the pan in the fryer and cook at 360 degrees F for 10 minutes. Serve hot and enjoy!

Nutrition: calories 272, fat 4, fiber 3, carbs 14, protein 4

Tiger Shrimp Mix

Preparation time: 5 minutes
Cooking time: 10 minutes
Servings: 2

Ingredients:

- 20 tiger shrimp, peeled and deveined
- Salt and black pepper to taste
- ½ teaspoon Italian seasoning
- 1 tablespoon extra virgin olive oil
- ¼ teaspoon smoked paprika

Directions:

Add all the ingredients to a bowl and toss. Put the shrimp in the air fryer's basket and cook at 380 degrees F for 10 minutes. Divide into bowls and serve.

Nutrition: calories 219, fat 6, fiber 4, carbs 14, protein 15

Hot Shrimp Mix

Preparation time: 2 hours
Cooking time: 10 minutes
Servings: 4

Ingredients:

- 1 pound large shrimp, peeled and deveined
- 1 teaspoon red pepper flakes
- 2 tablespoons olive oil
- 1 teaspoon Tabasco sauce
- 2 tablespoons water
- 1 teaspoon basil, dried
- Salt and black pepper to taste
- 1 tablespoon parsley, chopped
- ½ teaspoon garlic powder
- ½ teaspoon sweet paprika

Directions:

In a bowl, mix the shrimp with all other ingredients except the parsley; toss to coat the shrimp well. Place shrimp in the fridge for 2 hours. Transfer the shrimp to your air fryer's basket and cook at 370 degrees F for 10 minutes. Divide into bowls, sprinkle with parsley, and serve with a side salad.

Nutrition: calories 210, fat 7, fiber 6, carbs 13, protein 8

Butter Shrimp Mix

Preparation time: 5 minutes
Cooking time: 10 minutes
Servings: 2

Ingredients:
- 8 large shrimp
- 4 garlic cloves, minced
- Salt and black pepper to taste
- 1 tablespoon rosemary, chopped
- 2 tablespoons butter, melted

Directions:
Add all the ingredients to a bowl and toss. Transfer the shrimp to your air fryer and cook at 360 degrees F for 10 minutes. Divide into bowls, serve, and enjoy!

Nutrition: calories 210, fat 11, fiber 12, carbs 16, protein 9

Salmon and Capers

Preparation time: 5 minutes
Cooking time: 12 minutes
Servings: 4

Ingredients:
- 4 salmon fillets, boneless
- 1 tablespoon capers, drained
- 1 tablespoon dill, chopped
- Salt and black pepper to taste
- Juice of 1 lemon
- 2 teaspoons olive oil

Directions:
In your air fryer, mix the capers, dill, salt, pepper, and the oil, and then rub the fish gently with this mixture. Cook at 360 degrees F for 6 minutes on each side. Divide the fish between plates, drizzle the lemon juice all over, and serve.

Nutrition: calories 280, fat 11, fiber 1, carbs 12, protein 18

Simple Snapper Mix

Preparation time: 5 minutes
Cooking time: 15 minutes
Servings: 4

Ingredients:

- 8 garlic cloves, minced
- 1 tablespoon lemon zest
- ⅓ cup olive oil
- 4 medium snapper fillets, boneless
- 1½ tablespoons green olives, pitted and sliced
- Juice of 2 limes
- Salt and black pepper to taste

Directions:
Add all the ingredients except the fish to a baking dish that fits your air fryer; mix well. Add the fish and toss gently, then place in the fryer. Cook at 360 degrees F for 15 minutes. Divide everything between plates and serve.

Nutrition: calories 191, fat 2, fiber 3, carbs 18, protein 12

Simple Trout Mix

Preparation time: 10 minutes
Cooking time: 13 minutes
Servings: 2

Ingredients:

- 2 trout fillets, boneless
- Salt and black pepper to taste
- 1 red chili pepper, chopped
- 1 tablespoon lemon juice
- 1 tablespoon olive oil
- 1 tablespoon garlic, minced

Directions:
Put the trout in your air fryer and add all other ingredients; rub the trout gently. Cook at 360 degrees F for 13 minutes. Divide between plates and serve.

Nutrition: calories 271, fat 4, fiber 2, carbs 15, protein 11

Cilantro Trout Fillets

Preparation time: 5 minutes
Cooking time: 12 minutes
Servings: 4

Ingredients:
- 4 trout fillets, boneless
- 4 garlic cloves, minced
- 1 cup black olives, pitted and chopped
- 3 tablespoons cilantro, chopped
- 1 tablespoon olive oil

Directions:
Add all of the ingredients to your air fryer and mix well. Cook at 360 degrees F for 6 minutes on each side. Divide everything between plates and serve.

Nutrition: calories 251, fat 7, fiber 3, carbs 16, protein 12

Salmon and Jasmine Rice

Preparation time: 5 minutes
Cooking time: 30 minutes
Servings: 2

Ingredients:
- 2 wild salmon fillets, boneless
- Salt and black pepper to taste
- ½ cup jasmine rice
- 1 cup chicken stock
- 1 tablespoon butter, melted
- ¼ teaspoon saffron

Directions:
Add all ingredients *except* the fish to a pan that fits your air fryer; toss well. Place the pain in the air fryer and cook at 360 degrees F for 15 minutes. Add the fish, cover, and cook at 360 degrees F for 12 minutes more. Divide everything between plates and serve right away.

Nutrition: calories 271, fat 8, fiber 9, carbs 15, protein 8

Salmon and Carrots

Preparation time: 5 minutes
Cooking time: 20 minutes
Servings: 2

Ingredients:

- 2 salmon fillets, boneless
- 3 garlic cloves, minced
- 1 tablespoon olive oil
- ¼ cup veggie stock
- 1 cup baby carrots
- Salt and black pepper to taste

Directions:
In your air fryer, mix all the ingredients. Cook at 370 degrees F for 20 minutes. Divide everything between plates and serve.

Nutrition: calories 200, fat 6, fiber 6, carbs 18, protein 11

Spicy Cod

Preparation time: 5 minutes
Cooking time: 10 minutes
Servings: 4

Ingredients:

- 4 cod fillets, boneless
- 2 tablespoons assorted chili peppers
- Juice of 1 lemon
- 1 lemon, sliced
- Salt and black pepper to taste

Directions:
In your air fryer, mix the cod with the chili pepper, lemon juice, salt, and pepper. Arrange the lemon slices on top and cook at 360 degrees F for 10 minutes. Divide the fillets between plates and serve.

Nutrition: calories 200, fat 4, fiber 8, carbs 16, protein 7

Air Fried Salmon

Preparation time: 10 minutes
Cooking time: 12 minutes
Servings: 4

Ingredients:

- 4 salmon fillets, boneless
- 1 lemon, sliced
- 1 white onion, chopped
- 3 tomatoes, sliced
- 4 thyme sprigs, chopped
- 4 cilantro sprigs, chopped
- 3 tablespoons olive oil
- Salt and black pepper to taste

Directions:

In your air fryer, mix the salmon with the oil, onions, tomatoes, thyme, cilantro, salt, and pepper. Top with the lemon slices and cook at 360 degrees F for 12 minutes. Divide everything between plates and serve.

Nutrition: calories 200, fat 5, fiber 5, carbs 16, protein 15

Salmon Steaks Mix

Preparation time: 5 minutes
Cooking time: 15 minutes
Servings: 6

Ingredients:

- 6 salmon steaks
- 2 tablespoons olive oil
- 2 garlic cloves, minced
- 2 tablespoons parsley, chopped
- 1 cup clam juice
- 2 tablespoons lemon juice
- Salt and white pepper to taste
- 1 teaspoon sherry
- ⅓ cup dill, chopped

Directions:

In a pan that fits your air fryer, mix the salmon with all the other ingredients. Place the pan in the fryer and cook at 370 degrees F for 15 minutes. Divide everything between plates and serve.

Nutrition: calories 261, fat 8, fiber 6, carbs 15, protein 14

Chinese Trout Bites

Preparation time: 5 minutes
Cooking time: 12 minutes
Servings: 4

Ingredients:

- 1 pound trout fillets, boneless and cut into cubes
- 1 garlic clove, crushed
- 1 shallot, sliced
- 1-inch ginger piece, chopped
- ⅓ cup sake
- ⅓ cup mirin
- ¼ cup miso
- 1 sweet onion, chopped
- 2 celery stalks, sliced
- 1 tablespoon rice vinegar
- 1 teaspoon mustard
- 1 teaspoon sugar

Directions:
Add all ingredients to a pan that fits your air fryer and toss. Place the pan in the fryer and cook at 370 degrees F for 12 minutes. Divide into bowls and serve.

Nutrition: calories 271, fat 11, fiber 7, carbs 16, protein 6

Simple Trout

Preparation time: 5 minutes
Cooking time: 20 minutes
Servings: 4

Ingredients:

- 4 whole trout
- 3 ounces breadcrumbs
- Juice of 1 lemon
- 1 tablespoon chives, chopped
- Salt and black pepper to taste
- 1 egg, whisked
- 1 tablespoon butter
- 1 tablespoon olive oil

Directions:
In a bowl, combine the breadcrumbs, lemon juice, salt, pepper, egg, and chives; stir very well. Coat the trout with the breadcrumb mix. Heat up your air fryer with the oil and the butter at 370 degrees F; add the trout and cook for 10 minutes on each side. Divide between plates and serve with a side salad.

Nutrition: calories 214, fat 8, fiber 8, carbs 17, protein 7

Mussels Bowls

Preparation time: 5 minutes
Cooking time: 12 minutes
Servings: 4

Ingredients:

- 2 pounds mussels, scrubbed
- 12 ounces black beer
- 1 tablespoon olive oil
- 1 yellow onion, chopped
- 8 ounces spicy sausage, chopped
- 1 tablespoon paprika

Directions:
Combine all the ingredients in a pan that fits your air fryer. Place the pan in the air fryer and cook at 400 degrees F for 12 minutes. Divide the mussels into bowls, serve, and enjoy!

Nutrition: calories 201, fat 6, fiber 7, carbs 17, protein 7

Mussels and Shrimp

Preparation time: 10 minutes
Cooking time: 15 minutes
Servings: 4

Ingredients:

- 12 mussels
- 1½ pounds large shrimp, peeled and deveined
- 2 tablespoons butter, melted
- 2 yellow onions, chopped
- 3 garlic cloves, minced
- ½ cup parsley, chopped
- 20 ounces canned tomatoes, chopped
- 8 ounces clam juice
- ½ teaspoon marjoram, dried
- 1 tablespoon basil, dried
- Salt and black pepper to taste

Directions:
Place all the ingredients in a pan that fits your air fryer; toss well. Put the pan into the fryer and cook at 380 degrees F for 15 minutes. Divide into bowls and serve right away.

Nutrition: calories 261, fat 7, fiber 7, carbs 16, protein 8

Clams and Potatoes

Preparation time: 5 minutes
Cooking time: 15 minutes
Servings: 4

Ingredients:
- 15 small clams, shucked
- 2 chorizo links, sliced
- 1 pound baby red potatoes, scrubbed
- 1 yellow onion, chopped
- 10 ounces beer
- 2 tablespoons cilantro, chopped
- 1 teaspoon olive oil

Directions:
In a pan that fits your air fryer, add all of the ingredients and toss. Place the pan in the fryer and cook at 390 degrees F for 15 minutes. Divide into bowls and serve.

Nutrition: calories 231, fat 6, fiber 8, carbs 16, protein 16

Parmesan Clams

Preparation time: 10 minutes
Cooking time: 12 minutes
Servings: 4

Ingredients:
- 24 clams, shucked
- 3 garlic cloves, minced
- 4 tablespoons butter, softened
- ¼ cup parsley, chopped
- ¼ cup parmesan cheese, grated
- 1 teaspoon oregano, dried
- 1 cup breadcrumbs

Directions:
In a bowl, combine the breadcrumbs, parmesan, oregano, parsley, butter, and garlic; mix well. Divide the breadcrumb mixture into the exposed clams. Put the clams in your air fryer and cook at 380 degrees F for 12 minutes. Serve and enjoy!

Nutrition: calories 100, fat 7, fiber 4, carbs 15, protein 6

Saffron Shrimp Mix

Preparation time: 10 minutes
Cooking time: 8 minutes
Servings: 4

Ingredients:
- 20 shrimp, peeled and deveined
- 2 tablespoons butter, melted
- Salt and black pepper to taste
- ¼ cup parsley, chopped
- ½ teaspoon saffron powder
- Juice of 1 lemon
- 4 garlic cloves, minced

Directions:
In a pan that fits your air fryer, mix the shrimp with all the other ingredients; toss well. Place the pan in the fryer and cook at 380 degrees F for 8 minutes. Divide between plates and serve hot.

Nutrition: calories 261, fat 7, fiber 9, carbs 16, protein 7

Shrimp and Corn

Preparation time: 10 minutes
Cooking time: 10 minutes
Servings: 4

Ingredients:
- 1½ pounds shrimp, peeled and deveined
- 2 cups corn
- A drizzle of olive oil
- ¼ cup chicken stock
- 1 tablespoon old bay seasoning
- Salt and black pepper to taste
- 1 teaspoon red pepper flakes, crushed
- 2 sweet onions, cut into wedges
- 8 garlic cloves, crushed

Directions:
Grease a pan that fits your air fryer with the oil. Add all other ingredients to the oiled pan and toss well. Place the pan in the fryer and cook at 390 degrees F for 10 minutes. Divide everything into bowls and serve.

Nutrition: calories 261, fat 7, fiber 6, carbs 17, protein 11

Simple Shrimp

Preparation time: 10 minutes
Cooking time: 10 minutes
Servings: 4

Ingredients:
- 1 pound shrimp, peeled and deveined
- 2 tablespoons olive oil
- 1 tablespoon red onion, chopped
- 1 cup chicken stock

Directions:
In a pan that fits your air fryer, mix all the ingredients. Place the pan in the fryer and cook at 380 degrees F for 10 minutes. Divide into bowls and serve.

Nutrition: calories 261, fat 6, fiber 8, carbs 16, protein 6

Shrimp and Tomatoes

Preparation time: 10 minutes
Cooking time: 15 minutes
Servings: 4

Ingredients:
- 2 pounds shrimp, peeled and deveined
- 1 pound tomatoes, peeled and chopped
- ¼ cup veggie stock
- Salt and black pepper to taste
- 4 tablespoons olive oil
- 4 onions, chopped
- 1 teaspoon coriander, ground
- Juice of 1 lemon

Directions:
In a pan that fits your air fryer, mix all the ingredients well. Place the pan in the fryer and cook at 360 degrees F for 15 minutes. Divide into bowls and serve; enjoy!

Nutrition: calories 161, fat 1, fiber 6, carbs 17, protein 7

Chili Tomato Shrimp

Preparation time: 10 minutes
Cooking time: 10 minutes
Servings: 4

Ingredients:
- 1 pound shrimp, peeled and deveined
- ½ teaspoon sugar
- 2 teaspoons vinegar
- 1 cup tomato juice
- Salt and black pepper to taste
- 1 teaspoon chili powder
- 1 yellow onion, chopped
- 2 tablespoons olive oil

Directions:
Place all of the ingredients into a pan that fits your air fryer and mix well. Put the pan in the fryer and cook at 370 degrees F for 10 minutes. Divide into bowls and serve.

Nutrition: calories 251, fat 7, fiber 7, carbs 18, protein 11

Pea Pods and Shrimp Mix

Preparation time: 10 minutes
Cooking time: 8 minutes
Servings: 4

Ingredients:
- 1 pound shrimp, peeled and deveined
- 2 tablespoons soy sauce
- ½ pound pea pods
- 3 tablespoons balsamic vinegar
- ¾ cup pineapple juice
- 3 tablespoons sugar

Directions:
In a pan that fits your air fryer, mix all the ingredients. Place the pan in the fryer and cook at 380 degrees F for 8 minutes. Divide into bowls and serve.

Nutrition: calories 251, fat 4, fiber 3, carbs 14, protein 5

Different Shrimp Mix

Preparation time: 10 minutes
Cooking time: 10 minutes
Servings: 4

Ingredients:

- 18 ounces shrimp, peeled and deveined
- Salt and black pepper to taste
- ½ tablespoon mustard seeds
- 1 tablespoon olive oil
- 1 teaspoon turmeric powder
- 2 green chilies, minced
- 2 onions, chopped
- 4 ounces curd, beaten
- 1-inch ginger, chopped

Directions:
In a pan that fits your air fryer, place and mix all the ingredients. Place the pan in the fryer and cook at 380 degrees F for 10 minutes. Divide into bowls and serve.

Nutrition: calories 251, fat 3, fiber 7, carbs 15, protein 8

Shrimp and Spaghetti

Preparation time: 10 minutes
Cooking time: 10 minutes
Servings: 4

Ingredients:

- 1 pound shrimp, cooked, peeled and deveined
- 2 tablespoons olive oil
- 1 garlic clove, minced
- 10 ounces canned tomatoes, chopped
- ¼ teaspoon oregano, dried
- 1 tablespoon parsley, finely chopped
- 1 cup parmesan cheese, grated
- 12 ounces spaghetti, cooked

Directions:
In a pan that fits your air fryer, add the shrimp with the oil, garlic, tomatoes, oregano, and parsley; toss well. Place the pan in the fryer and cook at 380 degrees F for 10 minutes. Add the spaghetti and the parmesan; toss well. Divide between plates, serve, and enjoy!

Nutrition: calories 271, fat 12, fiber 4, carbs 14, protein 5

Butter Flounder Fillets

Preparation time: 5 minutes
Cooking time: 12 minutes
Servings: 4

Ingredients:

- 2 pounds flounder fillets
- 4 tablespoons butter, melted
- Salt and black pepper to taste
- Juice of 1 lime

Directions:
Put the flounder fillets in your air fryer, and then add the melted butter, salt, pepper, and lime juice. Cook at 390 degrees F for 6 minutes on each side. Divide between plates, serve with a side salad, and enjoy.

Nutrition: calories 191, fat 6, fiber 7, carbs 15, protein 7

Tarragon Shrimp

Preparation time: 10 minutes
Cooking time: 12 minutes
Servings: 4

Ingredients:

- 2 tablespoons olive oil
- 2 garlic cloves, minced
- 1 yellow onion, chopped
- 2 tablespoons dry white wine
- ½ cup chicken stock
- Salt and black pepper to taste
- 1 pound shrimp, peeled and deveined
- ¾ cup parmesan cheese, grated
- ¼ cup tarragon, chopped

Directions:
In a pan that fits your air fryer, add all ingredients except the parmesan cheese and stir well. Place the pan in the air fryer and cook at 380 degrees F for 12 minutes. Add the parmesan and toss. Divide everything between plates and serve.

Nutrition: calories 271, fat 8, fiber 8, carbs 17, protein 11

Shrimp, Crab and Sausage Mix

Preparation time: 10 minutes
Cooking time: 20 minutes
Servings: 6

Ingredients:

- 2 tablespoons olive oil
- 1 cup yellow onions, chopped
- ½ cup celery, chopped
- 1 cup green bell pepper, chopped
- 4 garlic cloves, chopped
- 6 plum tomatoes, chopped
- ½ teaspoon onion powder
- ½ teaspoon garlic powder
- 1 teaspoon thyme, dried
- 1 teaspoon celery seeds
- 1 teaspoon sweet paprika
- 1 pound sausage, sliced
- 1 cup chicken stock
- 24 shrimp, peeled and deveined
- ½ pound crab meat
- Salt and black pepper to taste

Directions:

Heat up a pan with the oil over medium heat, then add the onions and celery; stir and cook for 1-2 minutes. Add the bell peppers, garlic, tomatoes, onion powder, garlic powder, thyme, celery seeds, and paprika; stir and cook for another 2 minutes. Add the sausage, stock, shrimp, crab, salt, and pepper, and place the pan into the fryer. Cook at 380 degrees F for 15 minutes. Divide into bowls and serve.

Nutrition: calories 261, fat 8, fiber 12, carbs 17, protein 6

Squid Mix

Preparation time: 5 minutes
Cooking time: 17 minutes
Servings: 4

Ingredients:

- 17 ounces squids, cleaned and cut into medium pieces
- ½ cup veggie stock
- 1½ tablespoons red chili powder
- Salt and black pepper to taste
- ¼ teaspoon turmeric powder
- 4 garlic cloves, minced
- ½ teaspoon cumin seeds
- 3 tablespoons olive oil
- ¼ teaspoon mustard seeds
- 1-inch ginger, minced

Directions:

Place all ingredients in a pan that fits your air fryer and mix well. Insert the pan into the fryer and cook at 380 degrees F for 17 minutes. Divide between plates and serve.

Nutrition: calories 251, fat 5, fiber 7, carbs 15, protein 6

Squid and Peas

Preparation time: 10 minutes
Cooking time: 20 minutes
Servings: 4

Ingredients:
- 1 pound squid, cleaned and cut
- 1 pound fresh peas
- ½ pound canned tomatoes, crushed
- 1 yellow onion, chopped
- 2 tablespoons white wine
- 1 tablespoon olive oil
- Salt and black pepper to taste

Directions:
In a pan that fits your air fryer, mix together all of the ingredients. Place the pan in the fryer and cook at 380 degrees F for 20 minutes. Divide between plates and serve.

Nutrition: calories 221, fat 7, fiber 8, carbs 16, protein 6

Garlicky Squid

Preparation time: 10 minutes
Cooking time: 25 minutes
Servings: 4

Ingredients:
- 1 pound squid, cleaned and cut into small pieces
- 10 garlic cloves, minced
- 1 teaspoon ginger piece, grated
- 2 green chilies, chopped
- 2 yellow onions, chopped
- ½ tablespoon lemon juice
- 1 tablespoon coriander powder
- ¾ tablespoon chili powder
- Salt and black pepper to taste
- 1 teaspoon mustard seeds, toasted
- ½ cup chicken stock
- 3 tablespoons olive oil

Directions:
Place all ingredients into a pan that fits your air fryer and toss. Put the pan in the air fryer and cook at 380 degrees F for 25 minutes. Divide between plates and serve.

Nutrition: calories 251, fat 6, fiber 5, carbs 15, protein 14

Shrimp and Chestnut Mix

Preparation time: 10 minutes
Cooking time: 15 minutes
Servings: 4

Ingredients:
- ½ pound shrimp, peeled and deveined
- 8 ounces water chestnuts, chopped
- ½ pound shiitake mushrooms, sliced
- 2 tablespoons olive oil
- 1 garlic clove, minced
- 1 teaspoon ginger, minced
- 3 scallions, chopped
- Salt and black pepper to taste

Directions:
In your air fryer, add all the ingredients and mix. Cook at 380 degrees F for 15 minutes. Serve hot and enjoy!

Nutrition: calories 190, fat 3, fiber 4, carbs 12, protein 4

Baby Shrimp Salad

Preparation time: 10 minutes
Cooking time: 12 minutes
Servings: 4

Ingredients:
- ½ cup yellow onion, chopped
- 1 cup green bell pepper, chopped
- 1 cup red bell pepper, chopped
- 1 pound baby shrimp, peeled and deveined
- 1 cup mayonnaise
- Salt and black pepper to taste
- 1 tablespoon olive oil
- 1 teaspoon sweet paprika

Directions:
In a pan that fits your air fryer, add all the ingredients *except* the mayo; toss well. Place the pan in the fryer and cook at 380 degrees F for 12 minutes. Cool the mixture down, and then add the mayo. Toss and serve.

Nutrition: calories 210, fat 8, fiber 2, carbs 15, protein 5

Trout and Almond Butter Sauce

Preparation time: 10 minutes
Cooking time: 15 minutes
Servings: 5

Ingredients:

- 4 trout fillets, boneless
- Cooking spray
- Salt and black pepper to taste

For the sauce:

- 1 cup almond butter
- 4 teaspoons soy sauce
- ¼ cup lemon juice
- 1 teaspoon almond oil
- ¼ cup water

Directions:

Put the fish fillets in your air fryer, season with salt and pepper, and grease with the cooking spray. Cook at 380 degrees F for 5 minutes on each side and divide between plates. Heat up a pan with the almond butter over medium heat; then add the soy sauce, lemon juice, almond oil, and the water. Whisk the sauce well and cook for 2-3 minutes. Drizzle the almond butter sauce over the fish and serve.

Nutrition: calories 280, fat 7, fiber 3, carbs 18, protein 11

Baked Cod

Preparation time: 5 minutes
Cooking time: 12 minutes
Servings: 4

Ingredients:

- 4 cod fillets, boneless
- Salt and black pepper to taste
- 2 tablespoons parsley, chopped
- A drizzle of olive oil
- ¾ teaspoon sweet paprika
- ½ teaspoon oregano, dried
- ½ teaspoon thyme, dried
- ½ teaspoon basil, dried
- Juice of 1 lemon
- 2 tablespoons butter, melted

Directions:

Add all ingredients to a bowl and toss gently. Transfer the fish to your air fryer and cook at 380 degrees F for 6 minutes on each side. Serve right away.

Nutrition: calories 216, fat 7, fiber 3, carbs 14, protein 9

Lime Salmon

Preparation time: 5 minutes
Cooking time: 12 minutes
Servings: 6

Ingredients:
- 2 salmon fillets, boneless
- 1 lime, sliced
- Juice of 1 lime
- ½ cup butter, melted
- ½ cup olive oil
- 3 garlic cloves, minced
- 2 shallots, chopped
- Salt and black pepper to taste
- 6 green onions, chopped

Directions:
In a bowl, mix the salmon with the lime juice, butter, oil, garlic, shallots, salt, pepper, and the green onions; rub well. Transfer the fish to your air fryer, top with the lime slices, and cook at 380 degrees F for 6 minutes on each side. Serve with a side salad.

Nutrition: calories 270, fat 4, fiber 2, carbs 12, protein 6

Salmon and Blackberry Sauce

Preparation time: 5 minutes
Cooking time: 12 minutes
Servings: 2

Ingredients:
- 2 salmon fillets, boneless
- 1 tablespoon honey
- ½ cup blackberries
- 1 tablespoon olive oil
- Juice of ½ lemon
- Salt and black pepper to taste

Directions:
In a blender, mix the blackberries with the honey, oil, lemon juice, salt, and pepper; pulse well. Spread the blackberry mixture over the salmon, and then place the fish in your air fryer's basket. Cook at 380 degrees F for 12 minutes, flipping the fish halfway. Serve hot, and enjoy!

Nutrition: calories 210, fat 8, fiber 4, carbs 14, protein 11

Shrimp and Zucchini Mix

Preparation time: 10 minutes
Cooking time: 8 minutes
Servings: 4

Ingredients:

- 2 red onions, cut into chunks
- 3 zucchinis, cut in medium chunks
- 1 pound shrimp, peeled and deveined
- 2 tablespoons olive oil
- ¼ cup tomato sauce
- Salt and black pepper to taste
- 1 garlic clove, minced
- 1 tablespoon lemon juice
- ½ cup parsley, chopped

Directions:

In a baking dish that fits your air fryer, mix all the ingredients except the parsley; toss well. Place the baking dish into the fryer and cook at 400 degrees F for 8 minutes. Add the parsley and stir. Divide everything between plates and serve.

Nutrition: calories 210, fat 7, fiber 4, carbs 15, protein 9

Air Fryer Poultry Recipes

Turmeric Chicken Legs

Preparation time: 5 minutes
Cooking time: 20 minutes
Servings: 4

Ingredients:

- 4 chicken legs
- 5 teaspoons turmeric powder
- 2 tablespoons ginger, grated
- Salt and black pepper to taste
- 4 tablespoons heavy cream

Directions:
Place all ingredients in a bowl and mix well. Transfer the chicken to your air fryer and cook at 380 degrees F for 20 minutes. Divide between plates and serve.

Nutrition: calories 300, fat 4, fiber 12, carbs 22, protein 20

Flavored Turkey Breast

Preparation time: 10 minutes
Cooking time: 50 minutes
Servings: 4

Ingredients:

- 2 turkey breasts, skinless, boneless and halved
- Salt and black pepper to taste
- 1 teaspoon garlic powder
- 1 teaspoon onion powder
- ½ teaspoon thyme, dried
- 1 teaspoon rosemary, dried
- 1 tablespoon lemon juice
- 2 tablespoons olive oil

Directions:
In a bowl, mix all the ingredients and rub the turkey well. Transfer to your air fryer's basket and cook at 370 degrees F for 25 minutes on each side. Serve hot with a side salad.

Nutrition: calories 271, fat 10, fiber 5, carbs 18, protein 15

Salsa Verde Chicken Breast

Preparation time: 10 minutes
Cooking time: 20 minutes
Servings: 4

Ingredients:

- 16 ounces salsa Verde
- 1 tablespoon avocado oil
- Salt and black pepper to taste
- 1 pound chicken breast, boneless and skinless
- 1½ cups cheddar cheese, grated
- ¼ cup parsley, chopped
- 1 teaspoon sweet paprika

Directions:

In a baking dish that fits your air fryer, place all ingredients except the cheese; toss well. Put the pan into the fryer and cook at 380 degrees F for 17 minutes. Sprinkle with the cheese and cook for 3-4 minutes more. Divide between plates and serve.

Nutrition: calories 280, fat 18, fiber 9, carbs 17, protein 14

Creamy Chicken Thighs

Preparation time: 10 minutes
Cooking time: 20 minutes
Servings: 4

Ingredients:

- 5 chicken thighs
- 1 tablespoon olive oil
- 2 garlic cloves, minced
- 1 tablespoon rosemary
- ½ cup heavy cream
- ¾ cup chicken stock
-
- 1 teaspoon chili powder
- ¼ cup cheddar cheese, grated
- ½ cup tomatoes, chopped
- 2 tablespoons basil, chopped
- Salt and black pepper to taste

Directions:

Season the chicken with salt and pepper and rub it with ½ tablespoon of the oil. Put the chicken in your air fryer's basket and cook at 350 degrees F for 4 minutes. Heat up a pan that fits your air fryer with the remaining ½ tablespoon of oil over medium heat. Add rosemary, garlic, chili powder, tomatoes, cream, stock, cheese, salt, and pepper; stir / combine. Bring the mixture to a simmer, take off the heat, and then add the chicken thighs and toss everything. Place the pan in the air fryer and cook at 340 degrees F for 12 minutes. Divide between plates, sprinkle the basil on top, serve, and enjoy.

Nutrition: calories 232, fat 9, fiber 12, carbs 27, protein 16

Chinese Chicken Thighs

Preparation time: 10 minutes
Cooking time: 30 minutes
Servings: 4

Ingredients:
- 4 chicken thighs
- 2 green chilies, chopped
- 1 tablespoon olive oil
- 1 bunch spring onions, chopped
- 1 tablespoon ginger, grated
- 1 tablespoon fish sauce
- 1 tablespoon soy sauce
- 1 teaspoon sesame oil
- 14 ounces water
- 1 tablespoon rice wine

Directions:
Heat up a pan that fits your air fryer with the olive and sesame oil over medium heat. Add the chilies, onions, ginger, fish sauce, soy sauce, rice wine, and the water; whisk, bring to a simmer, cook for 3-4 minutes, and then take off the heat. Add the chicken thighs and toss everything. Place the pan into the air fryer and cook at 370 degrees F for 25 minutes. Divide between plates and serve.

Nutrition: calories 280, fat 12, fiber 12, carbs 20, protein 13

Oregano Chicken Thighs

Preparation time: 5 minutes
Cooking time: 30 minutes
Servings: 4

Ingredients:
- 8 chicken thighs
- 2 tablespoons olive oil
- 4 teaspoons oregano, chopped
- ½ teaspoon sweet paprika
- Salt and black pepper to taste
- 2 garlic cloves, minced
- 1 red onion, chopped

Directions:
In a baking dish that fits your air fryer, place all of the ingredients and mix well. Transfer the dish to your air fryer and cook at 400 degrees F for 30 minutes, shaking halfway. Divide between plates and serve.

Nutrition: calories 264, fat 14, fiber 13, carbs 21, protein 15

Herbed Chicken

Preparation time: 5 minutes
Cooking time: 30 minutes
Servings: 8

Ingredients:
- 8 chicken thighs
- Salt and black pepper to taste
- 3 garlic cloves, minced
- 3 tablespoons butter, melted
- 1 cup chicken stock
- ¼ cup heavy cream
- ½ teaspoon basil, dried
- ½ teaspoon thyme, dried
- ½ teaspoon oregano, dried
- 1 tablespoon mustard
- ¼ cup cheddar cheese, grated

Directions:
In a baking dish that fits your air fryer, place all ingredients except the cheddar cheese; mix well. Transfer the dish to your air fryer and cook at 370 degrees F for 25 minutes. Sprinkle the cheese on top and cook for 5 more minutes. Divide everything between plates and serve.

Nutrition: calories 280, fat 11, fiber 13, carbs 22, protein 14

Honey Duck Breasts

Preparation time: 10 minutes
Cooking time: 20 minutes
Servings: 6

Ingredients:
- 6 duck breasts, boneless
- 4 tablespoons soy sauce
- 1 teaspoon olive oil
- 2 tablespoons honey
- Salt and black pepper to taste
- 20 ounces chicken stock
- 1 tablespoon ginger, grated
- 4 tablespoons hoisin sauce

Directions:
Place all of the ingredients in a bowl and toss well. Put the bowl in the fridge for 10 minutes. Transfer the duck breasts to your air fryer's basket and cook at 400 degrees F for 10 minutes on each side. Divide between plates and serve with a side salad.

Nutrition: calories 286, fat 9, fiber 1, carbs 20, protein 17

Duck and Sauce

Preparation time: 5 minutes
Cooking time: 25 minutes
Servings: 4

Ingredients:
- 2 duck breasts, skin scored
- Salt and black pepper to taste
- 1 tablespoon sugar
- 1 tablespoon olive oil
- 2 tablespoons cranberries
- 8 ounces white wine
- 1 tablespoons garlic, minced
- 2 tablespoons heavy cream

Directions:
Season the duck breasts with salt and pepper and put them in preheated air fryer. Cook at 350 degrees F for 10 minutes on each side and divide between plates. Heat up a pan with the oil over medium heat, and add the cranberries, sugar, wine, garlic, and the cream; whisk well. Cook for 3-4 minutes, drizzle over the duck, and serve.

Nutrition: calories 280, fat 11, fiber 32, carbs 19, protein 20

Chicken Wings and Endives

Preparation time: 10 minutes
Cooking time: 30 minutes
Servings: 4

Ingredients:
- 8 chicken wings, halved
- 6 endives, shaved
- 1 tablespoon olive oil
- 2 garlic cloves, minced
- ¼ cup white wine
- Salt and black pepper to taste
- 1 tablespoon rosemary, chopped
- 1 teaspoon cumin, ground

Directions:
Season the chicken wings with the salt, pepper, cumin, and rosemary. Place the wings in your air fryer's basket and cook at 360 degrees F for 10 minutes on each side; divide between plates. Heat up a pan with the oil over medium heat, and then add the garlic, endives, salt, pepper, and the wine; bring to a simmer. Cook for 8 minutes, spread over the chicken, and serve.

Nutrition: calories 270, fat 8, fiber 12, carbs 20, protein 22

Turkey and Parsley Pesto

Preparation time: 35 minutes
Cooking time: 35 minutes
Servings: 4

Ingredients:
- 1 cup parsley, chopped
- ½ cup olive oil
- ¼ cup red wine
- 4 garlic cloves
- A pinch of salt and black pepper
- A drizzle of maple syrup
- 2 turkey breasts, boneless, skinless and halved

Directions:
In a blender, mix the parsley, garlic, salt, pepper, oil, wine, and maple syrup; pulse to make a parsley pesto and then transfer to a bowl. Add the turkey breasts to the bowl and toss well. Then place the bowl in the fridge for 30 minutes. Drain the turkey breasts (retaining the parsley pesto), put them in your air fryer's basket and cook at 380 degrees F for 35 minutes, flipping the meat halfway. Divide the turkey between plates, drizzle the parsley pesto, all over and serve.

Nutrition: calories 274, fat 10, fiber 12, carbs 20, protein 17

Chicken Breasts and Veggies

Preparation time: 10 minutes
Cooking time: 20 minutes
Servings: 4

Ingredients:
- 2 pounds chicken breasts, skinless and boneless
- 2 tablespoons olive oil
- 1 red onion, chopped
- 2 garlic cloves, minced
- Salt and black pepper to taste
- 12 brown mushrooms, halved
- 1 red bell pepper, chopped
- 1 green bell pepper, roughly chopped
- 2 tablespoons cheddar cheese, shredded

Directions:
Season the chicken breasts with salt and pepper, and then rub with the garlic and 1 tablespoon of the oil. Place the chicken breasts in your preheated air fryer's basket, cook at 390 degrees F for 6 minutes on each side, and divide between plates. Heat up a pan with the remaining 1 tablespoon of the oil over medium heat; add the onions, stir, and cook for 2 minutes. Add the mushrooms and bell peppers, stir, and cook for 5-6 minutes more. Divide this next to the chicken, sprinkle the cheese all over, and serve.

Nutrition: calories 285, fat 12, fiber 11, carbs 20, protein 22

Chicken and Green Coconut Sauce

Preparation time: 10 minutes
Cooking time: 16 minutes
Servings: 4

Ingredients:

- 10 green onions, roughly chopped
- 1 tablespoon ginger, grated
- 4 garlic cloves, minced
- 2 tablespoons oyster sauce
- 3 tablespoons soy sauce
- 1 teaspoon Chinese five spice
-
- 10 chicken drumsticks
- 1 cup coconut milk
- Salt and black pepper to taste
- 1 teaspoon olive oil
- ¼ cup parsley, chopped
- 1 tablespoon lemon juice

Directions:
In a blender, mix the green onions with the ginger, garlic, soy sauce, oyster sauce, five spice, salt, pepper, oil, and coconut milk; pulse well. In a baking dish that fits your air fryer, mix the chicken with the green sauce, toss, and then place the dish in the air fryer. Cook at 370 degrees F for 16 minutes, shaking the fryer once. Divide between plates, sprinkle the parsley on top, drizzle the lemon juice all over, and serve.

Nutrition: calories 281, fat 11, fiber 12, carbs 22, protein 16

Simple Chicken Thighs

Preparation time: 5 minutes
Cooking time: 16 minutes
Servings: 6

Ingredients:

- 8 chicken thighs
- 1 tablespoon turmeric powder
- 1 tablespoon coriander, ground
- 1 tablespoon ginger, grated
- 1 tablespoon sweet paprika
- Salt and black pepper to taste
- 2 tablespoons olive oil
- 1 tablespoon lime juice

Directions:
Place all the ingredients in a bowl and toss well. Transfer the chicken thighs to your air fryer's basket and cook at 370 degrees F for 8 minutes on each side. Divide between plates and serve with a side salad.

Nutrition: calories 270, fat 11, fiber 11, carbs 17, protein 11

Chicken Breasts Delight

Preparation time: 5 minutes
Cooking time: 25 minutes
Servings: 6

Ingredients:
- 1 tablespoon olive oil
- 3½ pounds chicken breasts
- 1 cup chicken stock
- 1¼ cups yellow onion, chopped
- 1 tablespoon lime juice
- 2 teaspoons sweet paprika
- 1 teaspoon red pepper flakes
- 2 tablespoons green onions, chopped
- Salt and black pepper to taste

Directions:
Heat the oil up in a pan that fits your air fryer over medium heat. Add the onions, lime juice, paprika, green onions, pepper flakes, salt, and pepper. Stir the onion mixture and cook for 8 minutes. Add the chicken and the stock, toss, and simmer for 1 more minute. Transfer the pan to your air fryer and cook at 370 degrees F for 12 minutes. Divide between plates and serve.

Nutrition: calories 280, fat 11, fiber 13, carbs 27, protein 16

Tomato Chicken Mix

Preparation time: 10 minutes
Cooking time: 20 minutes
Servings: 6

Ingredients:
- 14 ounces tomato sauce
- 1 tablespoon olive oil
- 4 medium chicken breasts, skinless and boneless
- Salt and black pepper to taste
-
- 1 teaspoon oregano, dried
- 6 ounces mozzarella cheese, grated
- 1 teaspoon garlic powder

Directions:
Put the chicken in your air fryer and season with salt, pepper, garlic powder, and the oregano. Cook the chicken at 360 degrees F for 5 minutes; then transfer to a pan that fits your air fryer, greased with the oil. Add the tomato sauce, sprinkle the mozzarella on top, place the pan in the fryer, and cook at 350 degrees F for 15 minutes more. Divide between plates and serve.

Nutrition: calories 270, fat 10, fiber 16, carbs 16, protein 18

Chicken and Veggies

Preparation time: 10 minutes
Cooking time: 25 minutes
Servings: 4

Ingredients:
- 1 red onion, chopped
- 1 carrot, chopped
- 3 garlic cloves, minced
- 4 chicken breasts, boneless and skinless
- 1 celery stalk, chopped
- 1 cup chicken stock
- 2 tablespoons olive oil
- ½ teaspoon rosemary, dried
- 1 teaspoon sage, dried
- Salt and black pepper to taste

Directions:
In a pan that fits your air fryer, place all ingredients and toss well. Put the pan in the fryer and cook at 360 degrees F for 25 minutes. Divide everything between plates, serve, and enjoy!

Nutrition: calories 292, fat 12, fiber 16, carbs 19, protein 15

Japanese Chicken Thighs

Preparation time: 10 minutes
Cooking time: 30 minutes
Servings: 5

Ingredients:
- 2 pounds chicken thighs
- Salt and black pepper to taste
- 5 spring onions, chopped
- 2 tablespoons olive oil
- 1 tablespoon sherry wine
- ½ teaspoon white vinegar
- 1 tablespoon soy sauce
- ¼ teaspoon sugar

Directions:
Season the chicken with salt and pepper, rub with 1 tablespoon of the oil, and put it in the air fryer's basket. Cook at 360 degrees F for 10 minutes on each side and divide between plates. Heat up a pan with the remaining tablespoon of oil over medium-high heat, and add the spring onions, sherry wine, vinegar, soy sauce, and sugar; whisk. Cook for 10 minutes, drizzle over the chicken, and serve.

Nutrition: calories 271, fat 8, fiber 12, carbs 26, protein 17

Air Fried Whole Chicken

Preparation time: 10 minutes
Cooking time: 20 minutes
Servings: 8

Ingredients:

- 1 whole chicken, cut into medium pieces
- 3 tablespoons white wine
- 2 carrots, chopped
- 1 cup chicken stock
- 1 tablespoon ginger, grated
- Salt and black pepper to taste

Directions:

In a pan that fits your air fryer, mix all of the ingredients. Put the pan in the air fryer and cook at 370 degrees F for 20 minutes. Divide between plates and serve.

Nutrition: calories 220, fat 10, fiber 8, carbs 20, protein 16

Chicken Thighs and Rice

Preparation time: 5 minutes
Cooking time: 30 minutes
Servings: 4

Ingredients:

- 3 carrots, chopped
- 2 pounds chicken thighs, boneless and skinless
- ¼ cup red wine vinegar
- 4 garlic cloves, minced
- Salt and black pepper to taste
- 4 tablespoons olive oil
- 1 tablespoon garlic powder
- 1 tablespoon Italian seasoning
- 1 cup white rice
- 1 teaspoon turmeric powder
- 2 cups chicken stock

Directions:

In a pan that fits your air fryer, mix all of the ingredients and toss. Place the pan in the fryer and cook at 370 degrees F for 30 minutes. Divide between plates and serve.

Nutrition: calories 280, fat 12, fiber 12, carbs 16, protein 13

Glazed Chicken and Apples

Preparation time: 10 minutes
Cooking time: 20 minutes
Servings: 4

Ingredients:

- 3 apples, cored and sliced
- 2 tablespoons olive oil
- 1 tablespoon rosemary, chopped
- Salt and black pepper to taste
- 6 chicken thighs, skin-on
- ⅔ cup apple cider
- 1 tablespoon mustard
- 2 tablespoons honey

Directions:
Heat up a pan that fits your air fryer with 1 tablespoon of the oil over medium heat. Add the cider, honey, and mustard; whisk. Bring to a simmer and take off the heat. Add the chicken, apples, salt, pepper, and rosemary; toss. Place the pan in your air fryer and cook at 390 degrees F for 17 minutes. Divide between plates and serve.

Nutrition: calories 281, fat 11, fiber 12, carbs 28, protein 19

Lemon Chicken and Asparagus

Preparation time: 5 minutes
Cooking time: 15 minutes
Servings: 4

Ingredients:

- 2 tablespoons olive oil
- Juice of 1 lemon
- 1 teaspoon oregano, dried
- 3 garlic cloves, minced
- 1 pound chicken thighs
- Salt and black pepper to taste
- ½ pound asparagus, trimmed and halved
- 1 zucchini, roughly cubed
- 1 lemon, sliced

Directions:
In a pan that fits your air fryer, mix all of the ingredients. Place the pan in your air fryer and cook at 380 degrees F for 15 minutes. Divide between plates and serve.

Nutrition: calories 280, fat 8, fiber 12, carbs 20, protein 15

Turkey with Fig Sauce

Preparation time: 10 minutes
Cooking time: 30 minutes
Servings: 4

Ingredients:

- 2 turkey breasts, halved
- 1 tablespoon olive oil
- ½ teaspoon garlic powder
- ¼ teaspoon sweet paprika
- Salt and black pepper to taste
- 1 cup chicken stock
- 3 tablespoons butter, melted
- 1 shallot, chopped
- ½ cup red wine
- 4 tablespoons figs, chopped
- 1 tablespoon white flour

Directions:

Heat up a pan with the olive oil and 1½ tablespoons of the butter over medium-high heat. Add the shallots, stir, and cook for 2 minutes. Add the garlic powder, paprika, stock, salt, pepper, wine, and the figs; stir and cook for 7-8 minutes. Next add the flour, stir well, and cook the sauce for 1-2 minutes more; take off heat. Season the turkey with salt and pepper, and drizzle the remaining 1½ tablespoons of butter over them. Place the turkey in your air fryer's basket, and cook at 380 degrees F for 15 minutes, flipping them halfway. Divide between plates, drizzle the sauce all over, and serve.

Nutrition: calories 246, fat 12, fiber 4, carbs 22, protein 16

Simple Garlic and Lemon Chicken

Preparation time: 10 minutes
Cooking time: 15 minutes
Servings: 4

Ingredients:

- 4 chicken breasts, skinless and boneless
- 4 garlic heads, peeled, cloves separated and cut into quarters
- 2 tablespoons lemon juice
- Salt and black pepper to taste
- ½ teaspoon lemon pepper
- 1½ tablespoons avocado oil

Directions:

In a bowl, mix all of the ingredients and toss well. Transfer the chicken mixture to your air fryer and cook at 360 degrees F for 15 minutes. Divide between plates and serve with a side salad.

Nutrition: calories 240, fat 7, fiber 1, carbs 17, protein 18

Tarragon Chicken Breasts

Preparation time: 10 minutes
Cooking time: 15 minutes
Servings: 2

Ingredients:

- 2 chicken breasts, skinless and boneless
- 1 cup white wine
- ¼ cup soy sauce
- 2 garlic cloves, minced
- 8 tarragon sprigs, chopped
- Salt and black pepper to taste
- 1 tablespoon butter, melted

Directions:

In a bowl, mix the chicken with the wine, soy sauce, garlic, tarragon, salt, pepper, and the butter; toss well and set aside for 10 minutes. Transfer the chicken and its marinade to a baking dish that fits your air fryer and cook at 370 degrees F for 15 minutes, shaking the fryer halfway. Divide everything between plates and serve.

Nutrition: calories 271, fat 12, fiber 3, carbs 17, protein 15

Chicken and Pear Sauce

Preparation time: 10 minutes
Cooking time: 20 minutes
Servings: 6

Ingredients:

- 3 cups ketchup
- 1 cup pear jelly
- ¼ cup honey
- ½ teaspoon smoked paprika
- 1 teaspoon chili powder
- 1 teaspoon mustard powder
- Salt and black pepper to taste
- 1 teaspoon garlic powder
- 6 chicken breasts, skinless and boneless

Directions:
Season the chicken with salt and pepper, put it in preheated air fryer, and cook at 350 degrees F for 10 minutes. Heat up a pan with the ketchup over medium heat, add the pear jelly, honey, smoked paprika, chili powder, mustard powder, garlic powder, salt, and pepper; whisk and cook for 5-6 minutes. Add the chicken, toss, and cook for 4 minutes more. Divide everything between plates and serve.

Nutrition: calories 283, fat 13, fiber 7, carbs 19, protein 17

Honey Chicken and Dates

Preparation time: 10 minutes
Cooking time: 25 minutes
Servings: 6

Ingredients:

- 1 whole chicken, cut into medium pieces
- ¾ cup water
- ⅓ cup honey
- Salt and black pepper to taste
- ¼ cup olive oil
- 4 dates, chopped

Directions:
Put the water in a pot, bring to a simmer over medium heat. Add the honey, whisk, and take off the heat. Rub the chicken with the oil, season with salt and pepper, and place in your air fryer's basket. Add the dates and cook at 350 degrees F for 10 minutes. Brush the chicken with some of the honey mix, cook for 6 minutes more, flip again, brush one more time with the honey mix, and cook for 7 minutes more. Divide the chicken and the dates between plates and serve.

Nutrition: calories 270, fat 14, fiber 3, carbs 15, protein 20

Chicken and Leeks

Preparation time: 10 minutes
Cooking time: 30 minutes
Servings: 4

Ingredients:
- 4 chicken thighs, bone-in
- Salt and black pepper to taste
- 1 tablespoon olive oil
- 1 cup chicken stock
- 3 leeks, sliced
- 3 carrots, cut into thin sticks
- 2 tablespoon chives, chopped

Directions:
Heat up a pan that fits your air fryer over medium heat, add the stock, leeks and carrots, cover, and simmer for 20 minutes. Rub the chicken with olive oil, season with salt and pepper, put it in your air fryer, and cook at 350 degrees F for 4 minutes. Add the chicken to the leeks mix, place the pan in your air fryer, and cook for 6 minutes more. Divide between plates, serve, and enjoy!

Nutrition: calories 237, fat 10, fiber 4, carbs 19, protein 16

Chicken and Yogurt Mix

Preparation time: 1 hour
Cooking time: 15 minutes
Servings: 4

Ingredients:
- 17 ounces chicken meat, boneless and cubed
- 1 red bell pepper, deseeded and cubed
- 1 green bell pepper, deseeded and cubed
- 1 yellow bell pepper, deseeded and cubed
- 14 ounces yogurt
- Salt and black pepper to taste
- 3½ ounces cherry tomatoes, halved
- 1 tablespoon ginger, grated
- 2 tablespoons red chili powder
- 2 tablespoons coriander powder
- 2 teaspoons olive oil
- 1 teaspoon turmeric powder
- 2 tablespoons cumin powder
- 3 mint leaves, torn

Directions:
In a bowl, mix all of the ingredients, toss well, and place in the fridge for 1 hour. Transfer the whole mix to a pan that fits your air fryer and cook at 400 degrees F for 15 minutes, shaking the pan halfway. Divide everything between plates and serve.

Nutrition: calories 245, fat 4, fiber 5, carbs 17, protein 16

Air Fried Chicken Wings

Preparation time: 10 minutes
Cooking time: 45 minutes
Servings: 4

Ingredients:

- 16 chicken wings
- Salt and black pepper to taste
- ¼ cup butter, melted
- ¼ cup clover honey
- 4 tablespoons garlic, minced

Directions:

Put the chicken wings in your air fryer's basket and season with salt and pepper. Cook at 380 degrees F for 25 minutes, then at 400 degrees F for 5 minutes and put it in a bowl. Melt the butter in a pan over medium-high heat; then add the garlic, stir, and sauté for 5 minutes. Add salt, pepper, the air fried chicken and the honey; stir, and simmer for 10 minutes more over medium heat. Divide the chicken wings and the sauce between plates and serve.

Nutrition: calories 274, fat 11, fiber 3, carbs 19, protein 15

Tomato Duck Breast

Preparation time: 5 minutes
Cooking time: 20 minutes
Servings: 2

Ingredients:

- 1 smoked duck breast
- 1 teaspoon honey
-
- 1 tablespoon tomato paste
- ½ teaspoon apple vinegar

Directions:

In a bowl, mix the duck with the other ingredients and toss. Transfer the contents to your air fryer and cook at 370 degrees F for 10 minutes on each side. Cut the meat into halves, divide between plates, and serve.

Nutrition: calories 274, fat 11, fiber 3, carbs 22, protein 13

Turkey and Spring Onions Mix

Preparation time: 10 minutes
Cooking time: 30 minutes
Servings: 2

Ingredients:

- 2 small turkey breasts, boneless and skinless
- 2 red chilies, chopped
- 1 tablespoon olive oil
- 1 bunch spring onions, chopped
- 1 tablespoon oyster sauce
- 1 tablespoon soy sauce
- 1 cup chicken stock
- 1 tablespoon Chinese rice wine

Directions:
Add the oil to a pan that fits your air fryer and place it over medium heat. Then add the chilies, spring onions, oyster sauce, soy sauce, stock, and rice wine; whisk, and simmer for 3-4 minutes. Add the turkey, toss, and place the pan in the air fryer and cook at 380 degrees F for 30 minutes. Divide everything between plates and serve.

Nutrition: calories 280, fat 12, fiber 5, carbs 16, protein 14

Soy Sauce Chicken

Preparation time: 10 minutes
Cooking time: 40 minutes
Servings: 6

Ingredients:

- 1 whole chicken, cut into pieces
- 1 tablespoon ginger, grated
- 1 chili pepper, minced
- 2 teaspoons soy sauce
- 1 teaspoon sesame oil
- Salt and black pepper to taste

Directions:
In a bowl, mix the chicken with all the other ingredients and rub well. Transfer the chicken pieces to your air fryer's basket. Cook at 400 degrees F for 30 minutes, and then at 380 degrees F for 10 minutes more. Divide everything between plates and serve

Nutrition: calories 270, fat 8, fiber 4, carbs 20, protein 17

Butter and Parmesan Chicken

Preparation time: 10 minutes
Cooking time: 30 minutes
Servings: 4

Ingredients:

- 4 chicken breasts, boneless and skinless
- ¼ cup butter, melted
- ½ cup parmesan cheese, grated
- 1 cup corn flakes, crushed
- Salt and black pepper to taste
- 1 tablespoon olive oil

Directions:

In a bowl, mix all the ingredients and toss. Place the chicken in your air fryer's basket and cook at 360 degrees F for 15 minutes on each side. Divide between plates and serve.

Nutrition: calories 271, fat 9, fiber 4, carbs 19, protein 15

Duck Breast and Potatoes

Preparation time: 10 minutes
Cooking time: 30 minutes
Servings: 2

Ingredients:

- 1 duck breast, halved and scored
- 2 gold potatoes, cubed
- Salt and black pepper to taste
- 2 tablespoons butter, melted
- 1 ounce red wine

Directions:

Season the duck pieces with salt and pepper, put them in a pan, and heat up over medium-high heat. Cook for 4 minutes on each side, transfer to your air fryer's basket, and cook at 360 degrees F for 8 minutes. Put the butter in a pan and heat it up over medium heat; then add the potatoes, salt, pepper, and the wine, and cook for 8 minutes. Add the duck pieces, toss, and cook everything for 3-4 minutes more. Divide all between plates and serve.

Nutrition: calories 290, fat 13, fiber 4, carbs 10, protein 16

Balsamic Chicken

Preparation time: 10 minutes
Cooking time: 20 minutes
Servings: 4

Ingredients:
- 1 yellow onion, minced
- 4 chicken breasts, skinless and boneless
- ¼ cup balsamic vinegar
- 12 ounces canned tomatoes, chopped
- Salt and black pepper to taste
- ¼ cup cheddar cheese, grated
- ¼ teaspoon garlic powder

Directions:
In a baking dish that fits your air fryer, mix the chicken with the onions, vinegar, tomatoes, salt, pepper, and garlic powder. Sprinkle the cheese on top and place the pan in the air fryer; cook at 400 degrees F for 20 minutes. Divide between plates and serve.

Nutrition: calories 280, fat 11, fiber 2, carbs 19, protein 16

Simple Lemongrass Chicken

Preparation time: 10 minutes
Cooking time: 30 minutes
Servings: 4

Ingredients:
- 1 bunch lemongrass, trimmed
- 1 tablespoon ginger, chopped
- 4 garlic cloves, minced
- 2 tablespoons fish sauce
- 3 tablespoons soy sauce
- 10 chicken drumsticks
- 1 cup coconut milk
- Salt and black pepper to taste
- 1 teaspoon butter, melted
- ¼ cup parsley, chopped
- 1 yellow onion, chopped
- 1 tablespoon lemon juice

Directions:
In a blender, combine the lemongrass, ginger, garlic, soy sauce, fish sauce, and coconut milk; pulse well. Put the butter in a pan that fits your air fryer and heat it up over medium heat; add the onions, stir, and cook for 2-3 minutes. Add the chicken, salt, pepper, and the lemongrass mix; toss well. Place the pan in the fryer and cook at 380 degrees F for 25 minutes. Add the lemon juice and the parsley and toss. Divide everything between plates and serve.

Nutrition: calories 251, fat 8, fiber 14, carbs 19, protein 6

Spiced Chicken

Preparation time: 10 minutes
Cooking time: 25 minutes
Servings: 4

Ingredients:

- 6 chicken thighs, boneless
- 2 tablespoons olive oil
- ½ teaspoon coriander, ground
- ½ teaspoon cumin, ground
- ½ teaspoon ginger powder
- ½ teaspoon turmeric, ground
- ½ teaspoon cinnamon, ground
- 1 teaspoon sweet paprika
- 2 yellow onions, chopped
- 5 garlic cloves, chopped
- ¼ cup white wine
- 1 cup chicken stock
- ¼ cup cranberries, dried
- Juice of 1 lemon
- ½ cup cilantro, chopped

Directions:

Heat up the oil in a pan that fits your air fryer over medium heat. Add all other ingredients except the chicken, lemon juice, and cilantro; stir and cook for 5 minutes. Then add the chicken and toss. Place the pan in the fryer and cook at 380 degrees F for 20 minutes. Add the lemon juice and the cilantro and toss. Divide between plates, serve, and enjoy!

Nutrition: calories 261, fat 12, fiber 7, carbs 15, protein 25

Turkey Chili

Preparation time: 10 minutes
Cooking time: 25 minutes
Servings: 4

Ingredients:

- 1 pound turkey meat, cubed and browned
- Salt and black pepper to taste
- 15 ounces canned lentils, drained
- 1 yellow onion, chopped
- 1 green bell pepper, chopped
- 3 garlic cloves, chopped
- 2½ tablespoons chili powder
- 1½ teaspoons cumin, ground
- 12 ounces veggie stock

Directions:

Add all of the ingredients to a pan that fits your air fryer and mix well. Place the pan in the fryer and cook at 380 degrees F for 25 minutes. Divide into bowls and serve hot.

Nutrition: calories 251, fat 8, fiber 8, carbs 15, protein 17

Mexican Turkey Mix

Preparation time: 5 minutes
Cooking time: 20 minutes
Servings: 4

Ingredients:
- 1 pound turkey meat, ground
- Salt and black pepper to taste
- 2 tablespoons olive oil
- 10 ounces tomato sauce
- 4 ounces mushrooms, sliced
- 1 tablespoon oregano, dried
- 1 teaspoon garlic, minced
- 1 teaspoon basil, dried
- 1 yellow onion, chopped
- 1 cup cheddar cheese, grated

Directions:
Heat up the oil in a pan that fits your air fryer over medium heat. Add the turkey, oregano, garlic, basil, and the onions; toss, and cook for 2-3 minutes. Then add the mushrooms and tomato sauce, toss, and cook for 2 minutes more. Place the pan in the fryer and cook at 370 degrees F for 16 minutes. Sprinkle the cheese all over, divide the mix between plates, and serve.

Nutrition: calories 261, fat 8, fiber 6, carbs 16, protein 16

Chicken and Peppercorns Mix

Preparation time: 5 minutes
Cooking time: 20 minutes
Servings: 4

Ingredients:
- 8 chicken thighs, boneless
- Salt and black pepper to taste
- ½ cup balsamic vinegar
- 1 teaspoon black peppercorns
- 4 garlic cloves, minced
- ½ cup soy sauce

Directions:
In a pan that fits your air fryer, mix the chicken with all the other ingredients and toss. Place the pan in the fryer and cook at 380 degrees F for 20 minutes. Divide everything between plates and serve.

Nutrition: calories 261, fat 7, fiber 5, carbs 15, protein 16

Fast Turkey Meatballs

Preparation time: 10 minutes
Cooking time: 15 minutes
Servings: 8

Ingredients:
- 1 pound turkey meat, ground
- 1 yellow onion, minced
- ¼ cup parmesan cheese, grated
- ½ cup panko breadcrumbs
- 4 garlic cloves, minced
- ¼ cup parsley, chopped
- Salt and black pepper to taste
- 1 teaspoon oregano, dried
- 1 egg, whisked
- ¼ cup milk
- 2 teaspoons soy sauce
- 1 teaspoon fish sauce
- Cooking spray

Directions:
In a bowl, mix together all of the ingredients (except the cooking spray), stir well, and then shape into medium-sized meatballs. Place the meatballs in your air fryer's basket, grease them with cooking spray, and cook at 380 degrees F for 15 minutes. Serve the meatballs with a side salad.

Nutrition: calories 261, fat 7, fiber 6, carbs 15, protein 18

Rosemary Chicken Breasts

Preparation time: 10 minutes
Cooking time: 25 minutes
Servings: 4

Ingredients:
- 4 garlic cloves, chopped
- 2 chicken breasts, skinless, boneless and halved
- 1 yellow onion, sliced
- 1 teaspoon rosemary, dried
- 1 tablespoon fresh rosemary, chopped
- 2 tablespoons butter, melted
- 1 cup chicken stock
- 1 tablespoon soy sauce
- Salt and black pepper to taste
- 2 tablespoons cornstarch mixed with 2½ tablespoons water

Directions:
Heat up the butter in a pan that fits your air fryer over medium heat. Add the onions, garlic, dried and fresh rosemary, stock, soy sauce, salt, and pepper; stir, and simmer for 2-3 minutes. Add the cornstarch mixture, whisk, cook for 2 minutes more, and take off the heat. Add the chicken, toss gently, and place the pan in the fryer; cook at 370 degrees F for 20 minutes. Divide between plates and serve hot.
Nutrition: calories 281, fat 8, fiber 5, carbs 15, protein 20

Chicken and Smoked Pancetta

Preparation time: 10 minutes
Cooking time: 25 minutes
Servings: 4

Ingredients:

- 2 chicken breasts, skinless, boneless, cubed
- 4 ounces smoked pancetta, chopped
- ½ cup chicken stock
- 2 scallions, chopped
- ½ bunch thyme, chopped
- Salt and black pepper to taste
- ½ bunch rosemary, chopped
- ½ fennel bulb, cut into matchsticks
- 4 carrots, cut into thin matchsticks
- Juice of 1 lemon
- A drizzle of olive oil

Directions:
Heat up the oil in a pan that fits your air fryer over medium heat. Add the scallions, pancetta, thyme, rosemary, salt, pepper, fennel, and carrots; toss and cook for 5 minutes. Add the lemon juice and the chicken, toss, and cook for 5 more minutes. Place the pan in the fryer and cook at 380 degrees F for 15 minutes. Divide everything between plates and serve.

Nutrition: calories 281, fat 11, fiber 5, carbs 17, protein 20

Turkey Wings and Orange Sauce

Preparation time: 10 minutes
Cooking time: 35 minutes
Servings: 4

Ingredients:

- 2 turkey wings
- 2 tablespoons butter, melted
- 1½ cups cranberries
- Salt and black pepper to taste
- 1 yellow onion, sliced
- 1 cup orange juice
- 1 bunch thyme, roughly chopped

Directions:
Place the butter in a pan that fits your air fryer and heat up over medium-high heat. Add the cranberries, salt, pepper, onions, and orange juice; whisk, and cook for 3 minutes. Add the turkey wings, toss, and cook for 3-4 minutes more. Transfer the pan to your air fryer and cook at 380 degrees F for 25 minutes. Add the thyme, toss, and divide everything between plates. Serve, and enjoy!

Nutrition: calories 291, fat 12, fiber 7, carbs 20, protein 22

Cinnamon Chicken Mix

Preparation time: 10 minutes
Cooking time: 35 minutes
Servings: 8

Ingredients:

- 1 whole chicken, cut into pieces
- 1 tablespoon olive oil
- 1½ tablespoons lemon zest
- 1 cup chicken stock
- 1½ teaspoons cinnamon powder
- Salt and black pepper to taste
- 2 teaspoons garlic powder
- 1 tablespoon coriander powder

Directions:
Place all of the ingredients in a bowl and mix well. Transfer the chicken to your air fryer's basket and cook at 370 degrees F for 35 minutes, shaking the fryer from time to time. Divide the chicken between plates and serve with a side salad.

Nutrition: calories 281, fat 7, fiber 8, carbs 20, protein 28

Hot Wings

Preparation time: 10 minutes
Cooking time: 17 minutes
Servings: 6

Ingredients:

- 12 chicken wings, cut into 24 pieces
- ¼ cup honey
- 4 tablespoons hot sauce
- Salt and black pepper to taste
- ¼ cup tomato sauce
- 1 tablespoon cilantro, chopped

Directions:
In a bowl, mix the chicken wings with the hot sauce, honey, salt, pepper, and tomato sauce; toss well. Transfer the chicken wings to your air fryer's basket and cook at 400 degrees F for 17 minutes. Divide between plates, sprinkle the cilantro on top, and serve.

Nutrition: calories 271, fat 7, fiber 6, carbs 14, protein 20

Chicken and Baby Carrots Mix

Preparation time: 5 minutes
Cooking time: 30 minutes
Servings: 4

Ingredients:
- 6 chicken thighs
- 1 teaspoon olive oil
- Salt and black pepper to taste
- 1 yellow onion, chopped
- ½ pound baby carrots, halved
- ½ teaspoon thyme, dried
- 2 tablespoons tomato paste
- ½ cup white wine
- 15 ounces canned tomatoes, chopped
- 1 cup chicken stock

Directions:
Put the oil into a pan that fits your air fryer and heat up over medium heat. Add the chicken thighs and brown them for 1-2 minutes on each side. Add all the remaining ingredients, toss, and cook for 4-5 minutes more. Place the pan in the air fryer and cook at 380 degrees F for 22 minutes. Divide the chicken and carrots mix between plates and serve.

Nutrition: calories 271, fat 11, fiber 7, carbs 17, protein 20

Cajun Chicken and Okra

Preparation time: 10 minutes
Cooking time: 30 minutes
Servings: 4

Ingredients:
- 1 tablespoon olive oil
- 1 pound chicken thighs, halved
- Salt and black pepper to taste
- 1 tablespoon Cajun spice
- 1 red bell pepper, chopped
- 1 yellow onion, chopped
- 4 garlic cloves, minced
- 1 cup chicken stock
- ½ pound okra

Directions:
Add the oil to a pan that fits your air fryer and heat up over medium heat. Then add the chicken and brown for 2-3 minutes. Next, add all remaining ingredients, toss, and cook for 3-4 minutes more. Place the pan into the air fryer and cook at 380 degrees F for 22 minutes. Divide everything between plates and serve.

Nutrition: calories 261, fat 11, fiber 6, carbs 19, protein 17

Chicken and Beans Chili

Preparation time: 10 minutes
Cooking time: 30 minutes
Servings: 4

Ingredients:
- 1½ cups canned kidney beans, drained
- 1 yellow onion, minced
- 2 garlic cloves, minced
- Salt and black pepper to taste
- 1 pound chicken meat, ground
- 1 tablespoon olive oil
- 2 carrots, chopped
- 4 ounces canned green chilies, chopped
- 1 teaspoon brown sugar
- 15 ounces canned tomatoes, chopped
- A handful of cilantro, chopped

Directions:
Heat up the oil in a pan that fits your air fryer oil over medium heat; then add the onion and the garlic. Stir and cook for 2-3 minutes. Add the chicken, salt, pepper, carrots, chilies, sugar, and the tomatoes. Stir, bring to a simmer, and cook for 2-3 minutes more. Add the beans, toss, and place the pan in the air fryer. Cook at 370 degrees F for 25 minutes. Divide into bowls, sprinkle the cilantro on top, and serve.

Nutrition: calories 300, fat 14, fiber 11, carbs 18, protein 22

Chicken and Beer Mix

Preparation time: 10 minutes
Cooking time: 30 minutes
Servings: 4
Ingredients:
- 1 yellow onion, minced
- 4 chicken drumsticks
- 1 tablespoon balsamic vinegar
- 1 chili pepper, chopped
- 15 ounces beer
- Salt and black pepper to taste
- 2 tablespoons olive oil

Directions:
Put the oil in a pan that fits your air fryer and heat up over medium heat. Add the onion and the chili pepper, stir, and cook for 2 minutes. Add the vinegar, beer, salt, and pepper; stir, and cook for 3 more minutes. Add the chicken, toss, and put the pan in the fryer and cook at 370 degrees F for 20 minutes. Divide everything between plates and serve.

Nutrition: calories 291, fat 11, fiber 7, carbs 18, protein 22

Chicken Curry

Preparation time: 10 minutes
Cooking time: 30 minutes
Servings: 4

Ingredients:
- 15 ounces chicken breast, skinless, boneless, cubed
- 1 tablespoon olive oil
- 1 yellow onion, sliced
- Salt and black pepper to taste
- 6 potatoes, peeled and cubed
- 5 ounces heavy cream
- 1 teaspoon curry powder
- ½ bunch coriander, chopped

Directions:
Heat up the oil in a pan that fits your air fryer over medium heat. Add the chicken, toss, and brown for 2 minutes. Then add the onions, curry powder, salt, and pepper; toss, and cook for 3 minutes. Next add the potatoes and the cream; toss well. Place the pan in the air fryer and cook at 370 degrees F for 20 minutes. Add the coriander and stir. Divide the curry into bowls and serve.

Nutrition: calories 221, fat 8, fiber 11, carbs 17, protein 20

Marinara Chicken

Preparation time: 10 minutes
Cooking time: 25 minutes
Servings: 6

Ingredients:
- 1 tablespoon olive oil
- 2 pounds chicken breasts, skinless, boneless and cubed
- Salt and black pepper to taste
- ¾ cup yellow onion, diced
- 1 cup green bell pepper, chopped
- ¾ cup marinara sauce
- ½ cup cheddar cheese, grated

Directions:
Heat up a pan that fits your air fryer with the oil over medium heat. Add the chicken, toss, and brown for 3 minutes. Add the salt, pepper, onions, bell peppers, and the marinara sauce; stir, and cook for 3 minutes more. Place the pan in the air fryer and cook at 370 degrees F for 15 minutes. Sprinkle the cheese on top, divide the mix between plates, and serve.

Nutrition: calories 283, fat 11, fiber 5, carbs 15, protein 16

Bleu Cheese Chicken Mix

Preparation time: 10 minutes
Cooking time: 20 minutes
Servings: 4

Ingredients:

- 1 pound chicken breasts, skinless, boneless and cut into thin strips
- 1 small yellow onion, sliced
- ½ cup buffalo sauce
- ½ cup chicken stock
- ¼ cup bleu cheese, crumbled

Directions:

In a pan that fits your air fryer, mix the chicken with the onions, buffalo sauce, and the stock. Toss everything and then place the pan in the fryer; cook at 370 degrees F for 20 minutes. Sprinkle the cheese on top, divide everything between plates, and serve.

Nutrition: calories 261, fat 11, fiber 8, carbs 14, protein 18

Chicken and Potatoes

Preparation time: 5 minutes
Cooking time: 20 minutes
Servings: 4

Ingredients:

- 4 gold potatoes, cut into medium chunks
- 1 yellow onion, thinly sliced
- 1 pound chicken thighs, boneless
- ½ cup chicken stock
- Salt and black pepper to taste

Directions:

In a pan that fits your air fryer, mix the chicken with the salt, pepper, onions, and the stock. Place the pan in the fryer and cook at 380 degrees F for 10 minutes. Add the potatoes, put the pan in the fryer again, and cook at 400 degrees F for 10 minutes more. Divide between plates and serve.

Nutrition: calories 281, fat 11, fiber 7, carbs 20, protein 16

Chicken and Chickpeas Mix

Preparation time: 10 minutes
Cooking time: 25 minutes
Servings: 4
Ingredients:

- 5 ounces bacon, cooked and crumbled
- 2 tablespoons olive oil
- 1 cup yellow onion, chopped
- 8 ounces canned chickpeas, drained
- 2 carrots, chopped
- 1 tablespoon parsley, chopped
- Salt and black pepper to taste
- 2 pounds chicken thighs, boneless
- 1 cup chicken stock
- 1 teaspoon balsamic vinegar

Directions:
Heat up a pan that fits your air fryer with the oil over medium heat. Add the onions, carrots, salt and pepper; stir, and sauté for 3-4 minutes. Add the chicken, stock, vinegar, and chickpeas; then toss. Place the pan in the fryer and cook at 380 degrees F for 20 minutes. Add the bacon and the parsley and toss again. Divide everything between plates and serve.

Nutrition: calories 300, fat 8, fiber 11, carbs 20, protein 22

Chicken and Squash

Preparation time: 10 minutes
Cooking time: 25 minutes
Servings: 4
Ingredients:

- 3 garlic cloves, minced
- 2 tablespoons olive oil
- 2 red chilies, minced
- 2 tablespoons green curry paste
- A pinch of cumin, ground
- ¼ teaspoon coriander, ground
- ½ cup basil, chopped
- 14 ounces coconut milk
- 6 cups squash, cubed
- 8 chicken drumsticks
- Salt and black pepper to taste
- ½ cup cilantro, chopped

Directions:
Heat up a pan that fits your air fryer with the oil over medium heat. Add the garlic, chilies, curry paste, cumin, coriander, salt, and pepper; stir, and cook for 3-4 minutes. Add the chicken pieces and the coconut milk, and stir. Place the pan in the fryer and cook at 380 degrees F for 15 minutes. Add the squash, cilantro, and basil; toss, and cook for 5-6 minutes more. Divide into bowls and serve. Enjoy!
Nutrition: calories 299, fat 11, fiber 6, carbs 18, protein 20

Indian Chicken Mix

Preparation time: 10 minutes
Cooking time: 30 minutes
Servings: 4

Ingredients:

- 1 yellow onion, chopped
- 2 tablespoons butter, melted
- 4 garlic cloves, minced
- 1 tablespoon ginger, grated
- 1½ teaspoons paprika
- 1½ teaspoons coriander, ground
- 1 teaspoon turmeric powder
- Salt and black pepper to taste
- 15 ounces canned tomatoes, crushed
- ¼ cup lemon juice
- 1 pound spinach, chopped
- 1½ pounds chicken drumsticks
- ½ cup cilantro, chopped
- ½ cup chicken stock
- ½ cup heavy cream

Directions:
Place the butter in a pan that fits your air fryer and heat over medium heat. Add the onions and the garlic, stir, and cook for 3 minutes. Add the ginger, paprika, coriander, turmeric, salt, pepper, and the chicken; toss, and cook for 4 minutes more. Add the tomatoes and the stock, and stir. Place the pan in the fryer and cook at 370 degrees F for 15 minutes. Add the spinach, lemon juice, cilantro, and the cream; stir, and cook for 5-6 minutes more. Divide everything into bowls and serve.
Nutrition: calorie 281, fat 9, fiber 7, carbs 17, protein 20

Sesame Chicken Mix

Preparation time: 10 minutes
Cooking time: 20 minutes
Servings: 4

Ingredients:

- 2 pounds chicken breasts, skinless, boneless and cubed
- ½ cup yellow onion, chopped
- Salt and black pepper to taste
- 1 tablespoon olive oil
- 2 garlic cloves, minced
- ½ cup soy sauce
- 2 teaspoons sesame oil
- ½ cup honey
- ¼ teaspoon red pepper flakes
- 1 tablespoon sesame seeds, toasted

Directions:
Heat up the oil in a pan that fits your air fryer oil over medium heat. Add the chicken, toss, and brown for 3 minutes. Add the onions, garlic, salt, and pepper; stir, and cook for 2 minutes more. Add the soy sauce, sesame oil, honey, and pepper flakes; toss well. Place the pan in the fryer and cook at 380 degrees F for 15 minutes. Top with the sesame seeds and toss. Divide between plates and serve.
Nutrition: calories 240, fat 11, fiber 5, carbs 18, protein 16

Marjoram Chicken

Preparation time: 10 minutes
Cooking time: 30 minutes
Servings: 6

Ingredients:

- 2 pounds chicken thighs
- Salt and black pepper to taste
- 1 tablespoon olive oil
- ½ teaspoon sweet paprika
- ¼ cup white wine
- 1 teaspoon marjoram, dried
- ¼ cup chicken stock

Directions:
Heat up a pan that fits your air fryer with the oil over medium heat. Add the chicken pieces and brown them for 5 minutes. Add all remaining ingredients and toss well. Place the pan in the fryer and cook at 390 degrees F for 25 minutes. Divide between plates and serve.

Nutrition: calories 231, fat 7, fiber 6, carbs 18, protein 20

Air Fryer Meat Recipes

Spiced Pork Chops

Preparation time: 5 minutes
Cooking time: 15 minutes
Servings: 4

Ingredients:

- 4 medium pork chops
- Salt and black pepper to taste
- 1 tablespoon olive oil
- 2 tablespoons sweet paprika
- 2 tablespoons onion powder
- 2 tablespoons garlic powder
- 2 tablespoons oregano, dried
- 1 tablespoon cumin, ground
- 1 tablespoon rosemary, dried

Directions:
In a bowl, mix all of the ingredients and rub the pork chops well. Put the pork chops in your air fryer's basket and cook at 400 degrees F for 15 minutes, flipping them halfway. Divide between plates, serve, and enjoy.

Nutrition: calories 281, fat 8, fiber 7, carbs 17, protein 19

Chinese Pork and Broccoli Mix

Preparation time: 5 minutes
Cooking time: 15 minutes
Servings: 4

Ingredients:

- 1 pound pork stew meat, cut into strips
- 1 pound broccoli florets
- ⅓ cup oyster sauce
- 2 teaspoons olive oil
- 1 teaspoon soy sauce
- 1 garlic clove, minced

Directions:
In a bowl, mix the pork with all the other ingredients and toss well. Put the mixture into your air fryer and cook at 390 degrees F for 15 minutes. Divide into bowls and serve.

Nutrition: calories 281, fat 12, fiber 7, carbs 19, protein 20

French Beef Mix

Preparation time: 5 minutes
Cooking time: 15 minutes
Servings: 2

Ingredients:

- 1 red onion, sliced
- 1 green bell pepper, cut in strips
- Salt and black pepper to taste
- 2 teaspoons Provencal herbs
- ½ tablespoon mustard
- 1 tablespoon olive oil
- 7 ounces beef fillets, cut into strips

Directions:
Place all the ingredients in a baking dish that fits your air fryer and mix well. Put the pan in the fryer and cook at 400 degrees F for 15 minutes. Divide the mixture between bowls and serve.

Nutrition: calories 291, fat 8, fiber 7, carbs 19, protein 20

Beef and Mushroom Mix

Preparation time: 5 minutes
Cooking time: 17 minutes
Servings: 2

Ingredients:

- 2 beef steaks, cut into strips
- Salt and black pepper to taste
- 8 ounces white mushrooms, sliced
- 1 yellow onion, chopped
- 2 tablespoons dark soy sauce
- 1 teaspoon olive oil

Directions:
In a baking dish that fits your air fryer, combine all ingredients; toss well. Place the pan in the fryer and cook at 390 degrees F for 17 minutes. Divide everything between plates and serve.

Nutrition: calories 285, fat 8, fiber 2, carbs 18, protein 20

Oregano Pork Chops

Preparation time: 5 minutes
Cooking time: 15 minutes
Servings: 4

Ingredients:
- 2 tablespoons olive oil
- 4 pork chops
- Salt and black pepper to taste
- 4 garlic cloves, minced
- 2 tablespoon oregano, chopped

Directions:
Place all of the ingredients in a bowl and toss / mix well. Transfer the chops to your air fryer's basket and cook at 400 degrees F for 15 minutes. Serve with a side salad and enjoy!

Nutrition: calories 301, fat 7, fiber 5, carbs 19, protein 22

Crusted Rack of Lamb

Preparation time: 10 minutes
Cooking time: 20 minutes
Servings: 4

Ingredients:
- 2 tablespoons macadamia nuts, toasted and crushed
- 1 tablespoon vegetable oil
- 2 garlic cloves, minced
- 28 ounces rack of lamb
- Salt and black pepper to taste
- 1 egg, whisked
- 1 tablespoon oregano, chopped

Directions:
In a bowl, mix the lamb with the salt, pepper, garlic, and the oil; rub the lamb well. In another bowl, mix the macadamia nuts with the oregano, salt, and pepper; stir. Put the egg in a third bowl. Dredge the lamb in the egg, then in the macadamia nuts mix. Place the lamb in your air fryer's basket and cook at 380 degrees F for 10 minutes on each side. Divide between plates and serve with a side salad.

Nutrition: calories 280, fat 12, fiber 8, carbs 20, protein 19

Coconut Pork Mix

Preparation time: 5 minutes
Cooking time: 15 minutes
Servings: 4

Ingredients:

- 1 teaspoon ginger, grated
- 2 teaspoons chili paste
- 2 garlic cloves, minced
- 14 ounces pork chops, cut into strips
- 1 shallot, chopped
- 7 ounces coconut milk
- 2 tablespoons olive oil
- 3 tablespoons soy sauce
- Salt and black pepper to taste

Directions:

In a baking dish that fits your air fryer, mix the pork with the ginger, chili paste, garlic, shallots, oil soy sauce, salt, and pepper; toss well. Place the pan in the fryer and cook at 400 degrees F for 12 minutes, shaking the fryer halfway. Add the coconut milk, toss, and cook for 3-4 minutes more. Divide everything into bowls and serve.

Nutrition: calories 283, fat 11, fiber 9, carbs 22, protein 14

Creamy Pork and Sprouts

Preparation time: 10 minutes
Cooking time: 25 minutes
Servings: 4

Ingredients:

- 1 pound pork tenderloin, cubed
- 2 tablespoons olive oil
- 2 tablespoons rosemary, chopped
- Salt and black pepper to taste
- 1 garlic clove, minced
- 1½ pounds Brussels sprouts, trimmed
- ½ cup sour cream
- Salt and black pepper to taste

Directions:

In a pan that fits your air fryer, mix the pork with the oil, rosemary, salt, pepper, garlic, salt, and pepper; toss well. Place the pan in the fryer and cook at 400 degrees F for 17 minutes. Next add the sprouts and the sour cream and toss. Place the pan in the fryer and cook for 8 more minutes. Divide everything into bowls and serve.

Nutrition: calories 280, fat 13, fiber 9, carbs 22, protein 18

Pork and Chives Mix

Preparation time: 10 minutes
Cooking time: 22 minutes
Servings: 6

Ingredients:

- 1 cup mayonnaise
- 2 garlic cloves, minced
- 1 pound pork tenderloin, cubed
- 2 tablespoons chives, chopped
- 2 tablespoons mustard
- ¼ cup tarragon, chopped
- Salt and black pepper to taste

Directions:
Place all ingredients *except* the mayo into a pan that fits your air fryer; mix well. Put the pan in the fryer and cook at 400 degrees F for 15 minutes. Add the mayo and toss. Put the pan in the fryer for 7 more minutes. Divide into bowls and serve.

Nutrition: calories 280, fat 12, fiber 2, carbs 17, protein 14

Beef and Wine Sauce

Preparation time: 10 minutes
Cooking time: 40 minutes
Servings: 6

Ingredients:

- 2 tablespoons butter, melted
- 3 garlic cloves, minced
- Salt and black pepper to taste
- 1 tablespoon mustard
- 3 pounds beef roast
- 1¾ cups beef stock
- ¾ cup red wine

Directions:
In a bowl, mix the beef with the butter, mustard, garlic, salt, and pepper; rub the meat thoroughly. Put the beef roast in your air fryer's basket and cook at 400 degrees F for 15 minutes. Heat up a pan over medium-high heat and add the stock and the wine. Then add the beef roast and place the pan in the fryer; cook at 380 degrees F for 25 minutes more. Divide into bowls and serve.

Nutrition: calories 300, fat 11, fiber 4, carbs 18, protein 22

Lamb Chops and Dill

Preparation time: 10 minutes
Cooking time: 20 minutes
Servings: 6

Ingredients:
- 1 pound lamb chops
- 2 yellow onions, chopped
- 1 tablespoon olive oil
- 1 garlic clove, minced
- 3 cups chicken stock
- 2 tablespoons sweet paprika
- Salt and black pepper to taste
- 1½ cups heavy cream
- 2 tablespoons dill, chopped

Directions:
Put the lamb chops in your air fryer and season with the salt, pepper, garlic, and paprika; rub the chops thoroughly. Cook at 380 degrees F for 10 minutes. Transfer the lamb to a baking dish that fits your air fryer. Then add the onions, stock, cream, and dill, and toss. Place the pan in the fryer and cook everything for 7-8 minutes more. Divide everything between plates and serve hot.

Nutrition: calories 310, fat 8, fiber 10, carbs 19, protein 25

Mustard Pork Chops

Preparation time: 10 minutes
Cooking time: 15 minutes
Servings: 6

Ingredients:
- 2 pork chops
- ¼ cup olive oil
- 2 garlic cloves, minced
- 1 tablespoon mustard
- 1 teaspoon sweet paprika
- Salt and black pepper to taste

Directions:
Place all of the ingredients in a bowl, and coat the pork chops well. Transfer the pork chops to your air fryer's basket and cook at 400 degrees F for 15 minutes. Divide the chops between plates and serve

Nutrition: calories 284, fat 14, fiber 4, carbs 17, protein 28

Beef Roast and Grapes

Preparation time: 10 minutes
Cooking time: 40 minutes
Servings: 4

Ingredients:
- 1 pound beef roast meat, cubed
- 3 tablespoons olive oil
- Salt and black pepper to taste
- 1½ cups chicken stock
- ½ cup dry white wine
- 2 garlic cloves, minced
- 1 teaspoon thyme, chopped
- ½ red onion, chopped
- ½ pound red grapes

Directions:
Heat up the oil in a pan that fits your air fryer over medium-high heat. Add the beef, salt, and pepper; toss, and brown for 5 minutes. Add the stock, wine, garlic, thyme, and onions; toss and cook for 5 minutes more. Transfer the pan to your air fryer and cook at 390 degrees F for 25 minutes. Add the grapes, toss gently, and cook everything for 5-6 minutes more. Divide between plates and serve right away.

Nutrition: calories 290, fat 12, fiber 5, carbs 19, protein 28

Sage Pork Mix

Preparation time: 10 minutes
Cooking time: 50 minutes
Servings: 6

Ingredients:
- 2½ pounds pork loin, boneless and cubed
- ¾ cup beef stock
- 2 tablespoons olive oil
- ½ tablespoon smoked paprika
- 3 teaspoons sage, dried
- ½ tablespoon garlic powder
- 1 teaspoon basil, dried
- 1 teaspoon oregano, dried
- Salt and black pepper to taste

Directions:
In a pan that fits your air fryer, heat up the oil over medium heat. Add the pork, toss, and brown for 5 minutes. Add the paprika, sage, garlic powder, basil, oregano, salt, and pepper; toss and cook for 2 more minutes. Next add the stock and toss. Place the pan in the fryer and cook at 360 degrees F for 40 minutes. Divide everything between plates and serve.

Nutrition: calories 290, fat 11, fiber 6, carbs 20, protein 29

Beef Roast

Preparation time: 10 minutes
Cooking time: 55 minutes
Servings: 4

Ingredients:
- 3 tablespoons garlic, minced
- 1 tablespoon smoked paprika
- 3 tablespoons olive oil
- 2 pounds beef roast
- Salt and black pepper to taste

Directions:
In a bowl, combine all the ingredients and coat the roast well. Place the roast in your air fryer and cook at 390 degrees F for 55 minutes. Slice the roast, divide it between plates, and serve with a side salad.

Nutrition: calories 291, fat 12, fiber 9, carbs 20, protein 26

Tarragon Pork Loin

Preparation time: 10 minutes
Cooking time: 55 minutes
Servings: 6

Ingredients:
- 3 pounds pork loin roast, trimmed
- Salt and black pepper to taste
- 3 garlic cloves, minced
- 2 tablespoons tarragon, chopped
- 2 teaspoons sweet paprika
- ¼ cup olive oil

Directions:
In a bowl, mix the roast with all the other ingredients and rub well. Transfer the roast to your air fryer and cook at 390 degrees F for 55 minutes. Slice the roast, divide it between plates, and serve.

Nutrition: calories 290, fat 14, fiber 9, carbs 19, protein 22

Beef and Celery Mix

Preparation time: 10 minutes
Cooking time: 55 minutes
Servings: 6

Ingredients:
- 1 pound yellow onion, chopped
- 3 pounds beef roast
- 1 pound celery, chopped
- Salt and black pepper to taste
- 3 cups beef stock
- 16 ounces canned tomatoes, chopped
- 2 tablespoons olive oil

Directions:
Place all the ingredients into a baking dish that fits your air fryer and mix well. Put the pan in the fryer and cook at 390 degrees F for 55 minutes. Slice the roast, and then divide it and the celery mix between plates. Serve, and enjoy!

Nutrition: calories 300, fat 12, fiber 4, carbs 18, protein 20

Chinese Beef Mix

Preparation time: 5 minutes
Cooking time: 20 minutes
Servings: 4

Ingredients:
- 1 cup green onion, chopped
- 1 cup soy sauce
- ¼ cup sesame seeds, toasted
- 5 garlic cloves, minced
- Black pepper to taste
- 1 pound beef stew meat, cut into strips

Directions:
In a pan that fits your air fryer, place all ingredients and mix well. Place the pan in the fryer and cook at 390 degrees F for 20 minutes. Divide everything into bowls and serve.

Nutrition: calories 289, fat 8, fiber 12, carbs 20, protein 19

Pork and Bell Pepper Mix

Preparation time: 5 minutes
Cooking time: 20 minutes
Servings: 4

Ingredients:

- 1 pound pork, cut into strips
- 4 garlic cloves, minced
- 2 tablespoons olive oil
- 2 red bell peppers, cut in strips
- A pinch of salt and black pepper
- 2 tablespoons fish sauce
- ½ cup beef stock
- 4 shallots, chopped

Directions:

In a pan that fits your air fryer, place all the ingredients and toss. Place the pan in the fryer and cook at 400 degrees F for 20 minutes, shaking the fryer halfway. Divide everything between plates and serve.

Nutrition: calories 293, fat 12, fiber 12, carbs 20, protein 29

Lamb and Beans

Preparation time: 5 minutes
Cooking time: 30 minutes
Servings: 4

Ingredients:

- 1 carrot, chopped
- 1 yellow onion, sliced
- ½ tablespoon olive oil
- 3 ounces canned kidney beans, drained
- 8 ounces lamb loin, cubed
- 1 garlic clove, minced
- Salt and black pepper to taste
- 1 tablespoon ginger, grated
- 3 tablespoons soy sauce

Directions:

In baking dish that fits your air fryer, place all of the ingredients and mix well. Place the dish in the fryer and cook at 390 degrees F for 30 minutes. Divide everything into bowls and serve.

Nutrition: calories 275, fat 3, fiber 7, carbs 20, protein 18

Pork Chops and Spinach Mix

Preparation time: 5 minutes
Cooking time: 15 minutes
Servings: 4

Ingredients:
- 2 pork chops
- Salt and black pepper to taste
- 2 cups baby spinach
- 3 tablespoons spinach pesto
- ¼ cup beef stock

Directions:
Place the pork chops, salt, pepper, and spinach pesto in a bowl; toss well. Place the pork chops in the air fryer and cook at 400 degrees F for 4 minutes on each side. Transfer the chops to a pan that fits your air fryer, and add the stock and the baby spinach. Put the pan in the fryer and cook at 400 degrees F for 7 minutes more. Divide everything between plates and serve.

Nutrition: calories 290, fat 11, fiber 9, carbs 22, protein 19

Ground Beef Mix

Preparation time: 5 minutes
Cooking time: 20 minutes
Servings: 4

Ingredients:
- 1 tablespoon olive oil
- 1 pound ground beef
- 1 yellow onion, chopped
- Salt and black pepper to taste
- 2 garlic cloves, minced
- ½ teaspoon cumin
- ¼ cup tomato salsa
- 1 green bell pepper, chopped

Directions:
Heat up the oil in a pan that fits your air fryer over medium heat. Add the onion, garlic, bell peppers, and the cumin; stir, and sauté for 3 minutes. Add the meat, toss, cook for 3 minutes more, and take off the heat. Add the salsa, toss, and place the pan in the fryer; cook at 380 degrees F for 14 minutes more. Divide everything into bowls and serve.

Nutrition: calories 264, fat 11, fiber 4, carbs 20, protein 16

Smoked Pork Roast

Preparation time: 5 minutes
Cooking time: 55 minutes
Servings: 4

Ingredients:
- 2 pounds pork loin roast
- Salt and black pepper to taste
- 1 tablespoon olive oil
- 3 tablespoons smoked paprika
- 1 teaspoon liquid smoke
- 1 tablespoon brown sugar
- 2 tablespoons oregano, chopped

Directions:
Place all ingredients into a bowl, mix well, and be sure the pork is thoroughly coated. Transfer the roast to your air fryer and cook at 370 degrees F for 55 minutes. Slice the roast, divide it between plates, and serve.

Nutrition: calories 300, fat 12, fiber 9, carbs 22, protein 18

Pork and Cauliflower Mix

Preparation time: 5 minutes
Cooking time: 22 minutes
Servings: 4

Ingredients:
- 1 pound pork stew meat, cubed
- 1 cauliflower head, florets separated
- 2 tablespoons olive oil
- 1 teaspoon soy sauce
- 1 teaspoon sugar
- ⅓ cup balsamic vinegar
- 1 garlic clove, minced

Directions:
Place all the ingredients in a pan that fits your air fryer and mix well. Put the pan into the fryer and cook at 390 degrees F for 22 minutes. Divide into bowls, serve, and enjoy.

Nutrition: calories 270, fat 9, fiber 7, carbs 23, protein 20

Pork and Bell Peppers

Preparation time: 10 minutes
Cooking time: 22 minutes
Servings: 2

Ingredients:

- 1 sweet onion, chopped
- 1 red bell pepper, cut into strips
- 1 green bell pepper, cut into strips
- 1 yellow bell pepper, cut in strips
- Salt and black pepper to taste
- 1 tablespoon olive oil
- 7 ounces pork tenderloin, cut into strips

Directions:
Place all of the ingredients into a pan that fits your air fryer, and toss well. Put the pan in the fryer and cook at 390 degrees F for 22 minutes. Divide the mix between plates and serve.

Nutrition: calories 280, fat 13, fiber 7, carbs 21, protein 19

Beef and Peas

Preparation time: 5 minutes
Cooking time: 25 minutes
Servings: 2

Ingredients:

- 2 beef steaks, cut into strips
- Salt and black pepper to taste
- 14 ounces snow peas
- 2 tablespoons soy sauce
- 1 tablespoon olive oil

Directions:
Put all of the ingredients into a pan that fits your air fryer; toss well. Place the pan in the fryer and cook at 390 degrees F for 25 minutes. Divide everything between plates and serve.

Nutrition: calories 265, fat 11, fiber 4, carbs 22, protein 19

Fennel Pork Mix

Preparation time: 5 minutes
Cooking time: 15 minutes
Servings: 4

Ingredients:

- 3 tablespoons olive oil
- 2 pork chops
- Salt and black pepper to taste
- 1 teaspoon fennel seeds, roasted
- 1 tablespoon rosemary, chopped

Directions:
In a bowl, mix the pork chops with the oil, salt, pepper, fennel, and the rosemary; toss and make sure the pork chops are coated well. Transfer the chops to your air fryer and cook at 400 degrees F for 15 minutes. Divide the chops between plates and serve.

Nutrition: calories 281, fat 11, fiber 8, carbs 17, protein 20

Lamb Meatballs

Preparation time: 10 minutes
Cooking time: 12 minutes
Servings: 8

Ingredients:

- 4 ounces lamb meat, minced
- Salt and black pepper to taste
- 1 egg, whisked
- ½ tablespoon lemon zest
- 1 tablespoon oregano, chopped
- Cooking spray

Directions:
In a bowl, combine all of the ingredients except the cooking spray and stir well. Shape medium-sized meatballs out of this mix. Place the meatballs in your air fryer's basket, grease them with cooking spray, and cook at 400 degrees F for 12 minutes. Divide between plates and serve.

Nutrition: calories 294, fat 12, fiber 2, carbs 22, protein 19

Pork Meatloaf

Preparation time: 5 minutes
Cooking time: 20 minutes
Servings: 4

Ingredients:

- 1 pound ground pork meat
- 3 tablespoons breadcrumbs
- Cooking spray
- 1 egg, whisked
- 1 ounce chorizo, chopped
- Salt and black pepper to taste
- 1 tablespoon thyme, chopped
- 1 yellow onion, chopped

Directions:
Place all of the ingredients (except the cooking spray) in a bowl and stir / combine well. Transfer the mixture to a loaf pan, greased with cooking spray that fits your air fryer. Place the pan in the fryer and cook at 390 degrees F for 20 minutes. Slice and serve.

Nutrition: calories 290, fat 12, fiber 1, carbs 19, protein 26

Simple Pork Steaks

Preparation time: 5 minutes
Cooking time: 14 minutes
Servings: 4

Ingredients:

- 1 tablespoon sweet paprika
- 4 pork steaks
-
- Salt and black pepper to taste
- 1 tablespoon butter, melted

Directions:
Rub the pork steaks with the salt, pepper, butter, and paprika until thoroughly coated. Transfer the steaks to your air fryer's basket and cook at 390 degrees F for 7 minutes on each side. Divide the steaks between plates and serve.

Nutrition: calories 250, fat 12, fiber 5, carbs 18, protein 21

Sausage Mix

Preparation time: 5 minutes
Cooking time: 20 minutes
Servings: 4

Ingredients:
- 6 pork sausage links, halved
- 1 tablespoon olive oil
- Salt and black pepper to taste
- 1 tablespoon sweet paprika
- 1 red onion, sliced
- 1 tablespoon rosemary, chopped
- 2 garlic cloves, minced

Directions:
In a pan that fits your air fryer, mix all of the ingredients and toss. Place the pan in the fryer and cook at 360 degrees F for 20 minutes. Divide between plates and serve.

Nutrition: calories 280, fat 11, fiber 7, carbs 18, protein 18

Hot Pork Mix

Preparation time: 10 minutes
Cooking time: 17 minutes
Servings: 4

Ingredients:
- 1 pound pork tenderloin, cubed
- ½ teaspoon hot chili powder
- 1 teaspoon cinnamon powder
- 1 garlic clove, minced
- Salt and black pepper to taste
- 2 tablespoons olive oil
- 1 red onion, chopped
- 3 tablespoons parsley, chopped

Directions:
In a bowl, combine the chili, cinnamon, garlic, salt, pepper, and the oil. Then add the pork and rub it well with the mixture. Transfer the meat to your air fryer and cook at 280 degrees F for 12 minutes. Add the onions and cook for 5 minutes more. Divide everything between plates and serve with the parsley sprinkled on top.

Nutrition: calories 264, fat 12, fiber 1, carbs 19, protein 23

Beef, Arugula and Leeks

Preparation time: 10 minutes
Cooking time: 12 minutes
Servings: 4

Ingredients:
- 1 pound ground beef
- 3 leeks, roughly chopped
- Salt and black pepper to taste
- 1 tablespoon olive oil
- 2 tablespoons tomato paste
- 5 ounces baby arugula

Directions:
In a pan that fits your air fryer, mix the beef with the leeks, salt, pepper, oil, and the tomato paste; toss well. Place the pan in the fryer and cook at 380 degrees F for 12 minutes. Add the arugula and toss. Divide into bowls and serve.

Nutrition: calories 220, fat 12, fiber 3, carbs 18, protein 15

Garlicky Loin Roast

Preparation time: 5 minutes
Cooking time: 55 minutes
Servings: 4

Ingredients:
- 2 tablespoons panko breadcrumbs
- 1 tablespoon olive oil
- 3 garlic cloves, minced
- 1 pound pork loin roast
- Salt and black pepper to taste
- 1 tablespoon rosemary, chopped

Directions:
Place all ingredients except the roast into a bowl; stir / mix well. Spread the mixture over the roast. Place the roast in the air fryer and cook at 360 degrees F for 55 minutes. Slice the roast, divide it between plates, and serve with a side salad.

Nutrition: calories 300, fat 12, fiber 9, carbs 20, protein 28

Pork and Peanuts Mix

Preparation time: 5 minutes
Cooking time: 15 minutes
Servings: 4

Ingredients:

- 2 teaspoons chili paste
- 2 garlic cloves, minced
- 14 ounces pork chops, cubed
- 1 shallot, chopped
- 1 teaspoon coriander, ground
- 7 ounces coconut milk
- 2 tablespoons olive oil
- 3 ounces peanuts, chopped
- Salt and black pepper to taste

Directions:

Place all of the ingredients into a pan that fits your air fryer; mix well. Put the pan in the fryer and cook at 400 degrees F for 15 minutes. Divide into bowls and serve.

Nutrition: calories 283, fat 11, fiber 8, carbs 22, protein 18

Rubbed Steaks

Preparation time: 5 minutes
Cooking time: 14 minutes
Servings: 4

Ingredients:

- ¼ cup ancho chili powder
- 1 tablespoon dry mustard
- 2 tablespoons sweet paprika
- Salt and black pepper to taste
- 2 teaspoons ginger, grated
- 1 tablespoon oregano, dried
- 1 tablespoon coriander, ground
- 4 flank steaks
- Cooking spray

Directions:

In a bowl, mix all of the spices, and then rub the steaks well with the mixture. Put the steaks in your air fryer's basket, grease with cooking spray, and cook at 370 degrees F for 7 minutes on each side. Serve the steaks with a side salad, and enjoy!

Nutrition: calories 290, fat 12, fiber 10, carbs 22, protein 18

Milky Lamb

Preparation time: 5 minutes
Cooking time: 15 minutes
Servings: 4

Ingredients:
- 1 pound lamb chops
- 2 tablespoons olive oil
- 1 tablespoon rosemary, chopped
- 1 garlic clove, minced
- 1 tablespoon butter, melted
- 1 cup coconut milk
- Salt and black pepper to taste

Directions:
Season the lamb chops with salt and pepper, then put them in a pan that fits your air fryer. Add the oil, rosemary, garlic, butter, and milk to the pan; toss well Place the pan in the fryer and cook at 400 degrees F for 15 minutes. Divide the mix between plates and serve.

Nutrition: calories 281, fat 13, fiber 9, carbs 22, protein 19

Paprika Beef

Preparation time: 5 minutes
Cooking time: 26 minutes
Servings: 4

Ingredients:
- 1½ pounds beef fillet
- 3 teaspoons sweet paprika
- 2 tablespoons olive oil
- 1 tablespoon tomato paste
- ½ cup beef stock
-
- 1 tablespoon Worcestershire sauce
- 1 red onion, roughly chopped
- Salt and black pepper to taste

Directions:
In a bowl, mix the beef with all remaining ingredients; toss well. Transfer the mixture to a pan that fits your air fryer and cook at 400 degrees F for 26 minutes, shaking the air fryer halfway. Divide everything between plates and serve.

Nutrition: calories 304, fat 13, fiber 5, carbs 22, protein 18

Mustard Pork Chops

Preparation time: 5 minutes
Cooking time: 14 minutes
Servings: 6

Ingredients:
- 3 garlic cloves, minced
- 2 pounds pork chops
- 2 tablespoons chives, chopped
- 4 tablespoons mustard
- Salt and black pepper to taste

Directions:
In a bowl, mix the pork chops with the other ingredients and rub the chops well. Put the pork chops in your air fryer's basket and cook at 400 degrees F for 7 minutes on each side. Serve right away.

Nutrition: calories 260, fat 12, fiber 2, carbs 20, protein 19

Beef and Chives Marinade

Preparation time: 5 minutes
Cooking time: 55 minutes
Servings: 6

Ingredients:
- 2 tablespoons olive oil
- 2 tablespoons chives, minced
- 3 garlic cloves, minced
- Salt and black pepper to taste
- 2 pounds beef roast
- 1 cup balsamic vinegar

Directions:
In a bowl, mix the oil, vinegar, and spices (all ingredients except for the roast); whisk well. Add the roast and coat with the mixture. Transfer the roast to your air fryer's basket and cook at 390 degrees F for 55 minutes, flipping the roast halfway. Carve and serve right away.

Nutrition: calories 300, fat 9, fiber 4, carbs 19, protein 22

Cinnamon Beef

Preparation time: 5 minutes
Cooking time: 55 minutes
Servings: 6

Ingredients:
- 2 pounds beef roast
- Juice of 1 lemon
- 2 garlic cloves, minced
- 2 yellow onions, thinly sliced
- 1 tablespoon cilantro, chopped
- 1½ tablespoons cinnamon powder
- Salt and black pepper to taste
- 1 cup beef stock

Directions:
In a baking dish that fits your air fryer, mix the roast with all other ingredients and toss well. Place the dish in your fryer and cook at 390 degrees F for 55 minutes, flipping the roast halfway. Carve the roast, divide between plates, and serve with the cooking juices drizzled on top; enjoy!

Nutrition: calories 261, fat 11, fiber 7, carbs 20, protein 18

Basil Beef Roast

Preparation time: 5 minutes
Cooking time: 55 minutes
Servings: 6

Ingredients:
- 1½ pounds beef roast
- 2 carrots, sliced
- 1 cup beef stock
- 2 garlic cloves, minced
- 1 tablespoon basil, dried
- Salt and black pepper to taste

Directions:
In a pan that fits your air fryer, combine all ingredients well. Place the pan in the fryer and cook at 390 degrees F for 55 minutes. Slice the roast, divide it and the carrots between plates, and serve with cooking juices drizzled on top.

Nutrition: calories 281, fat 7, fiber 9, carbs 20, protein 27

Simple Beef Curry

Preparation time: 5 minutes
Cooking time: 35 minutes
Servings: 4

Ingredients:

- 2 pounds cubed beef
- 2 tablespoons olive oil
- 3 potatoes, diced
- 1 tomato, cubed
- 2½ tablespoons curry powder
- 2 yellow onions, chopped
- 2 garlic cloves, minced
- 10 ounces coconut milk
- Salt and black pepper to taste

Directions:

In a pan that fits your air fryer, heat up the oil over medium heat. Add the meat and brown it for 2-3 minutes. Then add the potatoes, tomato, curry powder, onions, garlic, salt, and pepper; toss, and cook for 2 more minutes. Transfer the pan to your air fryer and cook at 380 degrees F for 25 minutes. Add the coconut milk, toss, and cook for 5 minutes more. Divide everything into bowls, serve, and enjoy.

Nutrition: calories 300, fat 14, fiber 8, carbs 16, protein 20

Creamy Beef

Preparation time: 10 minutes
Cooking time: 45 minutes
Servings: 4

Ingredients:

- 1½ pounds cubed beef
- 1 red onion, chopped
- 2½ tablespoons vegetable oil
- 1½ tablespoons white flour
- 2 garlic cloves, minced
- 4 ounces brown mushrooms, sliced
- Salt and black pepper to taste
- 8 ounces sour cream
- 1 tablespoon cilantro, chopped

Directions:

In a bowl, mix the beef with the salt, pepper, and flour; toss. Heat up the oil in a pan that fits your air fryer over medium-high heat. Add the beef, onions, and garlic; stir, and cook for 5 minutes. Add the mushrooms and toss. Place the pan in the fryer and cook at 380 degrees F for 35 minutes. Add the sour cream and cilantro and toss; cook for 5 minutes more. Divide everything between plates and serve.

Nutrition: calories 300, fat 12, fiber 6, carbs 20, protein 13

Jalapeno Beef Mix

Preparation time: 5 minutes
Cooking time: 40 minutes
Servings: 6

Ingredients:

- 1½ pounds ground beef
- 1 red onion, chopped
- Salt and black pepper to taste
- 16 ounces canned white beans, drained
- 20 ounces canned tomatoes, chopped
- 1 cup beef stock
- 6 garlic cloves, chopped
- 7 jalapeno peppers, diced
- 2 tablespoons olive oil
- 3 tablespoons chili powder

Directions:

Heat up the oil in a pan that fits your air fryer over medium heat. Add the beef and the onions, stir, and cook for 2 minutes. Add all remaining ingredients and stir; cook for 3 minutes more. Place the pan in the air fryer and cook at 380 degrees F for 35 minutes. Divide everything into bowls and serve.

Nutrition: calories 300, fat 8, fiber 6, carbs 20, protein 17

Cumin Beef Mix

Preparation time: 5 minutes
Cooking time: 35 minutes
Servings: 4

Ingredients:

- 1 pound ground beef
- 1 yellow onion, chopped
- 2 tablespoons olive oil
- Salt and black pepper to taste
- 2 garlic cloves, minced
-
- 4 ounces canned kidney beans, drained
- 8 ounces canned tomatoes, chopped
- 2 teaspoons cumin, ground

Directions:

Heat up the oil in a pan that fits your air fryer over medium heat. Add the onion and the beef, stir, and cook for 2-3 minutes. Then add the garlic, salt, pepper, beans, tomatoes, and the cumin; toss, and cook for another 2 minutes. Transfer the pan to your air fryer and cook at 380 degrees F for 30 minutes. Divide everything into bowls and serve.

Nutrition: calories 281, fat 11, fiber 7, carbs 20, protein 15

Lamb and Carrots Mix

Preparation time: 10 minutes
Cooking time: 30 minutes
Servings: 6

Ingredients:

- 1½ pounds ground lamb
- ½ tablespoon olive oil
- Salt and black pepper to taste
- 1 cup beef stock
- 1 tablespoon red wine
- ½ teaspoon smoked paprika
- 1 yellow onion, chopped
- 4 garlic cloves, minced
- 4 carrots, grated

Directions:

Heat up a pan that fits your air fryer with the oil over medium heat; add the lamb, stir, and brown for 1-2 minutes. Add all remaining ingredients and toss well; cook for 2 more minutes. Transfer the pan to your air fryer and cook at 380 degrees F for 25 minutes. Divide the mix into bowls and serve.

Nutrition: calories 271, fat 12, fiber 6, carbs 17, protein 16

Pork and Celery Mix

Preparation time: 5 minutes
Cooking time: 35 minutes
Servings: 4

Ingredients:

- 2 tablespoons olive oil
- 1½ pounds pork stew meat, cubed
- 1 yellow onion, chopped
- 2 tablespoons red wine
- 2 garlic cloves, minced
- 2 cups beef stock
- ¼ cup tomato sauce
- Salt and black pepper to taste
- 3 celery stalks, chopped
- ½ bunch parsley, chopped

Directions:

In a pan that fits your air fryer, heat up the oil over medium heat. Add the pork and brown for 2-3 minutes. Next, add the onions, garlic, wine, salt, pepper, tomato sauce, and celery; stir, and cook for 2 minutes more. Place the pan in the fryer and cook at 380 degrees F for 30 minutes. Divide between plates and serve with the parsley sprinkled on top.

Nutrition: calories 291, fat 8, fiber 8, carbs 20, protein 16

Pork and Shallots Mix

Preparation time: 10 minutes
Cooking time: 35 minutes
Servings: 4

Ingredients:

- 3 ounces white mushrooms, sliced
- 1½ pounds pork stew meat, cubed
- 2 ounces canned tomatoes, cubed
- 16 ounces shallots, chopped
- ½ cup beef stock
- 2 ounces white wine
- 2 garlic cloves, minced
- 2 tablespoons chives, chopped
- Salt and black pepper to taste
- 2 tablespoons olive oil
- 1 tablespoon cilantro, chopped

Directions:
Heat up a pan that fits your air fryer with the oil over medium heat. Add the meat, stir, and brown for 2 minutes. Next, add the shallots, garlic, chives, salt, pepper, and mushrooms; toss, and cook for 2 minutes more. Then add the mushrooms, tomatoes, wine, and stock; stir well. Simmer for about 1 minute, and then transfer the pan to your air fryer; cook at 380 degrees F for 30 minutes. Add the cilantro and toss. Divide everything into bowls and serve.
Nutrition: calories 271, fat 11, fiber 4, carbs 19, protein 24

Beef Casserole

Preparation time: 10 minutes
Cooking time: 35 minutes
Servings: 4

Ingredients:

- 17 ounces small pasta, cooked
- 1 pound ground beef, browned
- 13 ounces mozzarella cheese, shredded
- 16 ounces tomato puree
- Salt and black pepper to taste
- 1 celery stalk, chopped
- 1 yellow onion, chopped
- 1 carrot, chopped
- Cooking spray

Directions:
Grease a baking dish that fits your air fryer with the cooking spray and spread the pasta on the bottom. Next layer the beef, tomato puree, celery, onion, and carrots. Season with salt and pepper and sprinkle the mozzarella on top. Place the dish in the air fryer and cook at 380 degrees F for 35 minutes. Divide between plates and serve.
Nutrition: calories 261, fat 11, fiber 7, carbs 18, protein 22

Beef and Tofu Mix

Preparation time: 10 minutes
Cooking time: 30 minutes
Servings: 6

Ingredients:

- 1 cup beef stock
- 2 pounds beef steak, cut into thin strips and browned
- Salt and black pepper to taste
- 1 yellow onion, thinly sliced
- 12 ounces extra firm tofu, cubed
- 1 chili pepper, sliced
- 1 scallion, chopped

Directions:
Mix all of the ingredients in a pan that fits your air fryer; toss well. Place the pan in the fryer and cook at 380 degrees F for 30 minutes. Divide between plates and serve.

Nutrition: calories 237, fat 8, fiber 6, carbs 18, protein 20

Marinated Beef

Preparation time: 10 minutes
Cooking time: 20 minutes
Servings: 4

Ingredients:

- 3 pounds chuck roast, cut into thin strips
- 1 tablespoon olive oil
- ½ cup soy sauce
- ½ cup black soy sauce
- 2 tablespoons fish sauce
- 5 garlic cloves, minced
- 3 red peppers, dried and crushed

Directions:
In a bowl, combine the beef with all ingredients; toss well and place in the fridge for 10 minutes. Transfer the beef to your air fryer's basket and cook at 380 degrees F for 20 minutes. Serve with a side salad.

Nutrition: calories 281, fat 11, fiber 6, carbs 17, protein 11

Pork and Cabbage

Preparation time: 10 minutes
Cooking time: 35 minutes
Servings: 6

Ingredients:

- 2½ pounds pork stew meat, cubed
- 2 teaspoons olive oil
- 2 bay leaves
- 3 garlic cloves, chopped
- 4 carrots, chopped
- 1 red cabbage head, shredded
- Salt and black pepper to taste
- ½ cup tomato sauce

Directions:
Heat up a pan that fits your air fryer with the oil over medium-high heat, add the meat, and brown it for 5 minutes. Add all remaining ingredients and toss. Place the pan in the fryer and cook at 380 degrees F for 30 minutes. Divide the mix between plates and serve.

Nutrition: calories 300, fat 12, fiber 6, carbs 19, protein 20

Great Pork Chops

Preparation time: 5 minutes
Cooking time: 20 minutes
Servings: 4

Ingredients:

- 4 pork chops
- 2 tablespoons olive oil
- 2 tablespoons white flour
- 1 yellow onion, minced
- 2 garlic cloves, minced
- 2 tablespoons tomato paste
- 1 teaspoon oregano, dried
- 4 ounces red wine
- Salt and black pepper to taste

Directions:
In a bowl, mix the pork chops with the flour, salt, and pepper; coat the chops well. Heat up the oil in a pan that fits your air fryer over medium heat. Add the pork chops and brown for 2-3 minutes. Add the onions, garlic, oregano, and wine; stir and cook for 2 more minutes. Add the tomato paste, toss, and then place the pan into the fryer. Cook at 380 degrees F for 14 minutes, and then divide between plates. Serve with a side salad, and enjoy!

Nutrition: calories 271, fat 11, fiber 5, carbs 19, protein 17

Fast Lamb Ribs

Preparation time: 5 minutes
Cooking time: 14 minutes
Servings: 4

Ingredients:
- 4 lamb ribs
- 4 garlic cloves, minced
- 1 cup veggie stock
- ½ teaspoon chili powder
- ¼ teaspoon smoked paprika
- 2 tablespoons extra virgin olive oil
- Salt and black pepper to taste

Directions:
In a bowl, combine all of the ingredients—except the ribs—and mix well. Then add the ribs and rub them thoroughly with the mixture. Transfer the ribs to your air fryer's basket and cook at 390 degrees F for 7 minutes on each side. Serve with a side salad.

Nutrition: calories 281, fat 7, fiber 9, carbs 17, protein 15

Greek Lamb Chops

Preparation time: 10 minutes
Cooking time: 14 minutes
Servings: 4

Ingredients:
- 4 lamb chops
- 1 tablespoon white flour
- 2 tablespoons olive oil
- Salt and black pepper to taste
- 1 teaspoon marjoram, dried
- 3 garlic cloves, minced
- 1 teaspoon thyme, dried
- ½ cup veggie stock
- 1 cup green olives, pitted and sliced

Directions:
Place all ingredients—*except* the olives—in a bowl and mix well. Then put in the fridge for 10 minutes. Transfer the lamb chops to your air fryer's basket and cook at 390 degrees F for 7 minutes on each side. Divide the lamb chops between plates, sprinkle the olives on top, and serve.

Nutrition: calories 271, fat 4, fiber 8, carbs 18, protein 11

Curry Pork Mix

Preparation time: 5 minutes
Cooking time: 30 minutes
Servings: 4

Ingredients:

- 1 pound pork stew meat, cubed
- 2 ounces coconut cream
- 3 tablespoons pure cream
- 3 tablespoons curry powder
- 2 tablespoons olive oil
- 1 yellow onion, chopped
- 1 tablespoon cilantro, chopped
- Salt and black pepper to taste

Directions:
In a bowl, mix the pork with the curry powder, salt, and pepper. Heat up a pan that fits your air fryer with the oil over medium-high heat; add the pork, toss, and brown for 3 minutes. Add the coconut cream, pure cream, and onions; toss. Place the pan in the fryer and cook at 380 degrees F for 25 minutes. Add the cilantro and toss. Divide everything into bowls and serve.

Nutrition: calories 271, fat 7, fiber 6, carbs 18, protein 18

BBQ Lamb Chops

Preparation time: 5 minutes
Cooking time: 15 minutes
Servings: 4

Ingredients:

- 4 lamb chops
- Salt and black pepper to taste
- 2 tablespoons flour
- 2 tablespoons olive oil
- 3 ounces red wine
- 2 garlic cloves, crushed
- 2 tablespoons tomato sauce
- 2 tablespoons bbq sauce
- 14 ounces canned tomatoes, chopped
- 2 tablespoons cilantro, chopped

Directions:
In a bowl, mix the lamb chops with salt, pepper, and the flour; toss and coat the lamb chops well. Heat up a pan that fits your air fryer with the oil over medium heat; add the lamb, toss, and brown for 2-3 minutes. Add the garlic, wine, tomato sauce, bbq sauce, and tomatoes; toss again. Place the pan in the fryer and cook at 400 degrees F for 12 minutes. Divide between plates and serve.

Nutrition: calories 261, fat 9, fiber 9, carbs 18, protein 20

Beef and Plums Mix

Preparation time: 10 minutes
Cooking time: 40 minutes
Servings: 6

Ingredients:

- 1½ pounds beef stew meat, cubed
- 3 tablespoons honey
- 2 tablespoons olive oil
- 9 ounces plums, pitted and halved
- 8 ounces beef stock
- 2 yellow onions, chopped
- 2 garlic cloves, minced
- Salt and black pepper to tastes
- 1 teaspoon turmeric powder
- 1 teaspoon ginger powder
- 1 teaspoon cinnamon powder

Directions:

In a pan that fits your air fryer, heat up the oil over medium heat. Add the beef, stir, and brown for 2 minutes. Add the honey, onions, garlic, salt, pepper, turmeric, ginger, and cinnamon; toss, and cook for 2-3 minutes more. Add the plums and the stock; toss again. Place the pan in the fryer and cook at 380 degrees for 30 minutes. Divide everything into bowls and serve.

Nutrition: calories 271, fat 11, fiber 6, carbs 19, protein 20

French Lamb Mix

Preparation time: 10 minutes
Cooking time: 20 minutes
Servings: 4

Ingredients:

- 1½ pounds lamb chops
- ½ pounds mushrooms, sliced
- 4 tomatoes, chopped
- 1 small yellow onion, chopped
- 6 garlic cloves, minced
- 2 tablespoons tomato paste
- 1 teaspoon olive oil
- Salt and black pepper to taste
- 1 teaspoon oregano, dried
- ½ teaspoon mint, dried
- A handful of cilantro, chopped

Directions:

Heat up a pan that fits your air fryer with the oil over medium heat. Add the lamb chops, salt, pepper, oregano, and mint; toss, and brown for 2-3 minutes. Add the mushrooms, onions, garlic, tomatoes, and tomato paste ,toss and cook for 2 more minutes. Place the pan in the fryer and cook at 400 degrees F for 12 minutes more. Add the cilantro and toss. Divide everything between plates and serve.

Nutrition: calories 271, fat 11, fiber 9, carbs 19, protein 12

Air Fryer Vegetable Recipes

Spinach and Cream Cheese Mix

Preparation time: 5 minutes
Cooking time: 8 minutes
Servings: 4

Ingredients:
- 14 ounces baby spinach
- 1 tablespoon olive oil
- 2 tablespoons milk
- 3 ounces cream cheese, softened
- Salt and black pepper to taste
- 1 yellow onion, chopped

Directions:
In a pan that fits your air fryer, mix all ingredients and toss gently. Place the pan in the air fryer and cook at 260 degrees F for 8 minutes. Divide between plates and serve.

Nutrition: calories 190, fat 4, fiber 2, carbs 13, protein 9

Balsamic Asparagus

Preparation time: 5 minutes
Cooking time: 5 minutes
Servings: 4

Ingredients:
- 1 asparagus bunch, trimmed and halved
- Salt and black pepper to taste
- 2 tablespoons lime juice
- 2 tablespoons olive oil
- 2 teaspoons balsamic vinegar
- 1 teaspoon oregano, dried

Directions:
In a bowl, combine all ingredients and toss. Put the asparagus in your air fryer's basket and cook at 400 degrees F for 5 minutes. Divide the asparagus between plates and serve.

Nutrition: calories 190, fat 3, fiber 6, carbs 8, protein 4

Cheesy Asparagus

Preparation time: 5 minutes
Cooking time: 6 minutes
Servings: 6

Ingredients:
- 14 ounces asparagus, trimmed
- 8 ounces cream cheese, softened
- 16 ounces cheddar cheese, grated
- ½ cup sour cream
- 3 garlic cloves, minced
- 1 teaspoon garlic powder

Directions:
In a pan that fits your air fryer, the mix asparagus with the cream cheese, sour cream, garlic powder, and garlic; toss. Sprinkle the cheddar cheese on top, and then place the pan in the fryer. Cook at 400 degrees F for 6 minutes. Divide between plates and serve.

Nutrition: calories 191, fat 8, fiber 2, carbs 12, protein 8

Simple Fennel Mix

Preparation time: 10 minutes
Cooking time: 12 minutes
Servings: 2

Ingredients:
- 2 fennel bulbs, trimmed and halved
- A drizzle of olive oil
- 2 garlic cloves, minced
- 1 tablespoon lime juice
- 1 teaspoon sweet paprika

Directions:
In a bowl, combine all ingredients and toss. Put the fennel in your air fryer's basket and cook at 400 degrees F for 12 minutes. Divide between plates and serve.

Nutrition: calories 131, fat 4, fiber 7, carbs 10, protein 8

Beets and Capers

Preparation time: 5 minutes
Cooking time: 20 minutes
Servings: 4

Ingredients:
- 4 beets, peeled and cut into wedges
- 2 tablespoons balsamic vinegar
- 1 tablespoon cilantro, chopped
-
- Salt and black pepper to taste
- 1 tablespoon olive oil
- 2 tablespoons capers

Directions:
Put the beet wedges in your air fryer's basket and cook at 400 degrees F for 20 minutes. Transfer the beet wedges to a salad bowl, and then add the remaining ingredients. Toss, serve, and enjoy.

Nutrition: calories 70, fat 1, fiber 1, carbs 6, protein 4

Sesame Seed Beets Mix

Preparation time: 10 minutes
Cooking time: 20 minutes
Servings: 6

Ingredients:
- 6 beets, peeled and quartered
- Salt and black pepper to taste
- 1 tablespoon sesame seeds, toasted
- 1 tablespoon red wine vinegar
- 1 tablespoon olive oil

Directions:
Put the beets in your air fryer's basket and cook at 400 degrees F for 20 minutes. Transfer the beets to a bowl, and add all remaining ingredients. Toss and serve.

Nutrition: calories 100, fat 2, fiber 4, carbs 7, protein 5

Beets and Kale Mix

Preparation time: 5 minutes
Cooking time: 20 minutes
Servings: 4

Ingredients:

- 1½ pounds beets, peeled and quartered
- 1 tablespoon olive oil
- 2 tablespoons balsamic vinegar
- ½ cup orange juice
- Salt and black pepper to taste
- 2 scallions, chopped
- 2 cups kale leaves

Directions:
Put the beets in your air fryer's basket and cook at 400 degrees F for 15 minutes. Add the kale leaves and cook for another 5 minutes. Transfer the beets and kale to a bowl and add all remaining ingredients. Toss, serve, and enjoy.

Nutrition: calories 151, fat 2, fiber 3, carbs 9, protein 4

Beet and Tomato Salad

Preparation time: 5 minutes
Cooking time: 25 minutes
Servings: 6

Ingredients:

- 8 small beets, trimmed, peeled and cut into wedges
- 1 red onion, sliced
- 1 tablespoon balsamic vinegar
- Salt and black pepper to taste
- 1 pint mixed cherry tomatoes, halved
- 2 ounces pecans, chopped
- 2 tablespoons olive oil

Directions:
Put the beets in your air fryer's basket, and add the salt, pepper, and 1 tablespoon of the oil. Cook at 400 degrees F for 15 minutes. Transfer the beets to a pan that fits your air fryer, and add the onions, tomatoes, pecans, and remaining 1 tablespoon of the oil; toss well. Cook at 400 degrees F for 10 more minutes. Divide between plates and serve.

Nutrition: calories 144, fat 7, fiber 5, carbs 8, protein 6

Cauliflower Mix

Preparation time: 5 minutes
Cooking time: 7 minutes
Servings: 4

Ingredients:

- 1 cauliflower head, florets separated
- 1 tablespoon peanut oil
- 6 garlic cloves, minced
- 1 tablespoon Chinese rice wine vinegar
- Salt and black pepper to taste

Directions:

Mix all ingredients in a bowl. Put the mixture in the fryer and cook at 400 degrees F for 7 minutes. Divide between plates and serve.

Nutrition: calories 141, fat 3, fiber 4, carbs 4, protein 2

Broccoli and Tomatoes

Preparation time: 5 minutes
Cooking time: 7 minutes
Servings: 4

Ingredients:

- 1 broccoli head, florets separated
- Salt and black pepper to taste
- 6 cherry tomatoes, halved
- ¼ cup scallions, chopped
- 1 tablespoon olive oil

Directions:

Put the broccoli florets in your air fryer's basket, and add the salt, pepper, and ½ tablespoon of the oil; toss well. Cook at 380 degrees F for 7 minutes. Transfer the broccoli to a bowl, and add the tomatoes, scallions, salt, pepper, and the remaining ½ tablespoon of oil. Toss and serve.

Nutrition: calories 111, fat 4, fiber 4, carbs 9, protein 2

Mustard Brussels Sprouts

Preparation time: 5 minutes
Cooking time: 15 minutes
Servings: 4

Ingredients:
- 1 pound Brussels sprouts, trimmed
- Salt and black pepper to taste
- 1 tablespoon mustard
- 1 tablespoon olive oil
- 2 tablespoons cilantro, chopped

Directions:
In a bowl, mix the sprouts with the salt, pepper, mustard, and the oil; toss well. Transfer the sprouts to your air fryer's basket and cook at 380 degrees F for 15 minutes. Divide the sprouts between plates, sprinkle the cilantro on top, and serve.

Nutrition: calories 122, fat 2, fiber 2, carbs 9, protein 4

Parmesan Broccoli

Preparation time: 5 minutes
Cooking time: 8 minutes
Servings: 4

Ingredients:
- 1 broccoli head, florets separated
- Juice of 1 lime
- Salt and black pepper to taste
- 2 tablespoons olive oil
- 3 tablespoons parmesan cheese, grated

Directions:
Put the broccoli in your air fryer's basket; add the salt, pepper, and the oil, and toss. Cook at 400 degrees F for 8 minutes. Transfer the broccoli to a bowl, add the lime juice and parmesan, toss, and serve.

Nutrition: calories 122, fat 3, fiber 6, carbs 8, protein 9

Red Cabbage and Carrots

Preparation time: 5 minutes
Cooking time: 8 minutes
Servings: 4

Ingredients:
- 1 red cabbage head, shredded
- 1 tablespoon olive oil
- 1 carrot, grated
- ¼ cup balsamic vinegar
- Salt and black pepper to taste

Directions:
Place all ingredients in a pan that fits your air fryer, and mix well. Put the pan in the fryer and cook at 380 degrees F for 8 minutes. Divide between plates and serve.

Nutrition: calories 100, fat 4, fiber 2, carbs 7, protein 2

Butter Carrots

Preparation time: 5 minutes
Cooking time: 15 minutes
Servings: 4

Ingredients:
- 1 pound carrots, cut into wedges
- A pinch of salt and black pepper
- 1 teaspoon sweet paprika
- ½ tablespoon butter, melted

Directions:
In a bowl, combine all of the ingredients and toss well. Put the carrots in your air fryer and cook at 350 degrees F for 15 minutes. Divide between plates and serve.

Nutrition: calories 90, fat 2, fiber 3, carbs 4, protein 4

Green Beans Mix

Preparation time: 5 minutes
Cooking time: 6 minutes
Servings: 4

Ingredients:

- 1 pound green beans, trimmed
- 2 tablespoons olive oil
- 3 garlic cloves, minced
- Salt and black pepper to taste
- 1 tablespoon balsamic vinegar

Directions:
Place all of the ingredients in a bowl, *except* the vinegar, and mix well. Put the beans in your air fryer and cook at 400 degrees F for 6 minutes. Divide the green beans between plates, drizzle the vinegar all over, and serve.

Nutrition: calories 101, fat 3, fiber 3, carbs 4, protein 2

Spicy Kale Mix

Preparation time: 5 minutes
Cooking time: 12 minutes
Servings: 6

Ingredients:

- 2 tablespoons olive oil
- 3 garlic cloves, minced
- 2½ pounds kale leaves
- Salt and black pepper to taste
- 2 tablespoons balsamic vinegar
- 1 tablespoon chili powder
- ½ teaspoon crushed red pepper

Directions:
In a bowl, mix the kale with salt, pepper, oil, red pepper, and chili powder; toss well. Transfer the kale to your air fryer and cook at 250 degrees F for 12 minutes. Put the kale leaves in a bowl, add the garlic and the vinegar, and toss. Serve, and enjoy!

Nutrition: calories 102, fat 4, fiber 8, carbs 4, protein 2

Eggplant Mix

Preparation time: 5 minutes
Cooking time: 15 minutes
Servings: 4

Ingredients:

- 4 eggplants, roughly cubed
- 2 tablespoons lime juice
- Salt and black pepper to taste
- 1 teaspoon oregano, dried
- 2 tablespoons olive oil

Directions:
Place all of the ingredients in a pan that fits your air fryer and mix / toss well. Put the pan into the fryer and cook at 400 degrees F for 15 minutes. Divide the eggplants between plates and serve.

Nutrition: calories 125, fat 5, fiber 2, carbs 11, protein 5

Hot Greek Potatoes

Preparation time: 5 minutes
Cooking time: 15 minutes
Servings: 4

Ingredients:

- 1½ pounds potatoes, peeled and cubed
- 1 tablespoon olive oil
- Salt and black pepper to taste
-
- 1 tablespoon hot paprika
- 2 tablespoons black olives, pitted and sliced
- 1 cup Greek yogurt

Directions:
In a bowl, mix the potatoes with the oil, salt, pepper, and paprika; toss well. Put the potatoes in your air fryer's basket and cook at 400 degrees F for 15 minutes. Place the potatoes in a serving dish, and add the yogurt and the black olives. Toss, serve, and enjoy.

Nutrition: calories 140, fat 3, fiber 4, carbs 10, protein 4

Coconut Mushroom Mix

Preparation time: 5 minutes
Cooking time: 8 minutes
Servings: 8

Ingredients:
- 1 pound brown mushrooms, halved
- 1 small yellow onion, chopped
- Salt and black pepper to taste
- 2 tablespoons olive oil
- 14 ounces coconut milk

Directions:
Add all ingredients to a pan that fits your air fryer and mix well. Place the pan in the fryer and cook at 400 degrees F for 8 minutes. Divide between plates and serve.

Nutrition: calories 202, fat 4, fiber 1, carbs 13, protein 4

Oregano Pearl Onions

Preparation time: 5 minutes
Cooking time: 10 minutes
Servings: 8

Ingredients:
- 1 pound pearl onions, trimmed
- 3 ounces feta cheese, crumbled
- 1 tablespoon olive oil
- A pinch of salt and black pepper
- 2 tablespoons oregano, chopped

Directions:
In a bowl, mix the onions with the salt, pepper, and oil. Transfer the contents to your air fryer and cook at 400 degrees F for 10 minutes. Transfer the onions to a bowl, add the oregano and the cheese, toss, and serve.

Nutrition: calories 140, fat 4, fiber 2, carbs 9, protein 5

Goat Cheese Brussels Sprouts

Preparation time: 5 minutes
Cooking time: 15 minutes
Servings: 8

Ingredients:
- 1 pound Brussels sprouts, trimmed
- 1 tablespoon olive oil
-
- Salt and black pepper to taste
- 3 ounces goat cheese, crumbled

Directions:
In a bowl, mix the sprouts with the oil, salt, and pepper; toss well. Put the sprouts in your air fryer's basket and cook at 380 degrees F for 15 minutes. Divide between plates, sprinkle the cheese on top, and serve.

Nutrition: calories 150, fat 3, fiber 4, carbs 4, protein 6

Tarragon Green Beans

Preparation time: 5 minutes
Cooking time: 7 minutes
Servings: 4

Ingredients:
- 1 pound green beans, trimmed
- 1 tablespoon tarragon, chopped
- Zest of 2 lemons
- 1 tablespoon olive oil
- Salt and black pepper to taste

Directions:
In a bowl, mix the green beans with the lemon zest, oil, salt, and pepper; toss well. Put the beans in your air fryer and cook at 400 degrees F for 7 minutes. Divide the beans between plates, sprinkle the tarragon on top, and serve.

Nutrition: calories 181, fat 7, fiber 4, carbs 9, protein 3

Balsamic Zucchini Mix

Preparation time: 5 minutes
Cooking time: 12 minutes
Servings: 4

Ingredients:

- 4 zucchinis, sliced
- Salt and black pepper to taste
- 2 tablespoons lime juice
- 2 tablespoons olive oil
- 2 teaspoons balsamic vinegar
- 1 teaspoon oregano, dried

Directions:
In a pan that fits your air fryer, mix all the ingredients well. Place the pan in the fryer and cook at 400 degrees F for 12 minutes. Divide the mix between plates and serve.

Nutrition: calories 100, fat 1, fiber 3, carbs 8, protein 4

Artichokes and Mayonnaise

Preparation time: 5 minutes
Cooking time: 15 minutes
Servings: 6

Ingredients:

- 14 ounces canned artichoke hearts
- A drizzle of olive oil
- 16 ounces parmesan cheese, grated
- 3 garlic cloves, minced
- ½ cup mayonnaise
- 1 teaspoon garlic powder

Directions:
In a pan that fits your air fryer, mix the artichokes with the oil, garlic, and garlic powder, and then toss well. Place the pan in the fryer and cook at 350 degrees F for 15 minutes. Cool the mix down, add the mayo, and toss. Divide between plates, sprinkle the parmesan on top, and serve.

Nutrition: calories 200, fat 11, fiber 3, carbs 9, protein 4

Coconut Artichokes

Preparation time: 5 minutes
Cooking time: 15 minutes
Servings: 2

Ingredients:
- 2 artichokes, washed, trimmed and halved
- 2 garlic cloves, minced
- ¼ cup coconut, shredded
- Juice of 1 lemon
- 1 tablespoon coconut oil, melted

Directions:
In a bowl, mix the artichokes with the garlic, oil, and lemon juice; toss well. Put the artichokes into your air fryer and cook at 360 degrees F for 15 minutes. Divide the artichokes between plates, sprinkle the coconut on top, and serve. Enjoy!

Nutrition: calories 213, fat 8, fiber 6, carbs 13, protein 6

Wrapped Asparagus

Preparation time: 5 minutes
Cooking time: 5 minutes
Servings: 4

Ingredients:
- 8 asparagus spears, trimmed
- 8 ounces prosciutto slices
- A pinch of salt and black pepper

Directions:
Wrap the asparagus in prosciutto slices and then season with salt and pepper. Put all in your air fryer's basket and cook at 400 degrees F for 5 minutes. Divide between plates and serve.

Nutrition: calories 100, fat 2, fiber 5, carbs 8, protein 4

Cajun Asparagus

Preparation time: 5 minutes
Cooking time: 5 minutes
Servings: 4

Ingredients:
- 1 teaspoon extra virgin olive oil
- 1 bunch asparagus, trimmed
- ½ tablespoon Cajun seasoning

Directions:
In a bowl, mix the asparagus with the oil and Cajun seasoning; coat the asparagus well. Put the asparagus in your air fryer and cook at 400 degrees F for 5 minutes. Divide between plates and serve.

Nutrition: calories 151, fat 3, fiber 4, carbs 9, protein 4

Squash Salad

Preparation time: 5 minutes
Cooking time: 12 minutes
Servings: 4

Ingredients:
- 1 butternut squash, cubed
- 2 tablespoons balsamic vinegar
- 1 bunch cilantro, chopped
- Salt and black pepper to taste
- 1 tablespoon olive oil

Directions:
Put the squash in your air fryer, and add the salt, pepper, and oil; toss well. Cook at 400 degrees F for 12 minutes. Transfer the squash to a bowl, add the vinegar and cilantro, and toss. Serve and enjoy!

Nutrition: calories 151, fat 4, fiber 7, carbs 11, protein 8

Creamy Squash Mix

Preparation time: 5 minutes
Cooking time: 12 minutes
Servings: 6

Ingredients:

- 1 big butternut squash, roughly cubed
- 1 cup sour cream
- Salt and black pepper to taste
- 1 tablespoon parsley, chopped
- A drizzle of olive oil

Directions:
Put the squash in your air fryer, add the salt and pepper, and rub with the oil. Cook at 400 degrees F for 12 minutes. Transfer the squash to a bowl, and add the cream and the parsley. Toss and serve.

Nutrition: calories 200, fat 7, fiber 6, carbs 11, protein 7

Orange Carrots

Preparation time: 5 minutes
Cooking time: 15 minutes
Servings: 4

Ingredients:

- 1½ pounds baby carrots
- 2 teaspoons orange zest
- 2 tablespoons cider vinegar
- ½ cup orange juice
- A handful of parsley, chopped
- A drizzle of olive oil

Directions:
Put the baby carrots in your air fryer's basket, add the orange zest and oil, and rub the carrots well. Cook at 350 degrees F for 15 minutes. Transfer the carrots to a bowl, and then add the vinegar, orange juice, and parsley. Toss, serve, and enjoy!

Nutrition: calories 151, fat 6, fiber 6, carbs 11, protein 5

Tomato Salad

Preparation time: 5 minutes
Cooking time: 5 minutes
Servings: 8

Ingredients:
- 1 red onion, sliced
- 2 ounces feta cheese, crumbled
- Salt and black pepper to taste
- 1 pint mixed cherry tomatoes, halved
- 2 ounces pecans
- 2 tablespoons olive oil

Directions:
In your air fryer, mix the tomatoes with the salt, pepper, onions, and the oil. Cook at 400 degrees F for 5 minutes. Transfer to a bowl and add the pecans and the cheese. Toss and serve.

Nutrition: calories 151, fat 4, fiber 6, carbs 9, protein 4

Tomato and Green Beans Salad

Preparation time: 5 minutes
Cooking time: 6 minutes
Servings: 4

Ingredients:
- 1 pound green beans, trimmed and halved
- 2 green onions, chopped
- 5 ounces canned green chilies, chopped
- 1 jalapeno pepper, chopped
-
- A drizzle of olive oil
- 2 teaspoons chili powder
- 1 teaspoon garlic powder
- Salt and black pepper to taste
- 8 cherry tomatoes, halved

Directions:
Place all ingredients in a pan that fits your air fryer, and mix / toss. Put the pan in the fryer and cook at 400 degrees F for 6 minutes. Divide the mix between plates and serve hot.

Nutrition: calories 200, fat 4, fiber 7, carbs 12, protein 6

Bell Peppers and Kale

Preparation time: 5 minutes
Cooking time: 15 minutes
Servings: 4

Ingredients:

- 2 red bell peppers, cut into strips
- 2 green bell peppers, cut into strips
- ½ pound kale leaves
- Salt and black pepper to taste
- 2 yellow onions, roughly chopped
- ¼ cup veggie stock
- 2 tablespoons tomato sauce

Directions:
Add all ingredients to a pan that fits your air fryer; mix well. Place the pan in the fryer and cook at 360 degrees F for 15 minutes. Divide between plates, serve, and enjoy!

Nutrition: calories 161, fat 7, fiber 6, carbs 12, protein 7

Garlic Parsnips

Preparation time: 5 minutes
Cooking time: 15 minutes
Servings: 4

Ingredients:

- 1 pound parsnips, cut into chunks
- 1 tablespoon olive oil
- 6 garlic cloves, minced
- 1 tablespoon balsamic vinegar
- Salt and black pepper to taste

Directions:
Add all of the ingredients to a bowl and mix well. Place them in the air fryer and cook at 380 degrees F for 15 minutes. Divide between plates and serve.

Nutrition: calories 121, fat 3, fiber 6, carbs 12, protein 6

Broccoli and Pomegranate

Preparation time: 5 minutes
Cooking time: 7 minutes
Servings: 4

Ingredients:
- 1 broccoli head, florets separated
- Salt and black pepper to taste
- 1 pomegranate, seeds separated
- A drizzle of olive oil

Directions:
In a bowl, mix the broccoli with the salt, pepper, and oil; toss. Put the florets in your air fryer and cook at 400 degrees F for 7 minutes. Divide between plates, sprinkle the pomegranate seeds all over, and serve.

Nutrition: calories 141, fat 3, fiber 4, carbs 11, protein 4

Bacon Cauliflower

Preparation time: 5 minutes
Cooking time: 12 minutes
Servings: 4

Ingredients:
- 1 cauliflower head, florets separated
- 1 tablespoon olive oil
- Salt and black pepper to taste
- ½ cup bacon, cooked and chopped
- 2 tablespoons dill, chopped

Directions:
Put the cauliflower in your air fryer and add the salt, pepper, and oil; toss well. Cook at 400 degrees F for 12 minutes. Divide the cauliflower between plates, sprinkle the bacon and the dill on top, and serve.

Nutrition: calories 200, fat 7, fiber 5, carbs 17, protein 7

Butter Broccoli

Preparation time: 5 minutes
Cooking time: 6 minutes
Servings: 4

Ingredients:

- 1 broccoli head, florets separated
- 1 tablespoon lime juice
- Salt and black pepper to taste
- 2 tablespoons butter, melted

Directions:
In a bowl, mix well all of the ingredients. Put the broccoli mixture in your air fryer and cook at 400 degrees F for 6 minutes.Serve hot.

Nutrition: calories 151, fat 4, fiber 7, carbs 12, protein 6

New Potatoes Mix

Preparation time: 5 minutes
Cooking time: 15 minutes
Servings: 4

Ingredients:

- 1 pound new potatoes, halved
- Salt and black pepper to taste
- 1½ tablespoons butter, melted
- 1 tablespoon dill, chopped

Directions:
Put the potatoes in your air fryer's basket, and add the salt, pepper, and butter; toss well. Cook at 400 degrees F for 15 minutes. Divide between plates, sprinkle the dill on top, and serve.

Nutrition: calories 171, fat 5, fiber 6, carbs 15, protein 8

Napa Cabbage Mix

Preparation time: 5 minutes
Cooking time: 12 minutes
Servings: 4

Ingredients:

- 1 napa cabbage, shredded
- 1 yellow onion, chopped
- 2 tablespoons tomato sauce
- ¼ teaspoon nutmeg, ground
- Salt and black pepper to taste
- 1 tablespoon parsley, chopped

Directions:
Add all of the ingredients to a pan that fits your air fryer and mix well. Place the pan in the fryer and cook at 300 degrees F for 12 minutes. Divide between plates and serve.

Nutrition: calories 154, fat 4, fiber 4, carbs 12, protein 5

Butter Cabbage Mix

Preparation time: 5 minutes
Cooking time: 12 minutes
Servings: 8

Ingredients:

- 1 green cabbage head, shredded
- ¼ cup butter, melted
- 1 tablespoon sweet paprika
- 1 tablespoon dill, chopped

Directions:
Mix all of the ingredients in a pan that fits your air fryer. Place the pan in the fryer and cook at 320 degrees F for 12 minutes. Divide everything between plates, serve, and enjoy!

Nutrition: calories 181, fat 4, fiber 6, carbs 15, protein 5

Turmeric Kale Mix

Preparation time: 5 minutes
Cooking time: 12 minutes
Servings: 2

Ingredients:
- 3 tablespoons butter, melted
- 2 cups kale leaves
- Salt and black pepper to taste
- ½ cup yellow onion, chopped
- 2 teaspoons turmeric powder

Directions:
Place all ingredients in a pan that fits your air fryer and mix well. Put the pan in the fryer and cook at 250 degrees F for 12 minutes. Divide between plates and serve.

Nutrition: calories 151, fat 4, fiber 5, carbs 15, protein 6

Spicy Cabbage

Preparation time: 5 minutes
Cooking time: 12 minutes
Servings: 4

Ingredients:
- 1 green cabbage head, shredded
- 1 tablespoon olive oil
- 1 teaspoon cayenne pepper
-
- A pinch of salt and black pepper
- 2 teaspoons sweet paprika

Directions:
Mix all of the ingredients in a pan that fits your fryer. Place the pan in the fryer and cook at 320 degrees F for 12 minutes. Divide between plates and serve right away.

Nutrition: calories 124, fat 6, fiber 6, carbs 16, protein 7

Easy Celery Root Mix

Preparation time: 5 minutes
Cooking time: 15 minutes
Servings: 4

Ingredients:
- 2 cups celery root, roughly cubed
- A pinch of salt and black pepper
- ½ tablespoon butter, melted

Directions:
Put all of the ingredients in your air fryer and toss. Cook at 350 degrees F for 15 minutes. Divide between plates and serve.

Nutrition: calories 124, fat 1, fiber 4, carbs 6, protein 6

Maple Glazed Corn

Preparation time: 5 minutes
Cooking time: 6 minutes
Servings: 4

Ingredients:
- 4 ears of corn
- 1 tablespoon maple syrup
- Black pepper to taste
- 1 tablespoon butter, melted

Directions:
Combine the black pepper, butter, and the maple syrup in a bowl. Rub the corn with the mixture, and then put it in your air fryer. Cook at 390 degrees F for 6 minutes. Divide the corn between plates and serve.

Nutrition: calories 100, fat 2, fiber 3, carbs 8, protein 3

Dill Corn

Preparation time: 5 minutes
Cooking time: 6 minutes
Servings: 4

Ingredients:
- 4 ears of corn
- Salt and black pepper to taste
- 2 tablespoons butter, melted
- 2 tablespoon dill, chopped

Directions:
In a bowl, combine the salt, pepper, and the butter. Rub the corn with the butter mixture, and then put it in your air fryer. Cook at 390 degrees F for 6 minutes. Divide the corn between plates, sprinkle the dill on top, and serve.

Nutrition: calories 100, fat 2, fiber 5, carbs 9, protein 6

Broccoli Casserole

Preparation time: 5 minutes
Cooking time: 15 minutes
Servings: 4

Ingredients:
- 2 tablespoons butter, melted
- 6 cups broccoli florets
- 2 garlic cloves, minced
- 1 cup chicken stock
- Salt and black pepper to taste
- 1 pound fettuccine pasta, cooked
- 2 green onions, chopped
- 1 tablespoon parmesan cheese, grated
- 3 tomatoes, chopped

Directions:
Use the butter to grease a baking dish that fits your air fryer. Add the broccoli, garlic, stock, salt, pepper, pasta, onions, and tomatoes; toss gently. Place the dish in the fryer and cook at 390 degrees F for 15 minutes. Sprinkle the parmesan on top, divide everything between plates, and serve.

Nutrition: calories 151, fat 6, fiber 5, carbs 12, protein 4

Mustard Greens Mix

Preparation time: 5 minutes
Cooking time: 12 minutes
Servings: 6

Ingredients:

- 1 pound collard greens, trimmed
- ¼ pound bacon, cooked and chopped
- A drizzle of olive oil
- Salt and black pepper to taste
- ½ cup veggie stock

Directions:
Place all ingredients in a pan that fits your air fryer and mix well. Put the pan in the fryer and cook at 260 degrees F for 12 minutes. Divide everything between plates and serve.

Nutrition: calories 161, fat 4, fiber 5, carbs 14, protein 3

Balsamic Mustard Greens

Preparation time: 5 minutes
Cooking time: 12 minutes
Servings: 4

Ingredients:

- 1 bunch mustard greens, trimmed
- 2 tablespoons olive oil
- ½ cup chicken stock
- 2 tablespoons tomato puree
- 3 garlic cloves, minced
- Salt and black pepper to taste
- 1 tablespoon balsamic vinegar

Directions:
Combine all ingredients in a pan that fits your air fryer and toss well. Place the pan in the fryer and cook at 260 degrees F for 12 minutes. Divide everything between plates, serve, and enjoy!

Nutrition: calories 151, fat 2, fiber 4, carbs 14, protein 4

Butter Endives

Preparation time: 5 minutes
Cooking time: 10 minutes
Servings: 4

Ingredients:
- 4 endives, trimmed and halved
- Salt and black pepper to taste
- 1 tablespoon lime juice
- 1 tablespoon butter, melted

Directions:
Put the endives in your air fryer, and add the salt, pepper, lemon juice, and butter. Cook at 360 degrees F for 10 minutes. Divide between plates and serve.

Nutrition: calories 100, fat 3, fiber 4, carbs 8, protein 4

Endives and Bacon

Preparation time: 5 minutes
Cooking time: 10 minutes
Servings: 4

Ingredients:
- 4 endives, trimmed and halved
- Salt and black pepper to taste
- 1 tablespoon olive oil
- 2 tablespoons bacon, cooked and crumbled
- ½ teaspoon nutmeg, ground

Directions:
Put the endives in your air fryer's basket, and add the salt, pepper, oil, and nutmeg; toss gently. Cook at 360 degrees F for 10 minutes. Divide the endives between plates, sprinkle the bacon on top, and serve.

Nutrition: calories 151, fat 6, fiber 8, carbs 14, protein 6

Air Fryer Dessert Recipes

Avocado Cake

Preparation time: 10 minutes
Cooking time: 30 minutes
Servings: 4

Ingredients:
- 1 tablespoon butter, melted
- 1 egg, whisked
- ⅓ cup brown sugar
- 2 avocados, peeled, pitted and mashed
- 1 cup white flour
- 1 teaspoon baking powder
- ½ teaspoon cinnamon powder
- Cooking spray

Directions:
Place all of the ingredients (except the cooking spray) in a bowl; mix / whisk well. Pour this mixture into a cake pan greased with cooking spray. Place the pan in your air fryer and cook at 350 degrees F for 30 minutes. Cool down, slice, and serve.

Nutrition: calories 202, fat 4, fiber 1, carbs 14, protein 7

Oreo Cheesecake

Preparation time: 10 minutes
Cooking time: 20 minutes
Servings: 8

Ingredients:
- 1 pound cream cheese, softened
- ½ teaspoon vanilla extract
- 2 eggs, whisked
- 4 tablespoons sugar
- 1 cup Oreo cookies, crumbled
- 2 tablespoons butter, melted

Directions:
In a bowl, mix the cookies with the butter, and then press this mixture onto the bottom of a cake pan lined with parchment paper. Place the pan in your air fryer and cook at 350 degrees F for 4 minutes. In a bowl, mix the sugar with the cream cheese, eggs, and vanilla; whisk until combined and smooth and spread this over the crust. Cook the cheesecake in your air fryer at 310 degrees F for 15 minutes. Place the cheesecake in the fridge for a couple of hours before serving.

Nutrition: calories 195, fat 12, fiber 4, carbs 20, protein 7

Cherry Cream Pudding

Preparation time: 5 minutes
Cooking time: 55 minutes
Servings: 4

Ingredients:

- 2 cups cherries, pitted and halved
- 4 egg yolks
- 1½ cups whipping cream
- ½ cup raisins
- ¼ cup sugar
- ½ cup chocolate chips.

Directions:
Place all ingredients in a bowl and mix well. Transfer the mixture to a greased pan that fits your air fryer. Cook at 310 degrees F for 55 minutes. Cool down and serve.

Nutrition: calories 212, fat 8, fiber 2, carbs 13, protein 7

Amaretto Cream

Preparation time: 5 minutes
Cooking time: 12 minutes
Servings: 8

Ingredients:

- 1 cup sugar
- ½ cup butter, melted
- 1 cup heavy cream
- 12 ounces chocolate chips
- 2 tablespoons amaretto liqueur

Directions:
Place all of the ingredients in a bowl and stir. Pour the mixture into small ramekins and place in the air fryer. Cook at 320 degrees F for 12 minutes. Refrigerate / freeze for a while… best when served really cold.

Nutrition: calories 190, fat 2, fiber 1, carbs 6, protein 3

Cinnamon Rolls

Preparation time: 2 hours
Cooking time: 10 minutes
Servings: 8

Ingredients:
- 1 pound bread dough
- ¾ cup brown sugar
- 1½ tablespoons cinnamon, ground
- ¼ cup butter, melted

Directions:
Roll the dough on a floured working surface, shape a rectangle, and brush with the butter. In a bowl, combine the cinnamon and sugar, and then sprinkle this over the dough. Roll the dough into a log, seal, cut into 8 pieces, and leave the rolls to rise for 2 hours. Place the rolls in your air fryer's basket and cook at 350 degrees F for 5 minutes on each side. Serve warm, and enjoy!

Nutrition: calories 200, fat 11, fiber 2, carbs 15, protein 4

Simple Nutmeg Pumpkin Pie

Preparation time: 10 minutes
Cooking time: 35 minutes
Servings: 8

Ingredients:
- 1 pie crust
- 3½ ounces pumpkin flesh, chopped
- 1 teaspoon nutmeg, ground
- 3 ounces water
- 1 egg, whisked
- 1 tablespoon sugar

Directions:
Put the water in a pot and bring to a boil over medium-high heat. Add the pumpkin, egg, sugar, and the nutmeg; stir, and allow to boil for 20 minutes. Remove the mixture from the heat and blend using an immersion blender. Put the pie crust in a lined pan that fits your air fryer and spread the pumpkin mix all over. Place the pan in the fryer and cook at 360 degrees F for 15 minutes. Slice and serve warm.

Nutrition: calories 212, fat 5, fiber 2, carbs 15, protein 7

Cinnamon Pears

Preparation time: 5 minutes
Cooking time: 15 minutes
Servings: 4

Ingredients:
- 2 pears, halved
- ½ teaspoon cinnamon powder
- 2 tablespoons sugar

Directions:
Put the pears in your air fryer, and sprinkle the cinnamon and the sugar all over. Cook at 320 degrees F for 15 minutes. Serve these pears warm, and enjoy!

Nutrition: calories 210, fat 2, fiber 1, carbs 12, protein 3

Butter Donuts

Preparation time: 10 minutes
Cooking time: 15 minutes
Servings: 4

Ingredients:
- 8 ounces flour
- 1 tablespoon brown sugar
- 1 tablespoon white sugar
- 1 egg
- 2½ tablespoons butter
- 4 ounces whole milk
- 1 teaspoon baking powder

Directions:
Place all of the ingredients in a bowl and mix well. Shape donuts from this mix and place them in your air fryer's basket. Cook at 360 degrees F for 15 minutes. Arrange the donuts on a platter and serve them warm.

Nutrition: calories 190, fat 8, fiber 1, carbs 14, protein 3

Cinnamon Apples

Preparation time: 5 minutes
Cooking time: 15 minutes
Servings: 4

Ingredients:
- 3 tablespoons butter, melted
- 4 apples, peeled, cored and cut into wedges
- 3 tablespoons cinnamon sugar

Directions:
In a pan that fits your air fryer, mix the apples with the sugar and the butter; toss. Place the pan in the fryer and cook at 370 degrees F for 15 minutes. Serve warm.

Nutrition: calories 204, fat 3, fiber 4, carbs 12, protein 4

Lemon Cake

Preparation time: 5 minutes
Cooking time: 17 minutes
Servings: 6

Ingredients:
- 3½ ounces butter, melted
- 3 eggs
- 3 ounces brown sugar
- 3 ounces flour
- 1 teaspoon dark chocolate, grated
- ½ teaspoon lemon juice

Directions:
Mix all of the ingredients in a bowl. Pour the mixture into a greased cake pan, and place in the fryer. Cook at 360 degrees F for 17 minutes. Let cake cool before serving.

Nutrition: calories 220, fat 11, fiber 3, carbs 15, protein 7

Yogurt Cake

Preparation time: 5 minutes
Cooking time: 30 minutes
Servings: 8

Ingredients:
- 1½ cups white flour
- 1 teaspoon baking soda
- ¾ cup sugar
- 1 banana, mashed
- ½ teaspoon baking powder
- 2 tablespoons vegetable oil
- 1 cup Greek yogurt
- 8 ounces canned pumpkin puree
- Cooking spray
- 1 egg
- ½ teaspoon vanilla extract

Directions:
In a bowl, combine all ingredients (except the cooking spray) and stir well. Pour the mixture into a cake pan greased with cooking spray and put it in your air fryer's basket. Cook at 330 degrees F for 30 minutes. Cool down, slice, and serve.

Nutrition: calories 192, fat 7, fiber 7, carbs 12, protein 4

Zucchini Bread

Preparation time: 10 minutes
Cooking time: 40 minutes
Servings: 6

Ingredients:
- 3 cups zucchinis, grated
- 1 cup sugar
- 1 tablespoon vanilla extract
- 2 eggs, whisked
- 2 cups white flour
- 1 tablespoon baking powder
- 1 stick butter, melted

Directions:
Add all of the ingredients to a bowl and mix well. Pour the mixture into a lined loaf pan and place in the fryer. and cook at 320 degrees F for 40 minutes. Slice and serve warm.

Nutrition: calories 132, fat 6, fiber 7, carbs 11, protein 7

Cream of Tartar Bread

Preparation time: 10 minutes
Cooking time: 40 minutes
Servings: 6

Ingredients:
- ¾ cup sugar
- ⅓ cup butter
- 1 teaspoon vanilla extract
- 1 egg
- 2 zucchinis, grated
- 1 teaspoon baking powder
- 1½ cups flour
- ½ teaspoon baking soda
- ⅓ cup milk
- 1½ teaspoons cream of tartar

Directions:
Place all ingredients in a bowl and mix well. Pour the mixture into a lined loaf pan and place the pan in the air fryer. Cook at 320 degrees F for 40 minutes Cool down, slice, and serve.

Nutrition: calories 222, fat 7, fiber 8, carbs 14, protein 4

Orange Cake

Preparation time: 10 minutes
Cooking time: 20 minutes
Servings: 3

Ingredients:
- 1 egg
- 4 tablespoons sugar
- 2 tablespoons vegetable oil
- 4 tablespoons milk
- 2 tablespoons orange juice
- 4 tablespoons flour
- 1 tablespoon cocoa powder
- ½ teaspoon baking powder
- ½ teaspoon orange zest

Directions:
Place all of the ingredients in a bowl and mix well. Divide the mixture between 3 ramekins and place them in your air fryer. Cook at 320 degrees F for 20 minutes. Serve the cakes warm, and enjoy!

Nutrition: calories 191, fat 7, fiber 3, carbs 14, protein 4

Maple Apples

Preparation time: 10 minutes
Cooking time: 10 minutes
Servings: 4

Ingredients:

- 2 teaspoons cinnamon powder
- 5 apples, cored and cut into wedges
- ½ teaspoon nutmeg powder
- 1 tablespoon maple syrup
- 4 tablespoons butter
- ¼ cup brown sugar

Directions:
In a pan that fits your air fryer, mix the apples with the other ingredients and toss. Place the pan in the fryer and cook at 360 degrees F for 10 minutes. Divide into cups and serve.

Nutrition: calories 180, fat 6, fiber 8, carbs 19, protein 12

Pineapple and Carrot Cake

Preparation time: 10 minutes
Cooking time: 45 minutes
Servings: 6

Ingredients:

- 5 ounces flour
- ¾ teaspoon baking powder
- ½ teaspoon baking soda
- ½ teaspoon cinnamon powder
- 1 egg, whisked
- 3 tablespoons yogurt
- ½ cup sugar
- ¼ cup pineapple juice
- 4 tablespoons vegetable oil
- ⅓ cup carrots, grated
- ⅓ cup coconut flakes, shredded
- Cooking spray

Directions:
Place all of the ingredients (except the cooking spray) in a bowl, and mix well. Pour the mixture into a spring form pan, greased with cooking spray that fits your air fryer. Place the pan in your air fryer and cook at 320 degrees F for 45 minutes. Allow the cake to cool before cutting and serving.

Nutrition: calories 200, fat 6, fiber 7, carbs 12, protein 4

Rum Cheesecake

Preparation time: 10 minutes
Cooking time: 20 minutes
Servings: 6

Ingredients:
- 2 teaspoons butter, melted
- ½ cup graham cookies, crumbled
- 16 ounces cream cheese, softened
- 2 eggs
- ½ cup sugar
- 1 teaspoon rum
- ½ teaspoon vanilla extract

Directions:
Grease a pan with the butter and spread the cookie crumbs on the bottom. In a bowl, mix all the remaining ingredients and whisk well; then spread this mixture over the cookie crumbs. Place the pan in your air fryer and cook at 340 degrees F for 20 minutes. Let the cheesecake cool down, refrigerate, and serve cold.

Nutrition: calories 212, fat 12, fiber 6, carbs 12, protein 7

Strawberry Cream

Preparation time: 5 minutes
Cooking time: 15 minutes
Servings: 6

Ingredients:
- 1 teaspoon gelatin
- 8 ounces cream cheese
- 4 ounces strawberries
- 2 tablespoons water
- ½ tablespoon lemon juice
- ¼ teaspoon sugar
- ½ cup heavy cream

Directions:
Place all ingredients in your blender and pulse. Divide the mixture into 6 ramekins and place them in your air fryer. Cook at 330 degrees F for 15 minutes. Refrigerate (or place briefly in freezer) and serve the cream really cold.

Nutrition: calories 202, fat 8, fiber 2, carbs 6, protein 7

Coffee Cream

Preparation time: 5 minutes
Cooking time: 10 minutes
Servings: 6

Ingredients:

- 2 tablespoons butter
- 8 ounces cream cheese
- 3 tablespoons coffee
- 3 eggs
- ⅓ cup sugar
- 1 tablespoon caramel syrup

Directions:
Place all ingredients in your blender and pulse. Divide the mixture between 6 ramekins, and place in the fryer. Cook at 320 degrees F; bake for 10 minutes. Let cool down and then place in the freezer before serving.

Nutrition: calories 234, fat 13, fiber 4, carbs 11, protein 5

Cream Cheese Cookies

Preparation time: 10 minutes
Cooking time: 14 minutes
Servings: 12

Ingredients:

- 6 ounces vegetable oil
- 6 eggs
- 3 ounces cocoa powder
- 2 teaspoons vanilla extract
- ½ teaspoon baking powder
- 4 ounces cream cheese
- 5 tablespoons sugar

Directions:
Add all the ingredients to a blender and pulse a bit. Pour this mixture into a baking dish lined with parchment paper that fits your air fryer. Place the pan in the fryer at 320 degrees F, and bake for 14 minutes. Slice into rectangles and serve.

Nutrition: calories 178, fat 11, fiber 3, carbs 3, protein 5

Walnut Cookies

Preparation time: 5 minutes
Cooking time: 17 minutes
Servings: 4

Ingredients:
- 1 egg
- ⅓ cup cocoa powder
- ⅓ cup sugar
- 7 tablespoons butter, melted
- ½ teaspoon vanilla extract
- ¼ cup white flour
- ¼ cup walnuts, chopped
- ½ teaspoon baking powder

Directions:
Place all of the ingredients in a bowl and mix well (preferably using a mixer). Spread the mixture on a baking sheet lined with parchment paper that fits your air fryer. Place the baking sheet in the fryer and bake at 320 degrees F for 17 minutes. Let the cookies cool down, cut, and serve.

Nutrition: calories 203, fat 12, fiber 1, carbs 13, protein 6

Creamy Blackberry Mix

Preparation time: 5 minutes
Cooking time: 12 minutes
Servings: 4

Ingredients:
- 1 cup blackberries
- 2 eggs
- ½ cup heavy cream
- ½ cup butter, melted
- 5 tablespoons sugar
- 2 teaspoons vanilla extract
- 2 teaspoons baking powder

Directions:
Place all of the ingredients in a bowl and whisk well. Divide the mixture between 4 ramekins, and place the ramekins in the fryer. Cook at 320 degrees F for 12 minutes. Refrigerate, and serve cold.

Nutrition: calories 230, fat 2, fiber 2, carbs 14, protein 7

Chocolate Brownies

Preparation time: 5 minutes
Cooking time: 25 minutes
Servings: 12

Ingredients:

- 1 teaspoon vanilla extract
- ½ cup butter, melted
- 1 egg
- 4 tablespoons sugar
- 2 cups white flour
- ½ cup chocolate chips

Directions:

Place all the ingredients in a bowl and mix well. Spread the mixture into a pan that fits your air fryer. Place the pan in the fryer and bake at 330 degrees F for 25 minutes. Cool down, slice, serve, and enjoy!

Nutrition: calories 230, fat 12, fiber 2, carbs 12, protein 5

Yogurt and Cream Cheese Cake

Preparation time: 10 minutes
Cooking time: 30 minutes
Servings: 10

Ingredients:

- 6 eggs, whisked
- 1 mandarin orange, peeled and pureed
- 1 teaspoon vanilla extract
- 1 teaspoon baking powder
- 9 ounces white flour
- 6 tablespoons sugar
- 4 ounces cream cheese, softened
- 4 ounces yogurt

Directions:

In a food processor, add the mandarin puree, flour, 2 tablespoons of sugar, eggs, vanilla extract, and baking powder; pulse. Divide the mixture between 2 cake pans lined with parchment paper cook each in the air fryer at 330 degrees F for 15 minutes. In a bowl, combine the cream cheese, yogurt, and 4 tablespoons sugar; whisk well. Place one cake layer on a plate and top with half of the yogurt mix; spread evenly. Add the other cake layer on top of the first with the yogurt mix, and top this layer with the remaining yogurt mix, spreading it well. Slice, serve, and enjoy!

Nutrition: calories 231, fat 13, fiber 2, carbs 11, protein 5

Creamy White Chocolate Cheesecake

Preparation time: 10 minutes
Cooking time: 20 minutes
Servings: 8

Ingredients:
For the crust:
- 4 tablespoons butter, melted
- 1½ cups chocolate cookies, crumbled

For the filling:
- 24 ounces cream cheese, softened
- 2 tablespoons cornstarch
- 1 cup sugar
- 3 eggs, whisked
- 1 tablespoon vanilla extract
- ½ cup heavy cream
- 12 ounces white chocolate, melted

Directions:
Place the cookie crumbs and butter in a bowl, and stir well. Spread the cookie crumb mixture on the bottom of a cake pan lined with parchment paper and freeze for now. In another bowl, mix all other ingredients; whisk well. Spread this over the cake crust, put the pan in the fryer, and cook at 320 degrees F for 20 minutes. Let the cake cool down and put in the fridge for 1 hour before serving.

Nutrition: calories 261, fat 12, fiber 6, carbs 12, protein 6

Pumpkin Cake

Preparation time: 10 minutes
Cooking time: 25 minutes
Servings: 8

Ingredients:
- 1 cup white flour
- 1 teaspoon baking powder
- ¾ teaspoon pumpkin pie spice
- ¾ cup sugar
- Cooking spray
- ½ cup Greek yogurt
- 8 ounces canned pumpkin puree
- 1 egg, whisked

Directions:
Place all ingredients (other than the cooking spray) in a bowl and mix well. Grease a cake pan with cooking spray, pour the cake batter inside, and spread. Place the pan in the air fryer and cook at 330 degrees F for 25 minutes. Let the cake cool down, slice, and serve.

Nutrition: calories 214, fat 9, fiber 3, carbs 14, protein 8

Banana Bread

Preparation time: 10 minutes
Cooking time: 40 minutes
Servings: 6

Ingredients:
- 3 bananas, peeled and mashed
- 1 cup sugar
- 2 eggs, whisked
- 2 cups white flour
- 1 tablespoon baking powder
- 1 stick of butter, melted

Directions:
Place all the ingredients in a bowl and stir well. Pour this mixture into a lined loaf pan, and place in the air fryer. Cook at 340 degrees F for 40 minutes. Let the bread cool; then slice, serve, and enjoy!

Nutrition: calories 200, fat 5, fiber 3, carbs 13, protein 7

Pear Bread

Preparation time: 10 minutes
Cooking time: 40 minutes
Servings: 6

Ingredients:
- 1 cup sugar
- ⅓ cup butter, melted
- 1 teaspoon vanilla extract
- 1 egg, whisked
- 2 pears, peeled and chopped
- 1 teaspoon baking powder
- 1½ cups flour
- ⅓ cup almond milk
- Cooking spray

Directions:
Combine all of the ingredients (except the cooking spray) in a bowl and mix well. Spread the mixture into a loaf pan greased with cooking spray, and place the pan in the air fryer. Cook at 340 degrees F for 40 minutes. Cool the bread down, slice, and serve.

Nutrition: calories 211, fat 4, fiber 6, carbs 14, protein 6

Lemon Lava Cake

Preparation time: 10 minutes
Cooking time: 20 minutes
Servings: 4

Ingredients:

- 1 egg, whisked
- 4 tablespoons sugar
- 2 tablespoons butter, melted
- 4 tablespoons milk
- 4 tablespoons flour
- ½ teaspoon baking powder
- 1 teaspoon lemon zest
- 1 teaspoon lemon juice

Directions:
Mix all the ingredients in a bowl and pour into 4 small ramekins. Place the ramekins in your air fryer and cook at 320 degrees F for 20 minutes. Serve the cakes right away.

Nutrition: calories 213, fat 5, fiber 5, carbs 15, protein 6

Pear Delight

Preparation time: 5 minutes
Cooking time: 20 minutes
Servings: 4

Ingredients:

- 2 teaspoons cinnamon powder
- 4 pears, peeled and roughly cut into cubes
- 1 tablespoon maple syrup
- 4 tablespoons butter, melted
- ¼ cup brown sugar

Directions:
In a pan that fits your air fryer, place all the ingredients and toss. Place the pan in the air fryer and cook at 300 degrees F for 20 minutes. Divide into cups, refrigerate, and serve cold.

Nutrition: calories 200, fat 3, fiber 4, carbs 16, protein 4

Orange Stew

Preparation time: 10 minutes
Cooking time: 20 minutes
Servings: 3

Ingredients:
- 4 oranges, peeled and cut into segments
- 2¼ cups white sugar
- 2 cups orange juice

Directions:
In a pan that fits your air fryer, mix the oranges with the sugar and orange juice; toss. Place the pan in the fryer and cook at 320 degrees F for 20 minutes. Divide the orange stew into cups, refrigerate, and serve cold.

Nutrition: calories 171, fat 1, fiber 4, carbs 8, protein 2

Baked Pears

Preparation time: 5 minutes
Cooking time: 20 minutes
Servings: 4

Ingredients:
- 4 pears, peeled and halved
- 1 cup red wine
- ½ cup sugar

Directions:
In a pan that fits your air fryer, mix the pears with the wine and sugar. Place the pan in the fryer and cook at 340 degrees F for 20 minutes. Divide into bowls and serve.

Nutrition: calories 200, fat 1, fiber 4, carbs 12, protein 3

Liqueur Chocolate Cream

Preparation time: 5 minutes
Cooking time: 12 minutes
Servings: 4

Ingredients:
- 3½ ounces heavy cream
- 3½ ounces sweet dark chocolate, cut into chunks
- 1 teaspoon liquor

Directions:
In a heat-proof dish, mix the cream with the chocolate and the liqueur. Place the dish in the air fryer and cook at 300 degrees F for 12 minutes. Whisk the cream, divide it into cups, and serve.

Nutrition: calories 200, fat 3, fiber 4, carbs 11, protein 3

Apricot Cake

Preparation time: 10 minutes
Cooking time: 30 minutes
Servings: 4

Ingredients:
- 8 ounces apricots, chopped
- 1 cup white flour
- 3 teaspoons baking powder
- 1 cup sugar
- 1 teaspoon ginger powder
- 1 teaspoon cinnamon powder
- ½ cup butter, softened
- 3 tablespoons maple syrup
- 4 eggs, whisked

Directions:
Place all the ingredients in a bowl and stir well. Pour the mixture into a cake pan lined with parchment paper, and place the pan in the fryer. Cook at 340 degrees F for 30 minutes. Let the cake cool before slicing and serving. Enjoy!

Nutrition: calories 213, fat 3, fiber 6, carbs 15, protein 4

Spiced Banana Pudding

Preparation time: 10 minutes
Cooking time: 25 minutes
Serving: 6

Ingredients:

- 4 bananas, peeled and mashed
- 2 eggs, whisked
- 1 cup milk
- ¾ cup maple syrup
- 1 teaspoon cinnamon powder
- ½ teaspoon ginger powder
- ¼ teaspoon cloves, ground
- 1 tablespoon cornstarch

Directions:

In a bowl, mix all the ingredients; whisk well. Pour the mixture into a pudding mould, put it in the air fryer, and cook at 340 degrees F for 25 minutes. Serve the pudding warm; enjoy!

Nutrition: calories 200, fat 4, fiber 6, carbs 15, protein 4

Lime Tapioca Pudding

Preparation time: 10 minutes
Cooking time: 15 minutes
Servings: 6

Ingredients:

- 2 cups milk
- ⅓ cup tapioca pearls, rinsed
- ½ cup sugar
- Zest of 1 lime

Directions:

Place all ingredients in a heat-proof dish that fits your air fryer; whisk well. Put the dish in the fryer and cook at 320 degrees F for 15 minutes. Set the pudding aside for 10 minutes, divide into bowls, and serve.

Nutrition: calories 161, fat 3, fiber 5, carbs 14, protein 4

Strawberry Cake

Preparation time: 10 minutes
Cooking time: 35 minutes
Servings: 8

Ingredients:

- 1 pound strawberries, chopped
- 1 cup ricotta cheese
- ¼ cup sugar
- 1 tablespoon lemon juice
- 1 egg, whisked
- 1 teaspoon vanilla extract
- 3 tablespoons butter, melted
- 1 cup white flour
- 2 teaspoons baking powder

Directions:
Place all of the ingredients in a bowl and whisk well. Pour the mixture into a cake pan lined with parchment paper, and place in the air fryer. Cook at 340 degrees F for 35 minutes. Cool the cake down, slice, and serve.

Nutrition: calories 200, fat 4, fiber 4, carbs 16, protein 4

Almond and Cocoa Cake

Preparation time: 10 minutes
Cooking time: 40 minutes
Servings: 6

Ingredients:

- 1 teaspoon almond extract
- 1 cup ricotta cheese, softened
- ½ cup cocoa powder
- ½ cup sugar
- 3 tablespoons butter, melted
- 1 cup white flour
- 2 eggs, whisked
- 2 teaspoons baking powder
- ¼ cup almonds, sliced

Directions:
Place all of the ingredients in a bowl and stir well. Pour the mixture into a cake pan lined with parchment paper place the pan in the fryer, and cook at 330 degrees F for 40 minutes. Allow the cake to cool, slice, and serve.

Nutrition: calories 200, fat 4, fiber 5, carbs 15, protein 5

Creamy Pudding

Preparation time: 5 minutes
Cooking time: 25 minutes
Servings: 6

Ingredients:
- 2 cups fresh cream
- 6 egg yolks, whisked
- 6 tablespoons white sugar
- Zest of 1 orange

Directions:
Combine all ingredients in a bowl and whisk well. Divide the mixture between 6 small ramekins. Place the ramekins in your air fryer and cook at 340 degrees F for 25 minutes. Place in the fridge for 1 hour before serving.

Nutrition: calories 200, fat 3, fiber 5, carbs 15, protein 5

Brioche Pudding

Preparation time: 5 minutes
Cooking time: 30 minutes
Servings: 4

Ingredients:
- 4 egg yolks, whisked
- 3 cups brioche, cubed
- 2 cups half and half
- ½ teaspoon vanilla extract
- 1 cup sugar
- 2 tablespoons butter, melted
- 2 cups milk
- ½ cup raisins
- Zest of ½ lemon

Directions:
In a bowl, add all of the ingredients and whisk well. Pour the mixture into a pudding mould and place it in the air fryer. Cook at 330 degrees F for 30 minutes. Cool down and serve.

Nutrition: calories 251, fat 4, fiber 5, carbs 20, protein 5

Apple and Cinnamon Sauce

Preparation time: 10 minutes
Cooking time: 30 minutes
Servings: 6

Ingredients:
- 6 apples, peeled, cored and cut into wedges
- 1 tablespoon cinnamon powder
- 1 cup sugar
- 1 cup red wine

Directions:
In a pan that fits your air fryer, place all of the ingredients and toss. Place the pan in the fryer and cook at 320 degrees F for 30 minutes. Divide into cups and serve right away.

Nutrition: calories 200, fat 4, fiber 4, carbs 15, protein 3

Grape Stew

Preparation time: 5 minutes
Cooking time: 14 minutes
Servings: 4

Ingredients:
- 1 pound red grapes
- Juice and zest of 1 lemon
- 26 ounces grape juice

Directions:
In a pan that fits your air fryer, add all ingredients and toss. Place the pan in the fryer and cook at 320 degrees F for 14 minutes. Divide into cups, refrigerate, and serve cold.

Nutrition: calories 151, fat 4, fiber 5, carbs 8, protein 4

Creamy Rice Pudding

Preparation time: 5 minutes
Cooking time: 20 minutes
Servings: 6

Ingredients:
- 1 tablespoon butter, melted
- 7 ounces white rice
- 16 ounces milk
- 1/3 cup sugar
- 1 tablespoon heavy cream
- 1 teaspoon vanilla extract

Directions:
Place all ingredients in a pan that fits your air fryer and stir well. Put the pan in the fryer and cook at 360 degrees F for 20 minutes. Stir the pudding, divide it into bowls, refrigerate, and serve cold.

Nutrition: calories 230, fat 4, fiber 6, carbs 17, protein 5

Honey Blackberry Pudding

Preparation time: 10 minutes
Cooking time: 30 minutes
Servings: 6

Ingredients:
- 1 pound ricotta cheese, softened
- 6 ounces blackberries
- 2 ounces honey
- 4 eggs
- ¼ cup sugar
- ¼ teaspoon vanilla extract
- Zest of ½ orange

Directions:
Place all the ingredients in a bowl; whisk well. Divide the mixture between 6 ramekins and place them in the air fryer. Cook at 300 degrees F for 30 minutes. Cool down, serve, and enjoy!

Nutrition: calories 191, fat 3, fiber 6, carbs 13, protein 5

Banana and Rice Pudding

Preparation time: 10 minutes
Cooking time: 20 minutes
Servings: 6

Ingredients:
- 1 cup brown rice
- 3 cups milk
- 2 bananas, peeled and mashed
- ½ cup maple syrup
- 1 teaspoon vanilla extract

Directions:
Place all the ingredients in a pan that fits your air fryer; stir well. Put the pan in the fryer and cook at 360 degrees F for 20 minutes.
Stir the pudding, divide into cups, refrigerate, and serve cold.

Nutrition: calories 161, fat 5, fiber 4, carbs 16, protein 5

Orange Marmalade

Preparation time: 10 minutes
Cooking time: 20 minutes
Servings: 4

Ingredients:
- 4 oranges, peeled and chopped
- 3 cups sugar
- 1½ cups water

Directions:
In a pan that fits your air fryer, mix the oranges with the sugar and the water; stir. Place the pan in the fryer and cook at 340 degrees F for 20 minutes. Stir well, divide into cups, refrigerate, and serve cold.

Nutrition: calories 161, fat 4, fiber 4, carbs 12, protein 4

Strawberry Jam

Preparation time: 5 minutes
Cooking time: 25 minutes
Servings: 6

Ingredients:
- Juice of 2 limes
- 4 cups sugar
-
- 1 pound strawberries, chopped
- 2 cups water

Directions:

In a pan that fits your air fryer, mix the strawberries with the sugar, lime juice and the water; stir. Place the pan in the fryer and cook at 340 degrees F for 25 minutes. Blend the mix using an immersion blender, divide into cups, refrigerate, and serve cold.

Nutrition: calories 161, fat 2, fiber 4, carbs 15, protein 2

Cranberry Jam

Preparation time: 5 minutes
Cooking time: 20 minutes
Servings: 8

Ingredients:
- 2 pounds cranberries
- 4 ounces black currant
- 2 pounds sugar
- Zest of 1 lime
- 3 tablespoons water

Directions:

In a pan that fits your air fryer, add all the ingredients and stir. Place the pan in the fryer and cook at 360 degrees F for 20 minutes. Stir the jam well, divide into cups, refrigerate, and serve cold.

Nutrition: calories 176, fat 2, fiber 3, carbs 15, protein 1

Sweet Plum Stew

Preparation time: 10 minutes
Cooking time: 30 minutes
Servings: 8

Ingredients:

- 1½ pounds plums, pitted and chopped
- 2 tablespoons lime juice
- 1 cup white sugar
- ½ cup water

Directions:

In a pan that fits your air fryer, mix the plums with the other ingredients; stir. Place the pan in the fryer and cook at 330 degrees F for 30 minutes. Divide the stew into cups, refrigerate, and serve cold.

Nutrition: calories 171, fat 1, fiber 3, carbs 16, protein 6

Apple Jam

Preparation time: 10 minutes
Cooking time: 20 minutes
Servings: 8

Ingredients:

- 8 apples, peeled, cored and blended
- 1 cup apple juice
- 1 teaspoon cinnamon powder

Directions:

In a pan that fits your air fryer, mix the apples with the cinnamon and apple juice; stir. Place the pan in the fryer and cook at 340 degrees F for 20 minutes. Blend using an immersion blender. Divide the jam into cups and serve.

Nutrition: calories 141, fat 2, fiber 4, carbs 14, protein 3

Conclusion

Cooking with an air fryer is the latest innovation in terms of modern cooking. Air fryers are a kitchen appliance that will most certainly ease your job in the kitchen. As you can see, you do not need to spend long hours in the kitchen anymore. You don't even need to be an expert, or even experienced, cook in order to make the best, most succulent, and delicious meals for you and all your loved ones.

All you need is an air fryer, the best ingredients, and the perfect air fryer cooking guide. This way you can create some of the most amazing culinary feasts in a matter of minutes.

Don't just take our word for this! You simply need to get your own air fryer as soon as possible, and a copy of this great air fryer cooking journal, and start this culinary journey that will definitely impress you and those for whom you cook.

Air fryers have become more and more popular over the last few years, and you should definitely consider purchasing one as soon as possible! It will be one of your best investments.

Get an air fryer today and start cooking in a new and fun way! Enjoy so many rich, delicious meals… and have fun cooking!

Recipe Index

A

Air Fried Beans Mix, 89
Air Fried Cauliflower Mix, 80
Air Fried Chicken Wings, 174
Air Fried Corn, 107
Air Fried Mushroom Mix, 22
Air Fried Salmon, 144
Air Fried Whole Chicken, 168
Air Fryer Lamb, 61
Almond and Cocoa Cake, 263
Amaretto Cream, 246
Apple and Cinnamon Sauce, 265
Apple and Dates Dip, 125
Apple Bran Granola, 44
Apple Jam, 269
Apple Oatmeal, 42
Apricot Cake, 261
Artichoke Rice, 89
Artichokes and Mayonnaise, 231
Avocado Cake, 245

B

Baby Shrimp Salad, 155
Bacon Cauliflower, 237
Baked Cod, 156
Baked Pears, 260
Balsamic Asparagus, 220
Balsamic Chicken, 177
Balsamic Mustard Greens, 243
Balsamic Zucchini Slices, 105
Banana and Rice Pudding, 267
Banana Bread, 258
Banana Chips, 103
Basil and Cilantro Crackers, 105
Basil Beef Roast, 210
BBQ Lamb Chops, 218
Beans and Quinoa Stew, 63
Beans Mix, 91
Beans Oatmeal, 44
Beef and Celery Mix, 198
Beef and Chives Marinade, 209
Beef and Mushroom Mix, 191
Beef and Peas, 202
Beef and Plums Mix, 219
Beef and Potato Stew, 52
Beef and Tofu Mix, 215
Beef and Wine Sauce, 194
Beef Casserole, 214
Beef Dip, 115
Beef Meatball Sandwiches, 50
Beef Meatballs and Sauce, 49
Beef Roast, 197
Beef Roast and Grapes, 196
Beef, Arugula and Leeks, 206
Beet and Tomato Salad, 223

Beets and Capers, 222
Beets and Kale Mix, 223
Bell Pepper and Lettuce Side Salad, 97
Bell Peppers and Kale, 236
Black Bean Burritos, 36
Black Beans Lunch Mix, 63
Black Beans Mix, 90
Blackberries and Cornflakes Mix, 18
Bleu Cheese Chicken Mix, 186
Bourbon Lunch Burger, 60
Breakfast Biscuits, 27
Breakfast Cauliflower Mix, 38
Breakfast Chicken Burrito, 15
Breakfast Pancakes, 35
Breakfast Potatoes Mix, 26
Breakfast Rice Pudding, 33
Breakfast Sausage Rolls, 26
Breakfast Spinach Pie, 40
Brioche Pudding, 264
Broccoli and Pomegranate, 237
Broccoli and Tomatoes, 224
Broccoli Bites, 113
Broccoli Casserole, 242
Broccoli Risotto, 88
Broccoli Spread, 124
Brown Lentils Mix, 102
Brussels Sprouts Side Dish Delight, 76
Butter and Parmesan Chicken, 176
Butter Broccoli, 238
Butter Cabbage Mix, 239
Butter Carrots, 226
Butter Donuts, 248
Butter Endives, 244
Butter Flounder Fillets, 152
Butter Shrimp Mix, 140
Butternut Puree, 93
Butternut Squash Stew, 72
Buttery Carrot Dip, 124
Buttery Onion Dip, 122

C

Cajun Asparagus, 233
Cajun Chicken and Okra, 183
Carrot Oatmeal, 43
Carrot Puree, 92
Carrots and Cauliflower Breakfast Mix, 19
Cauliflower and Mushroom Risotto, 79
Cauliflower Mix, 224
Cheese and Ham Patties, 30
Cheese Ravioli, 53
Cheesy Asparagus, 221
Cheesy Beef Meatballs, 109
Cheesy Hash Brown Mix, 17
Cheesy Mushroom Salad, 83
Cheesy Sausage and Tomatoes Dip, 118

Cheesy Spinach, 98
Cherry Cream Pudding, 246
Chicken and Baby Carrots Mix, 183
Chicken and Beans Casserole, 57
Chicken and Beans Chili, 184
Chicken and Beer Mix, 184
Chicken and Cabbage Curry, 70
Chicken and Cauliflower Bake, 58
Chicken and Chickpeas Mix, 187
Chicken and Green Coconut Sauce, 165
Chicken and Leeks, 173
Chicken and Mushroom Pie, 46
Chicken and Pear Sauce, 172
Chicken and Peppercorns Mix, 179
Chicken and Potatoes, 186
Chicken and Smoked Pancetta, 181
Chicken and Spinach Breakfast Casserole, 14
Chicken and Squash, 187
Chicken and Veggies, 167
Chicken and Yogurt Mix, 173
Chicken Breasts and Veggies, 164
Chicken Breasts Delight, 166
Chicken Curry, 185
Chicken Lunch Casserole, 54
Chicken Pizza Rolls, 47
Chicken Sticks, 108
Chicken Thighs and Rice, 168
Chicken Wings and Endives, 163
Chickpeas Stew, 64
Chili and Parsley Soufflé, 22
Chili Dip, 116
Chili Salmon Fillets, 130
Chili Tomato Salsa, 121
Chili Tomato Shrimp, 150
Chinese Beef and Cabbage Bowls, 55
Chinese Beef Mix, 198
Chinese Chicken Thighs, 161
Chinese Cod Fillets, 128
Chinese Pork and Broccoli Mix, 190
Chinese Pork Bites, 47
Chinese Trout Bites, 145
Chives Radish Snack, 106
Chocolate Brownies, 256
Chorizo Omelet, 27
Cilantro Trout Fillets, 142
Cinnamon Apples, 249
Cinnamon Beef, 210
Cinnamon Chicken Mix, 182
Cinnamon Pears, 248
Cinnamon Rolls, 247
Citrus Cauliflower Mix, 95
Clams and Potatoes, 147
Coconut Artichokes, 232
Coconut Cod Fillets, 137
Coconut Mushroom Mix, 229
Coconut Pork Mix, 193

Coconut Shrimp Snack, 108
Coconut Zucchini Mix, 56
Cod and Lime Sauce, 131
Cod and Warm Tomato Mix, 57
Cod Curry, 53
Cod Fillets and Kale Salad, 50
Cod Fillets with Leeks, 128
Cod Meatballs, 51
Cod Tortilla, 30
Coffee Cream, 254
Coriander Bites, 114
Corn Dip, 127
Corn Pudding, 25
Corn Stew, 71
Crab Bites, 112
Cranberry Dip, 122
Cranberry Jam, 268
Cream Cheese Cookies, 254
Cream of Tartar Bread, 251
Creamy Beef, 211
Creamy Blackberry Mix, 255
Creamy Cabbage Mix, 84
Creamy Chicken Thighs, 160
Creamy Leek Spread, 126
Creamy Mushroom Pie, 19
Creamy Peas Omelet, 31
Creamy Pork and Sprouts, 193
Creamy Potato Lunch, 54
Creamy Potatoes, 73
Creamy Pudding, 264
Creamy Rice Pudding, 266
Creamy Risotto, 86
Creamy Shrimp and Mushrooms, 133
Creamy Squash Mix, 234
Creamy Tomatoes, 76
Creamy White Chocolate Cheesecake, 257
Crusted Rack of Lamb, 192
Cumin Beef Mix, 212
Curry Pork Mix, 218

D
Delicious Eggplant Stew, 65
Different Shrimp Mix, 151
Dijon Hot Dogs, 48
Dill Corn, 242
Duck and Sauce, 163
Duck Breast and Potatoes, 176

E
Easy Celery Root Mix, 241
Easy Coconut Shrimp, 138
Easy Eggplant Spread, 123
Easy Mushroom Fritters, 38
Easy Mushroom Mix, 82
Easy Salmon Fillets and Bell Peppers, 136
Eggplant and Zucchini Breakfast Mix, 41
Eggplant Mix, 228

Endives and Bacon, 244
Endives and Rice Mix, 100
English Tuna Sandwiches, 31

F
Fast Lamb Ribs, 217
Fast Mango Dip, 119
Fast Parsley Dip, 126
Fast Turkey Meatballs, 180
Fava Beans Mix, 96
Fennel Pork Mix, 203
Flavored Salmon Fillets, 132
Flavored Turkey Breast, 159
French Beef Mix, 191
French Carrots Mix, 78
French Lamb Mix, 219
Fruity Breakfast Casserole, 16

G
Garlic Parsnips, 236
Garlic Potatoes, 84
Garlicky Beets, 96
Garlicky Loin Roast, 206
Garlicky Squid, 154
Glazed Chicken and Apples, 169
Goat Cheese Brussels Sprouts, 230
Grape Stew, 265
Great Pork Chops, 216
Greek Cream Cheese Balls, 110
Greek Lamb Chops, 217
Greek Quinoa Salad, 69
Greek Sandwiches, 45
Green Beans and Shallots, 74
Green Beans Lunch Stew, 64
Green Beans Mix, 227
Green Beans Omelet, 29
Ground Beef Mix, 200

H
Herbed Chicken, 162
Herbed Omelet, 34
Herbed Potatoes Mix, 99
Herbed Tomatoes Breakfast Mix, 41
Herbed Tuna, 132
Honey Blackberry Pudding, 266
Honey Chicken and Dates, 172
Honey Chicken Thighs, 67
Honey Duck Breasts, 162
Hot Dip, 120
Hot Greek Potatoes, 228
Hot Pork Mix, 205
Hot Shrimp Mix, 139
Hot Wings, 182

I
Indian Chicken Mix, 188
Indian Red Potatoes, 102
Italian Chicken Mix, 67
Italian Eggplant Sandwich, 24

Italian Mozzarella Sticks, 111
Italian Mushroom Mix, 75

J
Jalapeno Beef Mix, 212
Japanese Chicken Thighs, 167
Japanese Pork Mix, 58

K
Kale Crackers, 111
Kale Sandwich, 35

L
Lamb and Beans, 199
Lamb and Carrots Mix, 213
Lamb Chops and Dill, 195
Lamb Meatballs, 203
Lemon Cake, 249
Lemon Chicken and Asparagus, 169
Lemon Lava Cake, 259
Lemony Apple Bites, 104
Lemony Artichokes, 95
Lemony Endives Appetizer, 114
Lentils Lunch Cakes, 49
Lentils Lunch Curry, 65
Lentils Snack, 107
Lentils Spread, 115
Lime Corn, 83
Lime Salmon, 157
Lime Tapioca Pudding, 262
Liqueur Chocolate Cream, 261
Lunch Baby Carrots Mix, 68
Lunch Broccoli Mix, 61
Lunch Green Beans Casserole, 66
Lunch Tomato and Okra Stew, 62

M
Maple Apples, 252
Maple Glazed Corn, 241
Maple Parsnips Mix, 78
Maple Salmon, 133
Marinara Chicken, 185
Marinated Beef, 215
Marjoram Chicken, 189
Mashed Cauliflower, 91
Mashed Sweet Potatoes, 87
Mayo Brussels Sprouts, 74
Mexican Turkey Mix, 179
Milky Lamb, 208
Mint and Cherries Rice, 88
Minty Cauliflower Spread, 119
Minty Peas, 94
Minty Shrimp Mix, 110
Mixed Peppers Side Dish, 77
Moroccan Eggplant Side Dish, 80
Mung Beans Mix, 101
Mushroom Salad, 118
Mussels and Shrimp, 146
Mussels Bowls, 146

Mustard Brussels Sprouts, 225
Mustard Greens Mix, 243
Mustard Pork Chops, 195
Mustard Pork Chops, 209

N

Napa Cabbage Mix, 239
New Potatoes Mix, 238

O

Old Bay Chicken Wings, 48
Onion and Chili Dip, 123
Orange Cake, 251
Orange Carrots, 234
Orange Marmalade, 267
Orange Stew, 260
Oregano Artichoke Omelet, 28
Oregano Chicken Thighs, 161
Oregano Pearl Onions, 229
Oregano Pork Chops, 192
Oreo Cheesecake, 245

P

Paprika Beef, 208
Parmesan Asparagus Mix, 93
Parmesan Breakfast Muffins, 23
Parmesan Broccoli, 225
Parmesan Clams, 147
Parsley Quinoa, 85
Parsnips and Carrots Fries, 81
Parsnips Mash, 92
Pea Pods and Shrimp Mix, 150
Pear Bread, 258
Pear Delight, 259
Pear Oatmeal, 32
Pepper Rolls, 109
Peppers and Lettuce Salad, 40
Pesto Breakfast Toast, 20
Pineapple and Carrot Cake, 252
Pineapple Rice, 90
Pistachio Crusted Cod, 134
Polenta Cakes, 21
Pork and Bell Pepper Mix, 199
Pork and Bell Peppers, 202
Pork and Cabbage, 216
Pork and Cauliflower Mix, 201
Pork and Celery Mix, 213
Pork and Chives Mix, 194
Pork and Peanuts Mix, 207
Pork and Shallots Mix, 214
Pork Bites, 103
Pork Chops and Spinach Mix, 200
Pork Meatloaf, 204
Potato Chips, 112
Potato Frittata, 28
Potatoes and Calamari Stew, 70
Pumpkin Cake, 257

Q

Quinoa and Spinach Pesto Mix, 68
Quinoa and Spinach Salad, 69

R

Red Cabbage and Carrots, 226
Roasted Cod and Parsley, 135
Roasted Peppers Frittata, 17
Roasted Rhubarb, 98
Rosemary Chicken Breasts, 180
Rosemary Shrimp Kabobs, 129
Rubbed Steaks, 207
Rum Cheesecake, 253

S

Saffron Rice, 87
Saffron Shrimp Mix, 148
Sage Pork Mix, 196
Salmon and Balsamic Orange Sauce, 134
Salmon and Blackberry Sauce, 157
Salmon and Capers, 140
Salmon and Carrots, 143
Salmon and Fennel, 135
Salmon and Jasmine Rice, 142
Salmon and Orange Vinaigrette, 137
Salmon Fillets and Pineapple Mix, 136
Salmon Steaks Mix, 144
Salsa Chicken Mix, 71
Salsa Verde Chicken Breast, 160
Sausage Bake, 15
Sausage Bites, 113
Sausage Mix, 205
Sausage Omelet, 20
Scallions and Shallots Dip, 127
Sea Bass Paella, 138
Sea Bass Stew, 59
Sesame Chicken Mix, 188
Sesame Seed Beets Mix, 222
Shrimp and Chestnut Mix, 155
Shrimp and Corn, 148
Shrimp and Spaghetti, 151
Shrimp and Tomatoes, 149
Shrimp and Veggie Mix, 130
Shrimp and Zucchini Mix, 158
Shrimp Pasta, 52
Shrimp, Crab and Sausage Mix, 153
Simple Air Fried Beets, 79
Simple Air Fried Fennel, 94
Simple Balsamic Cod Fillets, 129
Simple Beef Curry, 211
Simple Cabbage Mix, 97
Simple Cheese Toast, 29
Simple Chicken Thighs, 165
Simple Chicken, Kale and Mushroom Mix, 56
Simple Eggplant Mix, 75
Simple Fennel and Tomato Spread, 125
Simple Fennel Mix, 221
Simple Garlic and Lemon Chicken, 170

Simple Lemongrass Chicken, 177
Simple Lunch Turkey, 51
Simple Nutmeg Pumpkin Pie, 247
Simple Okra Lunch Salad, 66
Simple Pork Steaks, 204
Simple Pumpkin Oatmeal, 42
Simple Rosemary Potatoes, 81
Simple Scrambled Eggs, 18
Simple Shrimp, 149
Simple Snapper Mix, 141
Simple Trout, 145
Simple Trout Mix, 141
Simple Zucchini Fries, 77
Smoked Bacon and Bread Mix, 16
Smoked Pork Roast, 201
Soy Sauce Chicken, 175
Spiced Banana Pudding, 262
Spiced Chicken, 178
Spiced Pork Chops, 190
Spiced Pumpkin Rice, 86
Spiced Tomato Party Mix, 120
Spicy Cabbage, 240
Spicy Cod, 143
Spicy Kale Mix, 227
Spinach and Cream Cheese Mix, 220
Squash Breakfast Mix, 33
Squash Dip, 117
Squash Salad, 233
Squid and Peas, 154
Squid Mix, 153
Strawberry Cake, 263
Strawberry Cream, 253
Strawberry Jam, 268
Strawberry Oatmeal, 43
Stuffed Peppers, 39
Sweet Plum Stew, 269
Sweet Potato Side Salad, 73

T
Tarragon Chicken Breasts, 171
Tarragon Green Beans, 230
Tarragon Pork Loin, 197
Tarragon Shrimp, 152
Thyme Potato Breakfast Mix, 14
Tiger Shrimp Mix, 139
Tofu and Bell Peppers Breakfast, 39
Tofu and Quinoa Bowls, 36
Tomato and Eggs Mix, 23
Tomato and Green Beans Salad, 235
Tomato Chicken Mix, 166
Tomato Dip, 116
Tomato Duck Breast, 174
Tomato Endives Mix, 101
Tomato Salad, 235
Tomatoes and Dates Salsa, 121
Trout and Almond Butter Sauce, 156
Turkey and Parsley Pesto, 164

Turkey and Spring Onions Mix, 175
Turkey Chili, 178
Turkey Wings and Orange Sauce, 181
Turkey with Fig Sauce, 170
Turmeric Cabbage Mix, 100
Turmeric Carrot Chips, 106
Turmeric Chicken Legs, 159
Turmeric Kale Mix, 240

V
Vanilla Oatmeal, 32
Vanilla Toast, 21
Veggie and Tofu Casserole, 37
Veggie Pudding, 55
Veggie Stew, 62

W
Walnut Cookies, 255
White Fish and Peas, 131
Wild Rice Mix, 85
Wrapped Asparagus, 232

Y
Yam Pudding, 37
Yellow Squash and Zucchini Mix, 82
Yogurt and Cream Cheese Cake, 256
Yogurt Cake, 250

Z
Zucchini and Chicken Breakfast Tortillas, 34
Zucchini and Mint Spread, 117
Zucchini Balls, 104
Zucchini Bread, 250

Made in the USA
Middletown, DE
17 December 2018